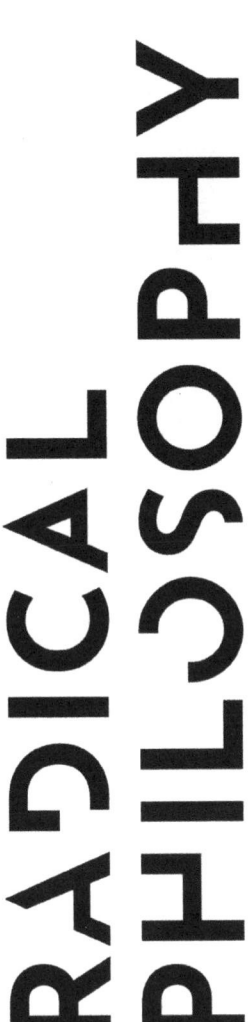

RADICAL PHILOSOPHY

2.05

Series 2 / Autumn 2019

Editorial collective
Claudia Aradau
Brenna Bhandar
Victoria Browne
David Cunningham
Peter Hallward
Stewart Martin
Lucie Mercier
Daniel Nemenyi
Hannah Proctor
Rahul Rao
Martina Tazzioli
Chris Wilbert

Engineers
Daniel Nemenyi
Alex Sassmanshausen

Cover image
Elisa Larvego, Archeology, 2010

Creative Commons BY-NC-ND
Radical Philosophy, Autumn 2019

ISSN 0300-211X
ISBN 978-1-9999793-4-8

What a body can do

Elsa Dorlin

On 11 Brumaire, Year XI [November 2, 1803], a Guadeloupe tribunal sentenced Millet de la Girardière to be placed in an iron cage in the square at Pointe-à-Pitre and left there until dead. The cage employed for this public torture is eight feet tall. The criminal confined therein straddles a sharp blade. His feet are shackled, and he must keep his legs straightened to avoid being wounded by the blade. A table is placed within his reach containing provisions and drinks to quench his thirst, but a guard is there night and day to prevent him from touching them. When the victim's forces start to become depleted he falls on the edge of the blade, which inflicts deep and cruel wounds upon him. Provoked by the pain, the wretch straightens himself, only to again fall down on the cutting blade, wounding himself horribly. This torture lasts three or four days.[1]

In this type of apparatus, the convict dies because he resists; because he tries, desperately, to escape death.* The atrocity of the torture lies in the way it transforms every movement by the body to protect itself from pain into a new agony. The slightest reflex of preservation becomes the impetus for the most unbearable suffering: this is what defines such modes of annihilation. What is remarkable is not the novelty of the torture, over which the modern colonial system certainly had no monopoly. The scene, along with the rhetorical device aimed at exhibiting its horror, resonates with another torture narrative, namely, the story of Damiens as described by Michel Foucault at the outset of *Discipline and Punish*. However, the two cases are entirely different.[2] As Foucault shows, the wounds inflicted on Damiens' body do not address the convict in his individuality, but aim instead to restore the all-powerful will of the sovereign and the subjugation of the community, which the crime had jeopardised. Mutilations by pliers and shears, scalding hot lead, boiling oil and molten wax, and the eventual dismemberment by horse ... throughout this entire atrocious ordeal, Damiens remains tied up, and there is nothing to suggest that he 'could' do anything. In other words, minimal as it may have been, his power [*puissance*] was in no way taken into account, precisely because it did not count.[3] If Damien's body is reduced to nothingness, this is because it is already nothing other than a theatre for staging the cohesion of a vengeful community ritualising the sovereignty of its king. What is thus exhibited is a complete absence of power, the better to express the magnificence of an absolutely sovereign power.

In the case of the torture of the iron cage, the onlooking public is still present. However, there is something else happening in the exposition of the torture victim's suffering. The technique appears to target the subject's capacity to (re)act, the better to dominate it. The repressive apparatus exhibits and excites the bodily reactions and vital reflexes of the condemned, constituting them as that which defines both the power [*puissance*] *and* the weakness of the subject. Repressive authority is no longer obliged to cast the powers that oppose it as absolutely impotent in order to affirm itself. On the contrary, the more this subjective power stages its repeated and desperate efforts to survive, the more repressive authority succeeds in governing it, while disappearing behind the passive and puppet-like figure of the hangman. This deadly government of the body is carried out with such an economy

---

* Editors' note: This article is a translation of the prologue, 'Ce que peut un corps', to Elsa Dorlin's book *Se Défendre: Une Philosophie de la violence* (Paris: La Découverte, 2017), 5–17. Subsequent chapters of the book address episodes in the history that determined which groups of people were authorised to bear weapons or defend themselves and which were constructed as defenceless, from the Early Modern period up to the present. The book also outlines a genealogy of 'self-defence', going back to techniques developed by black panthers or in the Warsow ghetto and exploring the history of feminist ju-jitsu and Krav maga. Kieran Aarons' full translation of the book is forthcoming from Verso in 2021. We have added a couple of subheadings and some paragraph breaks to the original text.

of means that the condemned appears to perish by his own hand alone. Everything has been worked out so that he will resist the sharp blade that threatens to fatally mutilate him: he must stand up straight in his stirrups, inside his cage.

In this way, the apparatus leads one to suppose that his life depends upon his strength, not only muscular and physical, but also 'mental': he must strain to stay alive, if he does not wish to suffer worse or die. At the same time, the sole purpose of this technology of torture is to destroy him, but in such a fashion that *the more he defends himself, the worse he will suffer*. The cruel comedy of the food placed around him attests to the fact that the torture plays precisely on the efficacy of vital movements so as to control them totally, the better to annihilate them. Just as his exhaustion will cause him to collapse onto the edge of the blade, his unbearable need to eat and drink will likewise become fatal to him. In addition, the initial impact point on his body will almost certainly be his genitals. It is almost as if power's work of encoding gender reaches its final completion here, given that the genitals, far more than any other part of the body, have become the ultimate site in which the subject's power of action lurks. When we defend them, we defend *ourselves*. That the apparatus strikes them first, indicates that it seeks to destroy that by which the subject – not the legal subject, but the *capable* subject – was instituted.

This murderous apparatus regards those subjected to it as *capable of doing something,* and it takes up, stimulates and solicits these vital impulses in their slightest forms so as to interpellate them as *in*-efficiency, to transmute them into impotence [*impuissance*]. It is a technology of power that produces a *subject* whose power of action has been 'aroused' the better to be seized upon in all its heteronomy. In spite of its being entirely directed toward the preservation of life, this power of action now finds itself reduced to being nothing but a mechanism of death in the service of the colonial penance machine. Here we see how an apparatus of domination can set out to persecute the very movement of *life*, targeting its vital impulse in its most muscular forms. The slightest gesture of defence or protection, the slightest movement aimed at the preservation and conservation of the self is enlisted in the annihilation as such of the body. By targeting the *power of the subject* as it is expressed in his impulse to defend his life and himself, this form of power

thereby constitutes self-defence as the very expression of corporeal life, as what a subject is, as 'what a life is'.[4]

From the iron cage to certain modern and contemporary torture techniques,[5] it is entirely possible to identify a common framework, a repertoire of techniques of power that can be distilled into the following adage: 'the more you defend yourself, the more you'll suffer, the more certain you are to die'. In certain circumstances, for certain bodies, to defend oneself is equivalent to dying from self-exhaustion: to put up a fight is to struggle in vain, to *become defeated*.[6] Such an *unhappy* mechanics of action has implications at the level of political mythology (what will our resistance accomplish?), as well as for our representations of the world and of ourselves (if every effort to save myself only leads to my ruin, what can I do?).

In all likelihood, it is lived experiences of this sort – i.e., not of our true power, but of the doubt thereof, the counter-effects of anxiety and fear engendered by failure and limitation – that ultimately become fundamental, in the sense that they are no longer the concrete experience of an exogenous enemy or threat of danger, however terrible, but rather the mirror refection of an action/reaction in oneself. The originality of such techniques resides precisely in this inexorable labour: the forcible incorporation of a deadly dimension of the *power of the subject* that engenders its own suspension as the sole recourse to stay alive. From this moment on, every affirmation of a movement of self-defence becomes at the same time a threat, a promise of death.

This economy of means, which transforms the body of the condemned (and of the assaulted more generally) into its own hangman, presents an outline of the modern subject in negative relief. It is certainly the case that this subject was defined by its capacity to defend itself (more on this below); however, this capacity for self-defence at the same time became a criterion for distinguishing between those accorded full subjectivity and everyone else. The latter included all those whose capacity for self-defence needed to be either diminished or annihilated, corrupted or delegitimated, and whose defensive bodies were exposed to the risk of death, the better to instil in them their incapacity to defend themselves, their radical *impotence*. Here it is not the body itself, but its power of action that the apparatus seeks both to target and to mobilise. This *defensive governance* exhausts, conserves, cares for, arouses and kills, following a complex mechanism. It defends some, while leaving others defenceless, accord to a carefully graduated metric. Here, to be *defenceless* does not mean that one is 'no longer able to wield political power'; rather, it is to be affected by a power of action that is no longer a polarised movement.[7] There is no greater danger of death than situations like this, wherein our power of action becomes twisted into an autoimmune reflex. It is no longer a question of directly obstructing the action of minorities, as in the case of sovereign repression, nor of simply leaving them to die, defenceless, as in the framework of biopower. It is a matter of *conducting certain subjects to annihilate themselves as subjects*, arousing their power of action so as to provoke them to exercise it at their own peril. It is a matter of producing beings who, the more they defend themselves, the more damaged they become.

Rodney King, 1991

March 3, 1991, Los Angeles. Rodney King, a 26-year-old African American taxi driver, is pursued by three police cruisers and a helicopter over a speeding violation. When he refuses to exit his vehicle, a gun is pointed at his face. A few seconds later, he complies and lays down on the pavement; he is then electrocuted with tasers and, as he tries to get up and protect himself to prevent a police officer from striking him, he is brutally beaten across his face and body by dozens upon dozens of baton-strikes. He is tied up and left unconscious, with his skull and jaw fractured in several places, open lacerations on his mouth and face, and a broken ankle, before an ambulance eventually arrived some minutes later to take him to hospital.

Such a detailed account of Rodney King's lynching is possible thanks to the amateur footage recorded by a witness named George Holliday, who filmed this would-be archive of contemporary domination from his apartment overlooking the freeway.[8] The video aired on television the same night, before circulating quickly around the globe. One year later, a trial began for the four police officers most directly involved in King's beating (there were more than twenty at the scene of the arrest) on charges of excessive use of force. It took place before a jury from which defence lawyers had struck every single African American (there were ten white jurors, one Latin American and one Asian). After nearly two months, the jury opted to acquit the officers. As soon as the verdict was announced, the famous 'L.A. riots' began: six days of urban revolt in which clashes with police and the army – veritable scenes of civil war – would leave 63 dead and more than 2000 demonstrators injured.

Beyond the verdict absolving [*qui blanchit*][9] the police officers, what is truly edifying is the argumentative rationale that succeeded in convincing the jury to exonerate the accused.[10] The strategy of the defence was to convince the jury that the officers were in danger. According to them, they felt aggressed, leaving them no choice but to defend themselves against a 'giant' (King was over 6'2') who struck them even while down on the ground, and seemed to be under the influence of a drug that made him 'insensitive to being hit'. During the second trial some months later, King would state that he was 'just trying to stay alive'.[11] It is this inversion of responsibilities that forms the decisive issue here. During the first trial, lawyers for the police produced and made use of one single and unique piece of evidence, namely, George Holliday's video. The same video that the public regarded precisely as proof of police brutality was called upon as evidence that, on the contrary, it was the police who were 'threatened' by Rodney King. In the courtroom, the video – as seen by the jurors and narrated by the police's legal team – was viewed as the scene of a legitimate defence, attesting to the 'vulnerability' of the police. How can such an interpretive gap be explained? How can the same images engender two versions of events, each with radically distinct victims depending on whether you happen to be a white juror in a courtroom or an *ordinary* spectator?[12]

This is the question posed by Judith Butler in a text composed just days after the announcement of the verdict. Rather than focusing on divergent judgments about 'who is the victim?', Butler draws our attention to the conditions under which certain visions determine individuals to judge that Rodney King is the victim of a lynching, *or* that the police are victims of an aggression. In accordance with the Fanonian perspective she adopts, Butler contends that the proper object of critique is not the logical relation between contradictory opinions, but the framework of intelligibility of perceptions that are themselves never immediate. The video should not be treated as a brute datum, as raw material for interpretation, but as the manifestation of a 'racially saturated field of visibility'.[13] In other words, the racial schematisation of perceptions defines both the production of the perceived and what it means to perceive: 'how do we account for this reversal of gesture and intention in terms of a racial schematisation of the visible field? Is this a specific transvaluation of agency proper to a racialised episteme? And does the possibility of such a reversal call into question whether what is 'seen' is not always already in part a question of what a certain racist episteme produces as the visible?'[14] What must be interrogated is this process by which perceptions come to be socially constructed, produced by a corpus that continues to constrain any possible act of knowledge.[15]

Independently of any posture of distress or expression of vulnerability, Rodney King is seen as the body of an aggressor, nourishing 'the phantasm of white racist aggression'.[16] Through the eyes of the white jurors sitting in the courtroom, Rodney King can *only* be seen as an 'agent of violence'. The same was true of those former male slaves (or descendants of slaves) throughout the entire segregationist period who, unjustly accused of sexual assault, were hunted down in the streets, dragged out of prison cells or their homes, tortured and executed. And the same remains true today for African American youths and young adults, who continue to be beaten and murdered in the streets. This perception of Rodney King as the body of an aggressor is both the condition and the continued effect of a projection of 'white paranoia'.[17]

Images never speak for themselves, particularly in a world in which the representation of violence has become such a central feature of visual culture.[18] At the very beginning of Holliday's video, Rodney King is seen standing with his arms outstretched toward a police officer who is trying to hit him. This protective gesture will be systematically regarded as a threatening posture, a blatant aggression. As Kimberlé Crenshaw and Gary Peller observe, the tactic employed by the police legal team consisted in *making* evidence out of the video by sequencing it into a multitude of stilled images disconnected one from another, thereby generating room for endless interpretations. By proliferating contradictory narratives about a scene that had become fragmented and isolated from the social context in which and through which it took place, police lawyers succeeded in blurring or 'disaggregating' the meaning of the sequence as a whole.[19] Whereas certain citizens (black as well as white) saw in the video overwhelming evidence of police

brutality, lawyers in the courtroom were able to claim that it offered no evidence of any excessive use of force: the officers had made a 'reasonable use' of violence. The moment where the police brutality reaches its peak, at the 81st second of the recording, had become a scene of legitimate defence against a madman.

The police perception of violence does not depend exclusively upon a framework of intelligibility drawn from the past. In fact, this framework is continually updated by material and discursive techniques of power that serve (among other things) to disaffiliate the perception of events from those social and political struggles that serve precisely to embed them in history, while crafting alternative frameworks for the apprehension and intelligibility of lived reality. By defending himself against police violence, Rodney King became indefensible. In other words, the more he defended himself, the more he was beaten, and the more he came to be perceived as the aggressor. This reversal of attack and defence, aggression and protection, within a framework that allows their terms and legitimate agents to be structurally assigned irrespective of the efficacy of their gestures, tends to transform such actions into anthropological markers, delineating a colour line that discriminates against the bodies and social groups that it forms thereby. This dividing line is never solely about distinguishing threatening/aggressive bodies from defensive bodies. Rather, it separates those who are agents (agents of their own defence) from those whose power of action has an entirely negative form, in the sense that they can only ever be agents of 'pure' violence.

Like any African American man arrested by a racist police force, Rodney King is therefore recognised as an agent, but only as an agent of violence, as a violent subject, to the exclusion of any other sort of action. Black men are always made responsible for this sort of violence: they are its cause and effect, its beginning and its end.[20] From this point of view, Rodney King's protective reflexes, the disordered gestures by which he struggled to stay alive (he flaps his arms, staggers, tries to get up, stands on his knees) were described as being under his 'total control' and as evidence of 'dangerous intent',[21] as if violence were the sole voluntary action possible for a black body, effectively excluding the very possibility of legitimate self-defence.[22] To attribute disqualified/disqualifying violent action and an entirely negative power of action exclusively to social groups constituted as 'at risk' also serves an important function, since it prevents police violence from being perceived as an aggression. Since bodies that have been made into minorities represent a threat, since they are a source of danger, the agents of every conceivable violence, the violence that is continuously exerted on them (beginning with that of the police and the state) need never appear as the filthy violence that it is: it is secondary, protective, defensive, an always-already legitimate response or reaction.

In the case of the torture in the iron cage, I have shown how targeting a body's power of action permits a certain technology of power to transform it into impotence (the more we struggle to escape suffering, the more wounded we become), with the result that the subject's defensive efforts to survive insidiously become the very mechanism of his negation. Self-defence is thus rendered irremediably impractical for the resisting body. In the case of Rodney King, another element also came into view. Here it is no longer simply about the power of action, but interpellation, the moral and political qualification whereby 'subjects of right' – or better, subjects with the right to defend themselves – come to be recognised. Rodney King cannot be perceived as a body defending itself; he is seen *a priori* as an agent of violence. The very possibility of defending oneself is the exclusive privilege of a dominant minority. In the case of the lynching of Rodney King, the state (through the intermediary of its armed representatives) is not regarded as violent but as reacting to violence: *it defends itself against violence*. On the other hand, for Rodney King, as for every other body victimised by this rhetoric of self-defence, the more he defended himself, the more indefensible he becomes.

Defenceless and indefensible

Millet de la Girardière could have defended himself but, by defending himself, he became defenceless. Rodney King defended himself but, by defending himself, he became indefensible. These two logics of subjection, which converge upon the same unhappy subjectivation, make up the principal concern of my book, *Self-Defence*, in the face of a technology of power that has never relied so heavily on such defensive logic to ensure its own perpetuation.

With this point of departure, we may begin to trace the outline of a certain apparatus of power, which I will call the defensive apparatus. How does it function? By targeting anything that expresses a force, a vital impulse, a movement polarised to defend itself, and then (for certain people) either marking out its trajectory and promoting its deployment through frameworks of legitimation, or else (for others) obstructing its realisation, its very possibility, by making its vital impulse uninhabitable and faltering, or dangerous and threatening, for oneself and others alike.

This double-edged defensive apparatus traces a line of demarcation between subjects who deserve to be defended and to defend themselves, and bodies driven back onto defensive tactics. For these vulnerable and violable bodies, only bare-knuckled subjectivities remain. Kept in check through violence, they live or survive only to the extent that they manage to equip themselves with defensive tactics. These subaltern practices constitute what I call self-defence [*autodéfense*] in the proper sense of the term, by contrast with the juridical concept of legitimate defence [*légitime défense*]. Unlike the latter, self-defence paradoxically has no subject – by which I mean that the subject it defends does not pre-exist this movement that resists the violence that targets it. In this sense, self-defence is part of what I propose to call the 'martial ethics of the self'.

Tracing this system back to its colonial origins makes it possible to question the supposedly monopolistic capture of violence by states laying claim to the legitimate use of physical force. Instead of a tendency towards monopoly, we may hypothesise an imperial economy of violence that paradoxically defends individuals who have always already been recognised as legitimate defenders of themselves. This economy maintains the legitimacy of the use of physical force for certain subjects, granting them powers of conservation and jurisdiction (vigilantism), or what amounts to a license to kill.

However, what is at issue is not merely the distinction, fundamental though it may be, between 'defended subjects' and 'defenceless subjects', between subjects who may defend themselves legitimately and those for whom this has been deemed illegitimate (and who are thereby rendered indefensible). There is an even more subtle threshold. For we must add that this government of the body intervenes at the level of the musculature itself. There is an art of governance that takes as its objects nerve impulses, muscular contractions, tensions of the kinaesthetic body and the discharge of hormonal fluids. It operates upon whatever excites or inhibits it, whatever allows it to act or counteracts it, restrains it or provokes it, reassures it or makes it tremble, whatever determines it to strike or not strike.

To begin from muscle rather than law: this is certain to change the way in which violence has come to be problematised by political thought. The focus of *Se Défendre* is on moments of the passage to defensive violence, moments that I did not feel could be rendered intelligible by subjecting them to a political and moral analysis centred around questions of legitimacy. At each of these moments, the stakes of the passage to defensive violence are nothing other than life itself: to not be shot down, first and foremost. Physical violence is thus understood here as vital necessity, as a praxis of resistance.

The history of self-defence is a polarised adventure marked by the continuous opposition of two antagonistic expressions of the defence of the 'self'. On the one hand, there is the dominant juridico-political tradition of legitimate defence, articulated to a myriad of practices of power with various modes of brutality. On the other hand, there is the submerged history of a 'martial ethics of self' that has traversed both political movements and contemporary counter-conducts, testifying to a surprising continuity of defensive resistance that has invested them with strength.

I propose to map out a constellational history of self-defence. My itinerary was assembled not by rounding up the most illustrative examples, but by exploring the memory of struggles for which the dominated body constitutes the principal archive: the syncretic knowledge and cultures of slave self-defence, feminist self-defence practices, the fighting techniques developed in eastern Europe by Jewish organisations against pogroms, etc.

By opening this archive, which includes many other stories as well, my aim is not to produce a work of history, but to practice a labour of genealogy. In our darkening sky, this constellation sparkles with echoes, addresses, testimonies and citational relations that connect its different points of light in a tenuous and subjective way. The major texts that form the philosophical backbone of the Black Panther Party for Self Defense pay homage to the insurgents of the Warsaw ghetto; queer self-defence patrols are in a citational relationship with black self-defence movements; the jiu-jitsu practiced by English internationalist anarchist suffragists was accessible to them in part due to an imperial policy for capturing the wisdom and know-how of the colonised, through their disarmament.

My own history and bodily experience served as the prism through which I listened, saw and read this archive. My theoretical and political culture has instilled in me a foundational idea, namely, that relations of power *in situ* can never fully depend upon confrontational encounters that are already collective, but everywhere involve lived experiences of domination transpiring in the intimacy of bedrooms, in subway station lobbies, beneath the apparent tranquillity of family reunions, etc. In other words, for some, the question of defence does not disappear when the moment of overt political mobilisation ends, but is part of a continuous experience, a phenomenology of violence. This feminist approach seizes upon something in the fabric of power relations that was traditionally construed as being either pre- or extra-political. Having made this shift, I intend to work not at the scale of constituted political subjects, but with the politicisation of subjectivities: in everyday life, in the intimacy of the enraged affects trapped within us, in the solitude of lived experiences of violence, where we continuously practice a nameless self-defence. From one day to the next, what does violence do to our lives, to our bodies, to our muscles? And what can our bodies both do and not do, in and through this violence?

Translated by Kieran Aarons

Elsa Dorlin teaches political and social philosophy at the University of Paris 8. Along with Se défendre: une philosophie de la violence *(2017), her books include* Sexe, genre et sexualités: introduction à la théorie féministe *(2008) and* La Matrice de la race: généalogie sexuelle et coloniale de la nation française *(2006).*

Notes

1. Joseph Elzéar Morénas, *Précis historique de la traite des Noirs et de l'esclavage colonial* (Paris: Firmin Didot, 1828), 251–252.

2. Michel Foucault, *Discipline and Punish*, trans. Alan Sheridan (New York: Vintage Books, 1977).

3. [Translator's note: The author frequently exploits the difference between the French term *puissance*, or 'power' in the sense of capacity, force, strength, or potential, and *pouvoir*, or 'power' understood as authority, influence, juridical right, and domination. With the exception of a small number of instances indicated with square brackets, the term *puissance* is always employed in a qualified form, as 'power of action' [*puissance d'agir*] or 'vital impulse' [*élan de puissance*]; where the term 'power' appears without further qualification, it translates *pouvoir*.]

4. Judith Butler, *Frames of War: When is Life Grievable?* (London and New York: Verso, 2009). [Translator's note: The citation refers to the French title of the book, which was translated as *Ce qui fait une vie. Essai sur la violence, la guerre et le deuil*.]

5. See the introduction by Grégoire Chamayou, in *Kubark: Le Manuel secret de manipulation mentale et de torture psychologique de la CIA* (Paris: Éditions Zones, 2012).

6. [Translator's note: The author here plays off a continuity of terms that cannot be reproduced in English: *se battre, c'est se débattre vainement, c'est être battu.e.*]

7. When he defines life, Georges Canguilhem notes that, 'far from being indifferent to the conditions that it confronts, life is that which fills out the concept of polarity in its true sense: life *is* polarity, or a polarised activity'. See Georges Canguilhem, *The Normal and the Pathological*, trans. Carolyn Fawcett (Boston: Reidel, 1978), 70–71.

8. The video is 9 minutes 20 seconds long. It is available here: https://www.youtube.com/watch?v=sb1WywIpUtY (Accessed 07.22.2019).

9. [Translator's note: ...*qui blanchit à proprement parler*: in French, the word *blanchir* means to 'clear of suspicion', but also more literally, 'to whiten', 'bleach', or 'launder'.]

10. A second trial took place in February of 1993 in Federal civil rights court, which ultimately sentenced two police officers im-plicated in the lynching to 32 months of prison time (the other two were acquitted again). During the trial, the judges granted that the police officers had acted within the legal scope of their duties during the first few minutes of the arrest, arguing that the first wave of beatings was justified by King's recalcitrant attitude. It was only on account of the 'useless' beatings that followed that the two were convicted.

11. See Seth Mydans, *The New York Times*, March 10, 1993.

12. I am using this expression deliberately, since George Holliday is white; in reality, it would be necessary to enter into detailed analysis of the mobilisation of national and international 'opinion' around the Rodney King case. What interests me here is the performative dimension of racial identity produced, among other things, by the courtroom and the temporality of the trial.

13. Judith Butler, 'Endangered/Endangering: Schematic Racism and White Paranoia', in *Reading Rodney King/Reading Urban Uprising*, ed. Robert Gooding-Williams (New York: Routledge, 1993), 15.

14. Butler, 'Endandered/Endangering', 16.

15. For example, in a study published in the *Journal of Health and Social Behavior* in 2005, the authors attempt to demonstrate on the basis of clinical research that African Americans feel more anger than Whites, and have fewer resources to manage their emotions in 'socially acceptable' ways. See J. Beth Mabry and K. Jill Kiekolt, 'Anger in Black and White: Race, Alienation, and Anger', *Journal of Health and Social Behavior* 46:1 (2005), 85–101. Such publications are part of a broader and continuously renewed production of racist knowledge, particularly in psychopathology, psychology and psychosociology. I would like to thank Paul Preciado for drawing my attention to this reference.

16. Butler, 'Endangered/Endangering', 20.

17. Ibid., 16.

18. The ontological status of evidence in the judicial system is a narrative construction. This becomes only more true wherever it is a question of visual evidence being considered as the recording of a fact. However, it is never an immediate truth that we grasp therein, but rather the manifestation of what is perceived as visible, sayable and therefore legitimate to constitute proof. The judicial field only offers a particularly rich terrain of investigation on which to grasp such gnoseological constructions of perception (schematisations) through socio-historical definitions. This hermeneutics is less about constructing evidence piece by piece than it is about deciding what counts as legally 'objective' evidence. This process is thus concealed by its claim to be guided solely by the 'naked truth' of facts. See Kimberlé Crenshaw and Gary Peller, 'Reel Time/Real Justice' in *Reading Rodney King/Reading Urban Uprising*, ed. Gooding-Williams, 56–70.

19. Crenshaw and Peller, 'Reel Time/Real Justice', 61. The authors describe a narrative technique of 'disaggregation'.

20. Butler, 'Endangered/Endangering', 20.

21. These were the terms used by the police officers during their hearings at the first trial.

22. 'Attributing violence to the object of violence is part of the very mechanism that recapitulates violence, and that makes the jury's 'seeing' into a complicity with that police violence.' Butler, 'Endangered/Endangering', 20.

The Centre for the Study of Democracy
and the Institute for Modern and Contemporary Culture present

French Politics

A Neighbour's "History of the Present"

26 September 2019
Introduction by Éric Fassin
University Paris 8 Vincennes Saint-Denis/LEGS

1. An Authoritarian Spiral in France?

10 October 2019	14 November 2019	4 December 2019 (Wed)
Sophie Wahnich	**Ninon Grangé**	**Fabien Jobard**
CNRS/TRAM	University Paris 8/LLCP	CNRS/CESDIP

2. French Universalism vs. Alien Identities?

30 January 2020	13 February 2020	March 2020 (TBC)
Silyane Larcher	**Sébastien Chauvin**	**Norman Ajari**
CNRS/IRIS	University of Lausanne/CEG	University Toulouse 2/ERRAPHIS

3. Can France Think of Itself as Postcolonial?

April 2020 (TBC)	11 June 2020
Elsa Dorlin	**Nacira Guénif-Souilamas**
University Paris 8	University Paris 8 /CEFEG

Once a month, on Thursdays, 5.30-7pm
Free events, open to all, but booking is
necessary
https://www.eventbrite.co.uk/e/seminar-series-french-politics-a-neighbours-history-of-the-present-tickets-63993628666

University of Westminster
309 Regent Street
W1B 2HW London

Contact: Emmanuel Jouai
e.jouai[a]my.westminster.ac.uk

With kind support from the French Embassy in the UK - Higher Education Research and Innovation Department (in association with "The Borders of Identity" seminar series supported by the Fonds d'Alembert 2019) and the Political Studies Association.

Hegel's racism for radicals

Rei Terada

Contemporary societies are not the first to confuse their desires not to be racist with their desires to minimise the scope of race. A few years ago, for instance, the University of California Humanities Research Institute summer workshop, 'Archives of the Non-Racial' (2014), noted that

> by the nineteenth century, the 'non-racial' emerged as an intellectual, political, and ethical category, assuming a variety of interpretations. Indexed to different intellectual, social, and political contexts, at times the non-racial has stood for the idea of 'a shared human nature.' At others, it has gestured toward the idea of 'abolition.' Sometimes it has meant the erasure of 'difference' and its substitution by 'sameness' alongside the commitment to a set of universal moral principles.[1]

This institutional description presents the 'non-racial' as divided into good, bad and neutral-sounding forms. At best, the 'non-racial' belongs to a vision of social relations beyond abolition; at worst, it is postracial in the cynical sense, a vision of sameness that disavows difference and, with it, racism.

Racial thinking, by contrast, is not ordinarily accorded a similar ambiguity and proximity; being unwelcome, it is presumed to belong to others, who are tasked with moving on from it. For oneself, it is an object of critique only. This presumption is held in common by the radical vision of heterogeneous social relations and the liberal vision of placid human sameness.

In this essay I will argue, in conversation with ongoing work in black studies, that this idea that racial thinking merely belongs to others is contradictory, that it is inherent to any deployment of the category of the 'non-racial', that it is characteristic of both liberalism *and* radicalism, and, further, that it is embedded deep in the philosophical sources of post-Enlightenment politics. In those sources racially subordinated people, especially black people, are called on to abjure a racial thinking that operates as a foil for proper political thought. This pattern continues today, as works from Paul Gilroy to Asad Haider exemplify; for Gilroy, racial thinking is the other of 'the goal of authentic democracy', while for Haider, it divides revolutionary black radicalism from 'expressions of racial ideology'.[2] Rather than being only a post-civil rights era symptom,[3] however, I want to argue that postraciality for this purpose of shoring up an 'authentic' politics has itself been with us for a long time: it arose alongside florid scientific racism and complements it.

The arrival of the 'non-racial' shows that the procedure of ascribing the 'non-racial' can itself only be postracial. It is postracial in two senses: in the pejorative sense, indicating the rhetorical erasure of an actually existing and persisting racial violence; and *postracial in a logical sense*, in that 'non-raciality' must carry assumptions about what 'race' is, and a responsibility for deciding what it looks like, in order to testify to its absence. In the postracial view, those assumptions always belong to other people, but such ascription does not hold up under examination. Rather, the idea that racial thinking is only something that comes from outside is part of the problem.

Postraciality depends on the availability of the concept of non-raciality, while the concept of non-raciality depends on the prior existence and identifiability of race. Otherwise, there's no way to tell the racial from the 'non-racial'. Postracial thinking exists wherever 'non-racial', in other words, postracial, in other words, conventionally racialising, categories are in use. In what follows, I'll explore this question within Hegel, taking the most radical interpretation of Hegel to be foundational for post-enlightenment politics. I will consider Hegel's criticism of both India and Africa for their supposed racialism; as we'll see the logic throughout is anti-black.

Radical negativity and the 'racial thinking' of others

As work in black studies has demonstrated, the major works of Kant and Hegel set the current terms of race.[4] They do so not only by playing race against a falsely transparent humanity, but by constructing what counts as real. One effect among many is that the real becomes aligned with the non-racial. In Hegel, historical relation functions as a medium of reality that entails that properly historical societies appear as 'non-racial' in their self-understanding, while non-historical societies, located in the medium of reality but without opening themselves to it, now appear as 'racial' in their self-understanding. A crucial characteristic that people now have, in this view, one that is symptomatic of their relation to historical reality, is their supposed practice of raciality and/or their incapacity to desire to be non-racial. Assigning non-raciality to historicity reassigns racial characteristics elsewhere – in fact, exactly where they are in systems of scientific racism, and to the same degrees. It also continues to be the case that blackness is placed inside and outside ethnic categories, as a kind of exemplary pure raciality that is more and less than Africanness. As we will see, Hegel attributes racialisation primarily to racialised people themselves. This line of thought terminates in the *political priority* of the non-racial.

These implications bear upon the radical, negative, non-teleological, 'left' Hegel specifically, and are for that reason especially pertinent as a matter for radical self-examination. The problem with the critical consensus that Hegel's dialectical subtlety triggers 'right' and 'left' interpretations is that left Hegelians often assume that anti-Hegelians are objecting to the rightist Hegel and that their own task is therefore to explain the resources that Hegel still offers to the left. This leaves no room for left criticism of left Hegelianism, and more to the point, threatens to close the logical space for racism in radical thought. At the most, as modelled by postracialism, radical thought finds left racism in other leftists making mistakes of conceptual exclusion. My goal here isn't to rehearse right/left arguments, and so I start with the following understandings:

(1) Hegel is radically historical rather than dogmatic. He is opposed to nature and essence, even as he preserves the extent to which communities may require some ideas of nature and essence. Further, his vision of history is neither progressive nor simply teleological, because

(2) Hegelian subjectivity and historicity centre self-division, aporia, disarticulation and negativity, and are radically non-identitarian;

(3) Hegel promotes radical openness to history as a structural necessity of relation; relation and speculation should be understood as the media of openness, and themselves incomplete and open;

(4) the speculative proposition is the container of relation in flux, and the model for all Hegelian propositions;

(5) relation in Hegel is grounded in non-relation, the Absolute of the system, and this Absolute is absolutely the opposite of the 'given.'

It is *in these philosophical choices* that I find Hegel's specific contribution to racial capitalism. They matter particularly much because they continue to characterise the preferences of left political theory. Despite their inadequacies, I cannot help preserving the ambiguity of the terms 'progressive', 'left' and 'radical' for the time being, not only because it is as difficult to say whether Hegel was radical or liberal as it is to say whether he was right or left, but because the structure of (post)racial thinking consolidated in Enlightenment philosophy affects the range of 'progressive' views from liberal to radical. I am concerned to make the point that radicals cannot distinguish themselves from liberals in this regard. The racism of radical circles is not a matter of inconsistency, but of the values affirmed above, which are often shared by positions that agree on little else.

Prosaic philosophical settings chosen by Hegel, Kant and others make it difficult to perceive the operation of race in radical circles; radical enlightenment philosophy integrally cultivates and encourages these difficulties. When instead we grasp that 'racial thinking' is not only used to subordinate others in open racism, but also projected, in a way that is itself racist, in order to cast them as *less political,* we may see more clearly that the set of radical Hegelian values can't be relied on to ensure its own enlightenment. Efforts to devote radical politics to anti-racism in general are likely to be recuperated into the idea that this will make anti-racism more properly political in comparison to the practice of other groups who are still stuck in racial thinking and its errors of ex-

clusion. Since such a radical stance is perfectly consistent with anti-blackness, a specific address to anti-blackness needs to become a radical platform in its own right.

Hegel's colonial opening

The frantic anti-blackness of Hegel's depiction of sub-Saharan Africa in *Lectures on the Philosophy of World History* is well-known. Building on that knowledge, we might explore Hegel's curious use of postracial ideals of relation there and in the less-discussed *Philosophy of Religion*. If Africa is 'savage', after all, it is because 'Africa proper' is 'self-enclosed'.[5] According to Hegel, North Africa, being coastal and oriented toward Europe, 'is not independent on its own account. ... Spain is said to belong to Africa. But it is just as correct to say that this part of Africa belongs to Europe.' Egypt, meanwhile, is riparian and associates with the Mediterranean.[6] Coastal rims, blue states of openness, 'benefit from the connecting aspect

of the sea'; indeed, water 'makes communication possible', 'enlivens' 'relations to the external world ... and for the ties of the soil and the limited circles of civil life with its pleasures and desires, it substitutes the element of fluidity, danger, and destruction.'[7] Quite explicitly, Hegel treats the sea as an embodiment of global relation as 'medium':

> through this supreme medium of communication, it also creates trading links between distant countries, a legal [*rechtlichen*] relationship which gives rise to contracts; and at the same time, such trade [*Verkehr*] is the greatest educational asset [*Bildungsmittel*], and the source from which commerce derives its world-historical significance.[8]

Offering humans access to one another, ocean channels accelerate the projects of 'all great and enterprising nations' and so, we can add in this mercantile context, enhances the values of relation and access themselves as properties of anything.[9] Thus, although North Africa

13

remains African because it does not yet 'stand on its own two feet', Hegel opines that it has access to influences that are likely to allow it to do so, as previous civilisations also did before they became historical.[10] Sub-Saharan Africa, in contrast, has no such access to relation, not even to other parts of Africa, such that the continent as a whole suffers from poor interrelation between its geographical regions. African sparsity of relation is explicitly the obverse of Europe's frustrated access to Africa: 'the Europeans … have not yet penetrated into the highland, where riches are to be found in the most inaccessible conditions.'[11] Such is Africa's geographical destiny as a 'highland' region.

If Hegel's geographical materialism predicts cultural backwardness for Africa, his theory of historical realisation, and particularly its emphasis on openness and negativity, predicts his geographical materialism. In order for Hegel's account of Africa to be what it is, it has to be able to indict African societies for being racial. That is, 'racial' practices are already a benchmark of the non-political. The key element of African societies' inferiority is their self-enclosure and 'government … patriarchal in character', by which Hegel means their reliance on kinship structures, or what he assumes are kinship structures.[12] Self-enclosure and kinship-centredness collapse into one: Hegel's causal logic here is that African societies, having no access to the foreign influences that would expand their scope, fall back into themselves and reproduce the prehistoric family unit.[13] Insofar as kinship structures are blood ties (Hegel does not explore the possibility of a difference between the two), Hegel's African societies are cast as racial in the way that later political science would criticise them for being 'tribal'. The series abstract-non-racial-open and familial-racial-closed renews the model of race that it finds in travel literature, not despite but through its greater abstraction.

Hegel's preference for open relationality, and use of it to reproduce racist accounts of Africans, is writ large in his philosophy altogether. Uncannily, it locates racial thinking in general in order to embody it in blackness specifically. The uncanniness is lost if Hegel is seen instead as conflicted or as merely excluding Africa. What if, instead, the anti-blackness of Hegel's imagination and enclosure of sub-Saharan Africa requires his postracialism? Hegel mentions, for example, that 'the original organisation that created social distinctions' in India 'immediately became set in stone as natural determinations (the castes).' In Hegel's account of India, 'distinctions imposed by nature' trap consciousness of social relations at the first available moment, the moment that locates value in natural origin. Such periods of entrapment, he explains, may occur whenever 'peoples may have had a long life without a state before they finally reach their destination.'[14]

In Hegel's account of Africa, by contrast, no impulse ever arises to make what is happening into a conscious social system, so that 'even the family ethos is lacking in strength.'[15] What Hegel imagines to precede incipient social organisation is a reproductive primal horde that, if it were to be systematised, would generate a natural order, as in the example of Hegel's imagination of caste; but Hegel's sub-Saharan Africa does not even get that far. These imaginations function as justifications for colonisation. Yet, Hegel's disapproval of 'natural' orders is taken to be something he gets right and as evidence for the extent to which he is not racist. As Joseph McCarney writes, defending Hegel from Robert Bernasconi's explanations of his racism, 'history is precisely, in one aspect at least, the escape of spirit from nature, its overcoming of all natural determinants such as common descent or blood relationship.'[16]

What is usually discussed as Hegel's development of abstract polity out of negativity, then, calls for the development of systems that promote access to racialized bodies, first in the name of stimulation and ultimately in the name of the objectively political. Philosophical relation after Hegel is not just interaction, but interaction valued in this way that bridges humanism and posthumanism (and therefore their opposed lines of left politics). A value on 'disaccustoming'[17] suggests customary racial locations as surely as myths of modernity suggest locations of the primitive, and representations of custom that one finds in contemporary political discourse are not conceivable outside it.[18]

Relation as coercion

In the informal pedagogy of the *Lectures on the Philosophy of World History*, which, readers are constantly reminded, are university lectures that were never published, prescribed relationality can take on the trivial appeal of breadth requirements. Relation must be affirmed in order to cultivate human potential.[19] But although the register and sophistication of arguments changes from text to lecture (e.g., from *Logic* to *World History*), Hegel's posthumanist and humanist ideas of relation are shaped by his radical negativity. Diverging political uses of Hegel are made possible by this speculative destabilisation of identity. At the same time, negativity generates the historical subject and, along with it, the nonhistorical actor, as nonraciality advances by saddling nonhistorical societies with racial practices whose 'depth' appears as the ambiguity of blackness. Negativity is especially able to legitimate the historical subject because the historical subject is shattered in it, displaying the objectivity of historical process. Not primarily a recognition of an other, it is more fundamentally a capacity to be dismembered, and therefore formed, by the Absolute. This capacity, it turns out, cannot be taken for granted. The negativity of the historical life that ensues affords a position from which to dismiss nonhistorical life.

From this perspective, the well-known stages of Hegel's argument appear as follows. As *Lectures on the Philosophy of Religion* points out, at first relation is both built on top of 'natural or necessary connection' and qualitatively distinct from it.[20] Even 'natural organisms' split internally before they 'engage with other things and thereby undergo a process of change.'[21] So, as mentioned above, for Hegel Indian society recognises natural or necessary connection only; relations can occur and be helpful for development, but they will remain incomplete. 'The precocious development of language and the progress and diffusion of nations [may] have acquired their significance and interest for concrete reasons, partly in so far as the nations in question have had contact with other states, and partly as they have begun to form constitutions of their own',[22] but no amount of linguistic and mercantile finesse will make them historical if they fail to be disturbed by non-relation that alienates the self. In qualitative distinction, something 'must be perceived as a non-given, something that holds itself back, something "foreign" to which spirit entertains no "positive" relation, and that means an absence of any determinate relation of positing: no positing relation at all. The relation to the "natural" is thus at first the aporetic relation to the relationless.'[23] Action begins with the non-given; what happens there is historically real, indeed the real movement of history. Equally crucially, the historical subject has to discover and internalise the disarticulation of non-relation: 'What has been reflection on our part must arise in the mind of the subject of this discipline [of the world] in the form of a consciousness that in himself he is miserable and null.'[24]

Non-relation, taken into the self as its negativity, connects the humanistic Hegel of organic growth to the radically anti-identitarian Hegel, the *Lectures* to the *Logic*. Internalised disturbance never stops and remains the live element of subsequent relationality and so of history. Exposure to non-relation, by definition an 'education' or 'discipline' in the historical real, a continuous disarticulation of the subject, is singularly catalytic, as its exposition in the vocabulary of the Absolute indicates. If Absolute non-relation itself lies beyond value, alienation by non-relation, with its monopoly on creating historical consciousness, is of maximal value. Since it exists only through contact with the "foreign" to which spirit entertains no "positive" relation', non-relation must be accessible;[25] such contact must be accessible. Ideally, it is available at any moment whatever. Yet, it is clear enough in Hegel's comparative history that not just any perceiver can actually perceive it. Not scarce as opportunity, still 'feel[ing oneself] as the negation of [one]self' remains precious, like 'thinking' in Heidegger and Arendt.[26] Non-relation that is not received as laceration of self isn't really received at all. The non-given mustn't be missed, it can't not be concerning, it can't be understood (which must be understood), and it can't be left entirely alone.[27] When the non-given is so received, spirit has started to work on 'the relation to the "natural"'.[28]

Here, non-relation taken up as such makes access possible to demand because the genuine abrasion of exposure to the Absolute pays for it. Immediately, the authenticity of non-relation is difficult to separate from the acquired taste for non-relation. A radically anti-identitarian movement of subjective undoing often walks in the tracks of subject-building, as Gayatri Spivak pointed out in her criticism of Deleuze in 1988.[29] They are two kinds of 'training',[30] humanist and posthumanist; yet also not even two, because while it's clear what posthumanists are fleeing, it's not clear where they can go. Contemporary criticism flees the identitarian moment of substituting an object of representation for the anorientation of non-relation – and why not? For example, it's problematic that Hegel substitutes pulp fiction images of Africa for something that he states he cannot comprehend ('because it is so totally different from our own culture, and so remote and alien in relation to our own mode of consciousness').[31] It can seem obviously better for Hegel to stay in non-relation, and in his famous formulations Hegel calls precisely for staying with the negative, which renews itself at every moment. Yet, Hegel also makes the 'openness' of the negative into the measure of authentic development *and then uses it to generate racist images of Africans who 'lack' it.*

Do we want to say here that Hegel is insincere, that he doesn't 'really' open up to non-relation, at least as soon as sub-Saharan Africa enters the picture? Or that there is a moment when insight does not yet turn into use, and that it might be extended indefinitely? Or can we say, more inconveniently, that there is a problem altogether with valuing exposure to non-relation in the way he does – namely, by making the perception of it criterial to reality as such, reality in general, however negatively understood? Can a measure of reality *not* be a weapon? For Hegel's conclusion is literally that, be-

cause within their own societies Africans supposedly do not experience the dismemberment of alienation, and rather encounter non-relation everywhere *but without being disturbed by it,* so then they remain at an irrational stage of racialism. This reasoning is more than a problem in Hegel and more than a matter of Eurocentrism, or of stereotypes. It's a specifically postracial Enlightenment technology that imputes racism elsewhere to demand colonial access (which figures as non-racial because it demands opening) to, and disposition over, the racial human. For radical philosophy, racism is *a priori* elsewhere. That's why the defence of racial hierarchisation by 'mention' – the criteria are not the radical writer's criteria – *redoubles* the contradiction of attributing raciality by postracial praise of the non-racial. Postracial reasoning as such creates racial elsewheres through complaints about over-valuation of kinship, attachment, and so forth on the part of the others of Europe: their lack of openness, their lack of access to and/or disinterest in relation, their failure to be properly disturbed by non-relation.

As part of the same train of thought, Hegel complains that Africans 'see nothing unbecoming' in being connected to Europeans only through slavery.[32] 'There is no slavery in the state that is rational; slavery is found only where spirit has not yet attained this point.'[33] Quite literally, for Hegel this lack of connection and its ill effect, blackness, is why Africans have to remain enslaved for a while longer.

Hegel's strong endorsement of radical negativity – for him the capacity to be torn within by non-relation, foundational of relational capacity – figures as black Africans' liminality to relation and imperviousness to non-relation. As Donna Jones suggests, this imputed imperviousness to disarticulation (historical subjectivity) entails that 'black people are not thought to die.'[34] Much as they can only merit the full force of slavery by proving to be slaveholders, what Hegel believes is African indifference to foreign stimulation allows them to be the objects of a peculiarly postracial racism. In this sense, I'm not sure that blacks are being correlated to the Real of the system, in which case their non-given status would have the history-authenticating function of non-relation itself. Postracially, they are lined up before the Real along with others, and singularly fail to notice it. Thus, life in sub-Saharan Africa 'consists of a series of contingent happenings and surprises' – by which fact itself, however, Africans in particular cannot, according to Hegel, be surprised.[35]

Hegel's deployment of non-relation and relation to verify the historicity of the globalised world adds a progressive twist to the more common idea, descending from the open admissions policy of Pauline Christianity, that persistent obstacles to relation must be resolved or classified as perverse. 'The Jewish religion', as recent anti-political theology tracks very well, lacks the 'latitudinarian tolerance' of international modernity.[36] As the historian of time Vanessa Ogle points out, nineteenth-century coordinators of time schemes, building global capital, quickly came to perceive 'peoples who do not partake' in the global effort as 'guilty of the crime of opposing it.'[37] Similarly, Christianity not only moralises, but invents particularity by offering itself as freedom from it.[38] Hegel stresses that he judges Judaism only by its lack of commitment to access: 'it is only a limitation in this respect and not a limitation of the religion [as such]'[39] – necessarily, or it would otherwise be Christianity! In this way Judaic 'particularity', Muslim 'excarnation'[40] and the provinciality of certain forms of Christianity are born only together with their vaunted open alternative, the historical real of global relation. The Christian structure of Hegel's anti-identitariansim is as well-known as his hostility to certain actually existing forms of Christianity *for still not being open enough.*

Radical philosophy might now re-read Hegel's history of religion and the nineteenth-century secularisation movements of which it is part for their contribution to a politics with both domestic European and transnational implications. On the domestic front, the 'latitudinarian tolerance' of religion at its best sharpens into '*political* union', passage from nation to people.[41] From here on, 'political' joins the growing list of hierarchising terms, as Cedric Robinson argues.[42] From here on, there are political (modern, historical, ultimately statist) societies and nonpolitical (primitive/past, nonhistorical, national at most) societies, or more accurately, in Robinson's phrase, 'political societies ... and those societies in which the question did not come up.'[43] Hegel aligns them with nonraciality and raciality, the political of course being nonracial. Political consciousness may now order more and less mature fractions of citizenry against the background of groups not sufficiently political, as were the racial societies of the past.

As practiced, the union of political citizens resembles the 'common participation' of the church whose inner relations are regulated by Spirit's 'authority for the truth and for the relation of each individual to the truth.'[44] Translated into political vocabulary, this means that social totality is regulated through each relation to the reality of history as evidenced in the real abstraction of global relations – individual, colonial and transnational. Notably, social relation maintains (sublates) individuality to get to a reflective version of collectivity. 'Independent subjectivity', Hegel specifies, is 'the soil on which grows the True';[45] in a more proverbial formulation, 'only what is free can have its determinations over against it as free.'[46] *Non-relation concerns being; but social relation assumes the existence of individuals*, even if in a local instance specific persons are not at issue. Otherwise, it would be difficult to discriminate communities organised without universal exchange from modern historical societies.

Collectivity is not at issue in my analysis of 'relation', and from Hegel's perspective it is never enough; *Hegel's theory of relation*, a particular theory of collectivity, is the issue, and in it relation accompanies the establishment of the individual unit and vice versa. For its part, the individual degrades into barbarism, Hegel writes, if relation does not occur. Complementarily, every time Hegel specifies that collectivity is not enough, is not yet political, he is acknowledging that societies can have every other kind of coordination and interest and still not be relational, historical or political. If, in view of the tendency for 'authentic' politicality to project the raciality of the insufficiently political, the political loses some lustre, that loss can enhance a radical view of the capacity of other ways of inhabiting well-being and justice. (In the last section, coming up, I'd like to contemplate these unintended acknowledgments.)

At the height of Hegel's secularisation of Christianity, 'the attributes of God are God's relation to the world',[47] and so, understood secularly, the attributes of human beings are social relations in the world in Hegel's by now quite specific sense:

> The way in which one human being is related to another – that is just what is human, that is human nature itself. When we are cognisant of how an object is related [to everything else], then we are cognisant of its very nature. To distinguish between the two [i.e., relation and nature] is to make misguided distinctions that collapse straightaway because they are productions of an understanding that does not know what it is doing.[48]

In a memorable footnote, Hegel compares the entity in relation to an element in chemical reaction: 'the acid is nothing else than the specific mode of its relation to the base – that is the nature of the acid itself.'[49]

The metaphor of acid is a fine articulation of how entities within social relation are not yet congealed into objects, a view that wholly avoids reification. A lot of radical philosophy is linked to this sentence; everyone will like it – I like it. And indeed maintaining a relational view of the world is for Hegel what it is for contemporary theory, a safeguard against reification. In the name of this safety, however, the relation becomes utter, and the entities in relation 'nothing else than' the relation. 'Nothing else' lays all attachments down at the door at considerable expense, so no complaint of easiness-on-the-self can be made. Inside the door, then, is the political, and it

sounds well-earned. But an outside, and exterior interiors, have now come into being. There, myriad phenomena, *which look from within relation like attachments and identities, but may be anything* from agricultural arts to diverting habits, now become evidence of nonpoliticality if they are really important to a community, i.e. if they happen to be preferred to the 'discipline of the world' in any friction between the two. This stigma of nonpoliticality, which can now be aimed, is, as a weapon, a kind of compensation for the historical subject's sacrificial self-nullification. It is a place where the aggression that cannot be turned against history goes. A 'progressive' race discourse begins to appear here, backed up by the clarity and force of belief in the real movement of history. It could never be biologically racist; it could only speak of a nonracial alliance to which anyone could belong, if they only cared to or knew how.

Blank reflections

Obviously, Hegel's view of 'racial' peoples isn't based on familiarity with non-European societies. He assumes that their practices are what his travel reading sounds like to him. Unlike Rousseau, he doesn't consider how his ideas would be evaluated within African and Asian social systems, even as he observes their existence. The situation would not necessarily be improved if he did, and, notably, epistemic critique per se also cannot improve it even as, at the same time, I have not reached the end of it. The end of it is the fact that Hegel's pejorative descriptions of imaginary societies indicate fictive alternative societies that Hegel also imagines in order to reject them. It is still merely studying what Hegel thinks to consider them, at the hallucinatory limit of his language. By gathering ideas that recur across his descriptions of various regions (reflecting the fact that the descriptions never describe actual regions), it is possible to piece together, as fantastic literature, what the societies of *World History* and *Philosophy of Religion* would look like if they were not being characterised as racial for not being statist. The blank pages of history aren't completely blank: this other fictional society is in Hegel's lectures ephemerally, a second apparition reflected in their medium, and so it is also something to consider.

Again and again, Hegel imagines a landscape populated by many and various groups, 'specialised in idiosyncrasies'.[50] The groups are polytheistic as an aggregate and also internally, which makes for a proliferation of values, powers and imaginations.[51] These polytheisms do not strive beyond the situations in which they find themselves, but seem to orient themselves with respect to a local environment and/or community, reflecting places and groups and, sometimes, particular persons. In general people inhabit societies of 'prosaic things' and 'understanding beings'.[52] Hegel supposes that there exists no further ordering of practices; 'hap and genius' account for what there is. These societies may have no arts, or may have merely 'beautiful' ones that stress sensory pleasures. They support themselves in subsistence economies, often nomadic ones; they live day to day without, as we have read, interpreting difficulty and radical contingency as discipline and disarticulation.[53] Their polities, as we have seen, Hegel imagines to be based on kinship structures. In these societies' idea of origin, springs of agency lie in objects. Hegel has read that in India the creation of the world involves 'going forth', meaning that agency lies in beings that go forth rather than in an original force that expresses them.[54] The gods themselves go forth, which implies that they are finite and that the origin is just any place at all.

This situation inhibits the development of value. Everything is 'special', so nothing is.[55] Instead, there is texture and variety to the point of incomprehensibility. Meaningfulness, one might say, exists instead of value. The sun and the mountains possess mentality and volition, and it becomes easy for people to 'relate themselves to the divine'.[56] Of this *accessibility,* which Hegel could be expected to admire if it were *facilitated by relation*, he remarks that it is 'an identity cheaply obtained. In fact it is everywhere.'[57] Crucially, and consistently with all the above, people in such societies 'let themselves be determined from without'[58] – even from without the human. Their authorities are themselves aleatory. Hegel is particularly fascinated by the 'oracles' that, he reads, were used in both Indian and Greek societies to 'allow the decision to be given from without':

> here no articulated answer was given. Their [oracles'] manifestation is some sort of external transformation, metallic forms, the rustling of trees, the blowing of the wind, visions, examinations of sacrificial animals, and contingencies of that sort. People needed such things in order to reach decisions.[59]

The societies he peripherally imagines are contradictorily long-lasting and slow to change and fragile and ephemeral. They may not leave much trace.

The story is problematic logically and politically, even as fiction; it is the negated, not entirely negated other of Hegel's philosophy of history in particular, which is to say that it is primitivist – the inside-out of what he organises, in ambiguous implication. Hegel's incidental images of other societies are able to do no more than raise the question of what he stands against. As such, whether such societies exist is not the main question to ask, but why, regardless of whether they exist or not, Hegel is so concerned to overcome these features of *possible* societies, and, moreover, what it means that the principles of radical history that he develops espouse their subordination as desirable, and their elimination as possible, practices. For this set of *principles* is racialised through and through in terms that black studies scholarship of the last thirty years makes amply available.

It is not simply that the values placed on characteristics of development and 'tradition', consciousness and 'immediacy', and so on down the line could be different, but that terms like tradition and immediacy come to be in the process of consolidating the historical in the first place, and do not function non-circularly at all. That's why translation into any terminology other than Hegel's own – 'prosaic activity' instead of 'immediacy', for example – illuminates the circularity of his assumptions even though there is no non-racist language to use instead. The momentary and unsatisfactory shift is enough to underline, with the disappearance of the non-racial, that it is not hunter-gatherer societies that need to be restored to Hegel's analysis, but the specialness of prescribed relation within it that needs to be understood as rendering *any* other principle and practice impossible, most of all future ones.

It is the vastness and unspecialness of the set {not-relation} that Hegel waves off. Christianity levels it once and for all, according to him. In his story the landscape (this too will have been an invention) in which everything matters is replaced with a thrilling sense that indeed – as exchange value allows – none of it needs to mean anything. Then there come the fatal moves of which capitalism is so fond, in which the fact that, indeed, none of it *needs* to mean anything means that none of it 'really' does mean anything. 'Nowhere are to be found such re-

volutionary utterances as in the Gospels; for everything that had been respected, is treated as a matter of indifference – as worthy of no regard.'[60]

Hegel breathlessly fetishises the radicality of this gesture in and of itself, focused on its power rather than its function. The same ecstasis greets the torn and disarticulated historical subject; its dismemberment is told and retold as a graphic dazzle. The 'severe' edge of the lines that caricature it mimic the 'discipline of the world'.[61] No one is a stranger to the elation of the gesture, and it can be a fine thing – for instance, to put it to work toward the destruction of all, under the name of racial capitalism, that made it possible to eliminate 'nonhistorical' life. But the gesture, and more than gesture, the strategies that align with it cannot but apotheosise historical mentality at the expense of something that then is not properly political. In its recurrent pattern, that something has been: the supposed racialism of 'primitive' societies, then racialised people's interest in racial identity, then critical conviction about the scope of a critique of antiblackness. Because the social forms that appear as essential, provincial, and so on – the contemporary ones as much as the antique – appear so within a set of values controlled by the global open, they are something else apart from that control. What they then are isn't necessarily better, but does have to be otherwise than what they seem to be in the grammar of their totalised antagonist. Like Hegel's unwittingly *possible* snapshots of polytheism and of Africans undisturbed by non-relation, the foils of political authenticity necessarily bear more possibilities, for better and worse, than can be seen from a postracial horizon.

Hegel's philosophy of history has appeal because it makes contingency and negativity into badges of honour, but it may look different if it is thought through that, in doing so, he makes them powerfully normative of political reality for all. Dismemberment's power to legitimate the historical subject is visible in the frequency with which contemporary Hegelians point to it, as though to say that no one would invent a subjectivity based on dismemberment. Rebecca Comay, for example, and Lacanian Marxism generally, endorses historical dislocation as Hegel's way of being 'dead right', and pathologises demurral from its affirmation.[62] These negative forms of historical legitimation, too, are forms of 'free association' that use a functionally postracial horizon to leave race shaped in the usual way in the middle ground. Because anyone can affirm historical dislocation, everyone who is anyone must.

In this way, contemporary historical subjectivity, too, no less than Hegel, selects a political society with a nonracial (postracial; conventionally racialised) horizon, whether or not that horizon is thought of as actually attainable. The complex that Hegel refines is not the only way to organise race in the early nineteenth century or now. It is the *progressive's* way of organising it and a key to radical racism thereafter, for, unlike reaction, radical political thought needs its racism to be postracial.

Rei Terada is Professor of Comparative Literature at the University of California, Irvine.   Her books include Looking Away: Phenomenality and Dissatisfaction, Kant to Adorno *(2009) and* Feeling in Theory: Emotion after the 'Death of the Subject' *(2001).*

The images in this article are by the artist Christina McPhee, and are reproduced here with her kind permission. McPhee's work moves from within a matrix of abstraction, shadowing figures and contingent effects. Her images emulate potential forms of life, in various systems and territories, and in real and imagined ecologies. (See www.christinamcphee.net*) In sequence, the three images are:* Second Person in Motion, *2016, ink, graphite, and watercolor on Rives BFK paper, 57.7 x 76.2 cm;* Persons of Interest, *2016, ink on Takefu washi paper, 63.5 x 96.5 cm;* Play of Context, *2016, ink on Takefu washi paper, 63.5 x 96.5 cm.*

Notes

1. UC Humanities Research Institute, accessed 10 August 2018, http://sect.uchri.org/apply/

2. Paul Gilroy, *Against Race: Imagining Political Culture Beyond the Color Line* (Cambridge, MA: Harvard UP, 2002), 12; Asad Haider, *Mistaken Identity: Race and Class in the Age of Trump* (London: Verso Books, 2018), 21. The rhetorical twist of Haider's recent book is that his exemplary radicals are black, and his main targets, those who take anti-blackness seriously, are multiracial. Only an antiracism that placed its faith in demographics, however, and hence really was identitarian, would be impressed by this. The pattern remains the same: focus on anti-blackness supposedly exemplifies racial thinking, and racial thinking is the foil to the authentically political.

3. See Barnor Hesse, 'Im/plausible deniability: racism's concep-

tual double bind', *Social Identities* 10 (2004), 9–29.

4. On Kant, see especially R.A. Judy, *(Dis)forming the American Canon: African-Arabic Slave Narratives and the Vernacular* (Minneapolis: University of Minnesota Press, 1993); Fred Moten, 'Black Kant (Pronounced Chant): A Theorizing Lecture', Kelly Writers House, 27 February 2007 (http://writing.upenn.edu/pennsound/x/Moten.php#2-27-07) and 'Knowledge of Freedom', *CR: The New Centennial Review* 4 (2004); and Denise Ferreira da Silva, '1 (life) ÷ 0 (blackness) = ∞ − ∞ or ∞ / ∞: On Matter Beyond the Equation of Value', *E-flux* 79 (2017) (unpaginated). Emmanuel Chukwudi Eze's 'The Color of Reason: The Idea of "Race" in Kant's *Anthropology*', in *Postcolonial Philosophy: A Critical Reader* (Oxford: Blackwell, 1997), J. Kameron Carter's discussion in *Race: A Theological Account* (Oxford: Oxford University Press, 2008), and Robert Bernasconi's 'Kant as an Unfamiliar Source of Racism', in *Philosophers on Race: Critical Essays*, ed. Julia K. Ward and Tommy L. Lott (Oxford: Blackwell, 2007), 145–66, show how Kant's construction of the human and of teleology position black people as unable to survive. Eze and Bernasconi, however, preserve the value of "moving beyond" race, Eze explicitly so. See Eze, *Achieving Our Humanity: The Idea of the Postracial Future* (New York: Routledge, 2001).

On Hegel, see especially Denise Ferreira da Silva, *Toward a Global Idea of Race* (Minneapolis: University of Minnesota Press, 2007). Hegel's racialisation is dialectical whereas Kant's is transcendental, and inclusive whereas Kant's emphasises limits. Kant's contribution ends in the 'void', absolutely alien space reserved to the noumenal; Hegel begins by confronting Absolute non-relation to set in motion a concrete, historically produced postracial reality, behind which (self-)racialised peoples lag. The Kant/Hegel opposition is a lose/lose situation. Hegel's role in the double bind can be seen in dialectics' treatment of its objects of analysis as racial *or not*. Although my focus in these pages is on the Hegelian-postracial strategy of inclusion, made possible by mandatory relation, in order to talk about it I'll sometimes need to describe its interaction with exclusion.

5. G.W.F. Hegel, *Lectures on the Philosophy of World History*, vol. 1, ed. and trans. Robert F. Brown and Peter C. Hodgson (Oxford: Oxford University Press, 2011), 196. Henceforward *PWH*. As usual, the question of which translation to use of Hegel's necessarily contested lectures, assembled from sets of student notes, is not really solvable. John Sibree's 1858 translation of the Introduction and Lectures together is still the only place to find English versions of certain material. See Hegel, *The Philosophy of History*, trans. John Sibree [Kitchener, Ontario: Batoche Books, 2001]. I use Brown and Hodgson, the most recent translation, where possible and fall back on Sibree as necessary; references to Sibree's edition are cited as Sibree, *PH*. Hugh Nisbet's less apologetic edition of the Introduction is sometimes indispensable. See Hegel, *Lectures on the Philosophy of World History. Introduction: Reason in History*, trans. H.B. Nisbet (Cambridge: Cambridge University Press, 1975), cited as Nisbet, *PWH*. As Nicholas Walker observes, Brown and Hodgson's claims to modernisation are problematic and 'in the last analysis most of the old and many of the new problems associated with this controversial work remain largely impervious to such textual and editorial changes and revisions' (Nicholas

Walker, review of Brown and Hodgson, *Notre Dame Philosophical Reviews*, 14 December 2011, https://ndpr.nd.edu/news/lectures-on-the-philosophy-of-world-history-vol-i-manuscripts-of-the-introduction-and-the-lectures-of-1822-3/). I find Brown and Hodgson's translation anodyne, but use it as a control.

6. Brown and Hodgson, *PWH*, 197.

7. Brown and Hodgson, *PWH*, 204, 194; G. W. F. Hegel, *Elements of the Philosophy of Right*, trans. H.B. Nisbet, ed. Allen Wood (Cambridge: Cambridge University Press, 1991), §247.

8. Hegel, *Elements of the Philosophy of Right*, §247.

9. Ibid., §247.

10. Brown and Hodgson, *PWH*, 197; Nisbet, *PWH*, 174.

11. Brown and Hodgson, *PWH*, 196–7; Nisbet, *PWH*, 173.

12. Nisbet, *PWH*, 185.

13. At this moment Hegel fails to extend to sub-Saharan Africans the dynamism he attributes to 'natural organisms' whose 'existence is not simply an immediate one which can be altered only by external influences' (Brown and Hodgson, *PWH*, 108).

14. Brown and Hodgson, *PWH*, 116, 114.

15. Nisbet, *PWH*, 184–5.

16. Joseph McCarney, 'Hegel's Racism? A Response to Bernasconi', *Radical Philosophy* 119 (2003), 32–5, 33.

17. Sibree, *PH*, 339.

18. To say so does not entail a pre-contact plenitude, a necessarily better society, as Hegel thinks Schlegel assumes in his writing on India (Nisbet, *PWH*, 132). Rather, it entails that while not every advocacy of liberation has to be political, history does. A political reply to the construction of caste that Hegel uses, and that is still in use, is Congress parliamentarian Shashi Tharoor's argument that the British regime codified caste out of scattered heterogeneous practices and solidified the term 'Hindu'. See Shashi Tharoor, *An Era of Darkness: The British Empire in India* (New Delhi: Aleph Book Company, 2016).

19. For typical apologetics on this point, see Timothy Brennan, *Borrowed Light: Hegel, Vico, and the Colonies* (Stanford: Stanford University Press, 2014), 98, 103.

20. G.W.F. Hegel, *Lectures on the Philosophy of Religion*, vol. 2, *Determinate Religion*, ed. Peter C. Hodgson, trans. R.F. Brown, P.C. Hodgson, and J.M. Stewart (Berkeley: University of California Press, 1987), 364. Henceforward *LPR*.

21. Brown and Hodgson, *PWH*, 109.

22. Nisbet, *PWH*, 138; see Brown and Hodgson, *PWH*, 117.

23. Werner Hamacher, *Premises: Essays on Philosophy and Literature from Kant to Celan*, trans. Peter Fenves (Cambridge, MA: Harvard University Press, 1997), 6–7.

24. Sibree, *PH*, 339.

25. Hamacher, *Premises*, 6.

26. Sibree, *PH*, 339.

27. In Kant this series would run: it can't not be thought, it can't be perceived, it can't not be limiting, it isn't really disturbing, the 'I' cannot but leave it alone. Both Fanon and Levinas transform this set of strictures by interpreting it from the perspective of the racial nonsubject. It then describes a set of impositions. I am pointing out the asymmetry of their readings with readings from the focal point of a subject confronting the racial other or that of the retrospect of historical subjectivity itself.

28. Hamacher, *Premises*, 7.

29. Gayatri Chakravorty Spivak, 'Can the Subaltern Speak?', in *Marxism and the Interpretation of Culture*, eds. Cary Nelson and Lawrence Grossberg (Urbana: University of Illinois Press, 1988), 271–314.

30. Hegel adds the etymology '[*trainés*, dragged]', recalling Adorno's complaint about being 'dragged along' by history (Sibree, *PH*, 339).

31. Nisbet, *PWH*, 176.

32. Sibree, *PH*, 116.

33. Brown and Hodgson, *PWH*, 197.

34. Donna Jones, 'Inheritance and Finitude: Toward a Literary Phenomenology of Time', *ELH* 85 (2018), 289–303, 300.

35. Nisbet, *PWH*, 176.

36. Sibree, *PH*, 215. See Brown and Hodgson, *LPR*, 372–374; a nationalisation of God is not exclusive to Judaism, but paradigmatic in it; when Christians act this way they are unnecessarily restricting Christianity (372).

37. Vanessa Ogle, *The Global Transformation of Time* (Cambridge, MA: Harvard University Press, 2015), 24.

38. Kathleen Biddick connects the consequences of supercession trenchantly to its contemporary legacies for anti-Semitism and Islamophobia in *Make and Let Die* (New York: Punctum Books, 2016), 81–105.

39. Brown and Hodgson, *LPR*, 374.

40. Biddick, *Make and Let Die*, 81–105.

41. Sibree, *PH*, 216.

42. Cedric Robinson, *Terms of Order: Political Science and the Myth of Leadership*, 2nd ed. (Chapel Hill: University of North Carolina Press, 2016).

43. Robinson, *Terms of Order*, 3.

44. Sibree, *PH*, 349, 350.

45. Ibid., 352.

46. Brown and Hodgson, *LPR*, 163.

47. Ibid., 326.

48. Ibid., 160.

49. Ibid., 162.

50. Sibree, *PH*, 338.

51. Brown and Hodgson, *LPR*, 366.

52. Sibree, *PH*, 216, 364.

53. Ibid., 352, 216.

54. Brown and Hodgson, *LPR*, 360.

55. In his comments on Hegel's account of pantheism, Peter Park notes that Hegel feels obliged to distinguish his own totalisation from pantheism. See Peter Park, *Africa, Asia, and the History of Philosophy: Racism in the Formation of the Philosophical Canon, 1780-1830* (Albany: SUNY Press, 2013), 146).

56. Sibree, *PH*, 215; Brown and Hodgson, *LPR*, 364.

57. Brown and Hodgson, *LPR*, 364.

58. Ibid., 356.

59. Ibid., 356.

60. Sibree, *PH*, 345.

61. On severity, see Gillian Rose, *Hegel Contra Sociology* [1981] (London: Verso, 2009), 55–62, 160–65.

62. Rebecca Comay, *Mourning Sickness: Hegel and the French Revolution* (Stanford: Stanford University Press, 2011), e.g. 116.

Spinoza's law

The epicurean definition of the law in the *Theological Political Treatise*

Dimitris Vardoulakis

In the first few pages of chapter 4 of his *Theological Political Treatise* (1670), Spinoza defines his conception of the law.[1] In fact, he defines the law twice, first in terms of compulsion or necessity and then in terms of use. I would like to investigate here these definitions, in particular the second one, as it is Spinoza's preferred one. The difficulty with understanding this definition is that it contains an expression, *ratio vivendi*, that is repeated several times in the first few pages of chapter 4, but, unless it is taken as a technical term referring to law as use, it is easy to mistake it as a casual expression that might mean different things each time. As a result, it is indispensable to turn to the Latin text to unlock the technical meaning of *ratio vivendi*.

This holds a few surprises. First, there is a historical surprise. Spinoza's definition of the law according to its use is typical of the epicurean understanding of the law. This suggests that his account of the law is aligned with the epicurean tradition.[2] Moreover, it raises the question of why this epicurean conception of legality has not been noted in jurisprudence. Second, Spinoza's conception of the law has the potential to make an intervention in contemporary definitions of legality, since it avoids both decisionism and positivism. Law defined as use can allow neither of exceptionalism nor of a conception of unalloyed legality that remains immune from social and political influences.

An important inference will follow these considerations: when law is determined through its use, any law is invalidated or delegitimated by the mere fact that it does not contribute to the well-being of the community. This has a radical political potential that I will touch upon

by way of conclusion. Spinoza's epicurean conception of the law will turn out to be of contemporary political relevance.

The two definitions of the law

The opening couple of sentences of chapter 4 of the *Theological Political Treatise* define the law in the course of drawing a distinction between divine and human law:

> The word law, taken in its absolute sense [*legis nomen absolute*], means that according to which each individual thing – either all in general or those of the same kind – acts in one and the same fixed and determinate manner, this manner depending either on Nature's necessity or on human will. A law which depends on Nature's necessity is one which necessarily follows from the very nature of the thing, that is, its definition; a law which depends on human will, and which could more properly be termed a statute [*jus*], is one which men ordain for themselves and for others with view to making life more secure and more convenient [*ad tutius, et commodius vivendum*]. (48/57)

It is striking what is elided in this distinction. Specifically, it does not say that the source or origin of divine law is revelation and that of human law is legitimacy or the sovereign as the one who has the authority to legislate. The two traditional sources of legality – a transcendent authority or the model of command and obedience – are absent from this definition.

The reason for these omissions is that these traditional avenues of approaching the law are not open to Spinoza. Revelation, according to chapter 1 of the *Theological Political Treatise*, is a communication with God that is mediated through the prophets' interpretation, which makes it a human construct. And the command and obedience model cannot account for divine law, since God or nature is understood in strictly impersonal terms by Spinoza. Instead of the traditional routes of approaching legality, Spinoza has recourse to a qualitative distinction between the absolute necessity of divine or natural law, and the dependence of human law on the will of a polity to preserve itself.

The evasion of the traditional way of understanding legality may solve Spinoza's problem of making legality fit his understanding of revelation, but it creates another, serious problem. The qualitative distinction between necessity and will may be challenged on the grounds that the human will cannot be separated in reality from the necessity of nature. What we will and do forms part of the concatenation of causes and effects that constitute the totality of nature – a point forcefully argued for in Part I of the *Ethics*.

To bypass this further problem, Spinoza concedes that it appears as if we are using the word 'law' as it applies to nature '*per translationem*', as a figure of speech or as a translation, of what is commonly understood by law, namely human law (49/58). The suggestion is that a more rigorous (*particularius*) definition of the law is required, which Spinoza promptly supplies: 'law should be defined … as a logic of living [*ratio vivendi*] that one prescribes to oneself or to others for some end [*finem*]' (49/58). The most notable feature of this more rigorous definition is the supposition of the use of instrumental reasoning as a defining feature of the law. The law concerns a certain rationality in how we conduct our lives, which is concerned with calculating the ends of our actions.

Alas, this second definition also creates more problems than it appears to solve. In particular, both the expression 'ratio vivendi' and the idea of the 'end' (*finis*) are problematic. What do they refer to? How can we understand the law as a logic of living irrespective of statute and political authority? And how can we reconcile the reference to ends here given Spinoza's fierce rejection of teleology in the appendix to Part I of the *Ethics*? In other words, for an understanding of Spinoza's second, rigorous definition of the law, we need to unravel how it is possible to understand law as broader than legitimacy as well as how law is related to means and ends relations.[3]

I will take these two issues in turn by focusing on the terms *ratio vivendi* and *finis* from the definition of the law. I will concentrate on the first few pages of chapter 4 of the *Theological Political Treatise*, because it is here that Spinoza specifically focuses on the definition of the law. It is worth reading the opening of chapter 4 very carefully, something which has rarely been done before.

Ratio vivendi: law and living

The term *ratio vivendi* in Spinoza's definition of the law is unusual: 'law should be defined … as a logic of living [*ratio vivendi*] that one prescribes to oneself or to others for some end' (49/58). This expression is not uncommon in the *Theological Political Treatise* – for instance, we find it in the title of chapter 13. But its critical use in the definition of the law is unusual.[4]

There are three distinct meanings of *ratio*: 1) it can be rationality or logic, as a translation of the Greek *logos*; 2) *ratio* can also mean proportion, just as in the English ratio; and, 3) it can mean rule or regulation. In fact, the second and third meaning are derivative of the first one: proportion is a kind of mathematical logic and rule is the application of rationality.[5]

Let us look next at how the expression *ratio vivendi* is translated in the major English editions. Shirley translates *ratio vivendi* as 'a rule of life'. Curley translates it as 'a principle of living'.[6] And Israel's edition renders it as 'a rule for living'.[7] These translations, even if they seem similar, in fact suggest significantly different meanings to the predicate of the law. Shirley's translation suggests that *ratio* refers to some externally imposed prescription; Curley's that it denotes a universal principle; and Israel's that *ratio* is more like an instruction for the conduct of one's life. Thus, all these renditions of *ratio vivendi* translate it in such a way as to make it amenable only to human, not to divine law – even though Spinoza provides a second definition that is meant to cover both.

The reason that these translations fail to include divine law in the second definition is that none of these translations entertains the possibility that *ratio* refers here to rationality, which is the primary meaning of *ratio* – and which is precisely the meaning I am trying to convey with my translation as 'logic of living'. The effect of not rendering *ratio vivendi* in such a way as to capture the idea that there is a *logic* to living, or that thought and life – mind and body – are intertwined, is to obscure an idea that is critical for Spinoza, namely, that there is no outside to the law. If the law is a *ratio vivendi* indicating that there is no life without thought, then *ratio vivendi* is a property not only of the law but also of human nature. What could this strange idea entail?

If we look for other uses of *ratio vivendi* in chapter 4, we note that the term and its cognates appears no less than nine times in the three opening pages of chapter 4, from 58 to 60 in the Gebhardt edition. Let us examine them in sequence:

1) The first use of the term occurs at the beginning where Spinoza asserts the distinction between divine and human law. Spinoza highlights the necessity of divine or natural law. Humans have no capacity to break or disobey divine law – nor do they have a say in how it operates. This is not the case with human law. 'The fact that people give up, or are compelled to give up, their natural right and bind themselves to live under certain *rationi vivendi*, depends on human will' (48/58). *Ratio vivendi* refers specifically to human law or specific statutes – notice the plural. It signifies the living arrangements that allow for the suspension of the law.

Spinoza immediately qualifies this distinction by noting that 'in an absolute sense, all things are determined by the universal laws of Nature' (48), whereby it may appear that a distinction between divine and human law is impossible. And yet, Spinoza insists on this distinction based on the transition from the monism contained in the idea that there is nothing outside the necessity to nature, on the one hand, to the primacy of practical judgment, on the other. Spinoza outlines this move in two steps. First, he argues that human law 'depends especially on the power of the human mind in the following respect, that the human mind, insofar as it is concerned with the perception of truth and falsity', has a capacity which 'can be quite clearly conceived without these human-made laws, whereas it cannot be conceived without Nature's necessary law' (48). This is the point that we learn in Part I of the *Ethics*, namely, that any form of knowledge presupposes a totality or what Spinoza calls substance, God or nature. Second, given that there is no usefulness in tracing every thought or every action back to its original causes, 'in terms of usefulness to life [*ad usum vitae*] it is better, indeed, it is necessary, to consider things as possible [*possibiles*]' (49/58). In other words, the impossibility of knowing the totality requires that we make practical judgments.[8]

So, the first use of *ratio vivendi* refers to human law in so far as it requires the operation of practical judgment as a result of the recognition of nothing existing outside nature or God. We already see that the standard translation of *ratio* as rule in the definition of the law is limited and it would not allow for the relation between monism and practical judgment in the first use of *ratio vivendi* in chapter 4.

2) The second use is in the definition of the law we saw already as the *ratio vivendi* prescribed toward certain ends. I will return to this definition after examining all the remaining uses of *ratio vivendi*.

3) Immediately after the definition of the law, Spinoza qualifies it by observing that such a conception of the law is obvious only to a minority whereas most people fail to perceive it since they '*nihil minus quam ex ratione vivunt*' (49/59). Instead of the participle 'vivendi', Spinoza uses here the indicative of the verb 'vivere', to live. Ratio is also in a prepositional phrase with 'ex' meaning according to. Here, then, Spinoza is referring to people who live with nothing like (*nihil minus*) rationality. Or, more simply, most people live without the capacity to make good practical judgments. In the sentence immediately after the definition, then, *ratio* clearly has the meaning of rationality – not that of rule.

4) Spinoza further explicates what it means for the law when people fail to exercise their *ratio* properly. He argues that since the majority do not understand the real meaning of the law, the legislators devise an expedient measure, namely, rewards for those following the law and punishments for those who do not. Due to this expediency, most people have a wrong understanding of the law as a *ratio vivendi* that is prescribed (*praescribitur*) by a sovereignty exterior to themselves (*ex aliorum imperio*) (49/59). Thus the logic of living of the law comes to be associated with the 'fear of the gallows', that is, with the sovereign prerogative of life and death. This, however, does not make one a 'just [*justus*]' person (49/59) because this conception of the law on the model of command and obedience is nothing but a trick or deception on the part of those who have power. Note that Spinoza does not outright reject this model, since it is still associated with *ratio vivendi*, that is, with a certain rationality concerned with the utility of the community.[9] In other words, Spinoza is not an anti-statist, nor an anarchist. Rather, his position is that political power (*imperium* or

summa potestas) cannot possibly be the precondition of the law. *Ratio vivendi* precedes legitimacy – not the other way round.

5 and 6) All uses up to now seem to suggest that *ratio vivendi* refers to human law. The fifth and sixth uses dispel this impression. Here Spinoza repeats the definition of the law (use 5) as a *ratio vivendi* used for a specific end, but now specifies that this applies both to human and divine law. It is only the end of this *ratio vivendi* that changes. For human law, it is the protection of life and the state (*rempublicam*), whereas for divine law it is the knowledge of God as the only supreme good (*solum summum bonum*) for the human (49/59). If the definition of the law above (in use 2) is consistent with the use here, then we cannot possibly translate *ratio* as rule, since no human rule can lead to the supreme good of Spinoza's divine law.

In other words, if both human and divine law are to be defined on a common basis that refers to instrumentality or utility, then *ratio vivendi* cannot refer to a restriction or a compulsion of living according to specified rules. Rather, for the human and divine law to have a common basis, *ratio* here must refer to rationality concerned with ends. I call this procedure the calculation of utility and I will return to it in the following section. Suffice it to say here that such a calculation may be linked to specific rules, but only to the extent that they are useful, that is, as effects of calculation. This means that for those who do not understand the real meaning of the law, *ratio* may be usefully misunderstood according to the command and obedience model – as we saw above in the fourth use. In other words, the misunderstanding of the law such as to confine it to a model that is applicable only to human law and that relies on command and obedience can still perform a positive function in society – for instance, so as to lead people to obey the law. But this misunderstanding is only an expedient and not definitional of the law. Prior to legitimacy, we have *ratio* as the calculation of utility. Prior to the command model of the law, there is practical judgment.

This priority of practical judgment shows that judgments about the utility of a community precede obedience, in which case no authority has legitimacy from the fact that it enjoys sovereignty. The priority of practical judgment implies that no constituted power is *ipso facto* legitimate, while it allows for the mobilization of utility

to contest any notion of authority. It also shows that authority is grounded on how it justifies itself—that is, it uses instrumental rationality to justify its actions so as to construct its legitimacy. In short, *justification precedes legitimation*.[10]

7, 8 and 9) Immediately after specifying that the *ratio vivendi* applies both to human and to divine law, Spinoza goes on to explain in what sense the divine law can be useful. This consists in the perfection of our intelligence (*intellectus*) as the means to secure our utility (*utile*), which is what the supreme good consists in (49–50/59). The supreme good consists in recognizing 'firstly, that without God nothing can be or be conceived, and secondly, that everything can be called into doubt as long as we have no clear and distinct idea of God' (50). In other words, the supreme good consists in the recognition that there is nothing outside God (or monism), which is the precondition for avoiding the distracting and distressing idea that there are deities who can intervene in the course of nature to punish or reward us. Recognition of monism, then, leads to the overcoming of fear and anxiety – it leads to blessedness (*beatitudo*).

Spinoza summarizes his discussion of the supreme good as follows:

the *ratio vivendi* that has regard to this end [*hunc finem*] [i.e. to the supreme good] can fitly be called the Divine Law. An enquiry as to what these means [*haec media*] are, and what *ratio vivendi* is required for this end [*hic finis*], and the fundamental principles of an optimal commonwealth and the *ratio vivendi* of human relations [*inter homines*] follow from it, belongs to a general treatise on Ethics. (50/60)

Here, the supreme good that is achieved by following the divine law is described in instrumental terms. The means and ends are provided by the *ratio vivendi* that is also responsible for good relations – social, political and ethical – amongst human beings. The supreme good has a *ratio vivendi* understood in terms of instrumentality. It is a living that rationalises conduct according to certain means and ends relations. *Ratio vivendi* as the predicate of both divine and human law can be translated as living under the guidance of calculating our utility or of forming practical judgments.

Spinoza concludes the discussion of the supreme good that can be derived from the *ratio vivendi* by saying that its proper exposition belongs to a treatise on ethics, that is, the *Ethics* whose writing Spinoza suspends in 1665 to compose the *Theological Political Treatise*. If we turn briefly to the discussion of the supreme good in the *Ethics*, we will discover more about its indissoluble relation to *phronesis* or practical knowledge.

In Part IV of the *Ethics* – that is, the part written immediately after the completion of the *Treatise* – Spinoza defines the supreme good (*summum bonum*) in Proposition 36 as follows: 'The greatest good of those who seek virtue is common to all, and can be enjoyed by all equally.' The Demonstration explains that virtue is to 'act according to the guidance of reason', which Spinoza supports with reference to Proposition 24 of Part IV: 'Acting absolutely from virtue is nothing else in us but acting, living, and preserving our being [*agere, vivere, suum esse conservare*] (these three signify the same thing) by the guidance of reason [*ex ductu rationis*], from the foundation of seeking one's own utility [*utile*].' From Propositions 36 and 24, then, we can say that the supreme good is to act, live and preserve oneself through the use of reason or rationality (*ratio*) insofar as *ratio* signifies both the virtue and the utility of human conduct. There is a coupling, then, of rationality and living, but the rationality here is not directed toward adequate ideas that are universally

true but toward practical knowledge and the calculation of one's utility. In other words, *ratio* here signifies the kind of instrumental rationality that I designate as the calculation of utility.

But why is this calculation of one's utility 'enjoyed by all equally'? Why does phronesis contributes to sociality? Spinoza addresses this in Proposition 35: 'Only insofar as men live according to the guidance of reason [*ex ductu rationis vivunt*], must they always agree in nature.' The demonstration relies on the principle that what advances the utility of one person contributes to the utility of others given that rationality is common is to all. Consequently, as the second Corollary puts it, 'when each one most seeks one's utility for oneself, then everyone contributes the most to everyone else's utility.' Or, as the Scholium puts it more succinctly, 'man is God to man.'[11] The exercise of the calculation of one's utility is not the same as egoistic self-interest. Rather, a proper exercise of the calculation of utility is a precondition of sociality. We share common ends because the process whereby we arrive at those ends – that is, *ratio* – is common to all. The calculation of utility as a guide to living is common to all. Nobody is excluded from *ratio vivendi*. And this also means – given that *ratio vivendi* is the predicate of the law – nobody is excluded from the law.

If we return now to the definition of the law, how can we understand *ratio vivendi* so as to encompass all the meanings we discovered? We can say that law is a 'logic of living that one prescribes to oneself or to others for some end.' Such a logic of living is a means toward the prosperity of both the individual and the community. This can take two forms that are not mutually exclusive. It can be either the blessedness that arises from monism, or the preservation of individual life and the life of the community that arises from human law. *Ratio vivendi* is, then, irreducible to the logic of authority that appeals to legitimacy so as to demand obedience. This does not mean that it may not be expedient to use authority, but authority relies on something prior to it, namely, this *ratio vivendi*, that can be understood as the calculation of utility. We will in the next section see that this calculation of utility can be understood as *phronesis* in the epicurean tradition in which it is regarded as the highest good for the humans and the cause of all virtues.

Spinoza's definition of the law in terms of the calculation of utility can be articulated as three interconnected ideas. First, Spinoza defines the law without recourse to a model of command and obedience, that is, the model that links legality with authority and legitimacy. Second, it entails that everyone is subject to the law, since everyone has the capacity to calculate their utility. This capacity is enough to place everyone within legality. Or, Spinoza rejects the possibility that one can find oneself outside the law. Third, if everyone is subject to the law, the account of the genesis of the law no longer requires an ante-legal or extra-legal origin, either in revelation or in some founding violence – that is, it does not require a political theological authority. We can understand the second and more precise definition of the law in chapter 4 of the *Theological Political Treatise* as the co-presence of these three ideas – the rejection of the command and obedience model as definitive of legality, the recognition that no one can be outside the law, and the anti-authoritarian thrust of the previous two positions.

It is worth underscoring that in this definition the calculation of utility contained in *ratio* is about living or *vivendi*. Thus, it is about the preservation of life for the individual and the community. It other words, in the *ratio vivendi* of human law, the calculation of utility encounters the conatus. Spinoza's law is about living and the pursuit of one's most vital ends.

Finem: phronesis and the law

Ivan Sergé notes that Spinoza's conception of the law is incompatible with Jewish, Aristotelian, Platonic and Stoic conceptions of legality.[12] I agree, but would like to add that this is because the definition of the law in terms of its use and utility is distinctively epicurean. It may appear strange to focus on the use and utility of the law in a time where instrumentality is largely seen as a key characteristic of neoliberalism, but we should remember that the means and ends relations were fundamental for a thinking of the ethical and the political for centuries – as for instance just a glance at the title of Cicero's most famous ethical treatise, *De finibus*, testifies.[13] This epicurean conception of the law is also incompatible with two main conceptions of legality that we can find in political philosophy in the last hundred years – namely, legal positivism and decisionism. Let us start with the epicurean connection before we turn to the contrast with the prevailing theories of law.

The connection between utility, use, law and justice is best described in Epicurus's *Principal Doctrines*, a collection of forty maxims or articles describing the key ideas of epicureanism, which are preserved in Diogenes Laertius. Articles 31 to 38 define legality in terms of utility.[14] Thus, article 33 says: 'There is no absolute justice [καθ' ἑαυτὸ δικαιοσύνη] but only a reciprocal agreement in specific places and times to prevent inflicting or suffering harm.'[15] No justice is absolute, and hence no laws are inviolable, because justice consist in calculating within specific circumstances what is good and what is bad. In article 36 Epicurus articulates the same idea in positive terms: 'justice is common to all [κοινὸν πᾶσιν] and it consists in calculating the utility [συμφέρον] that contributes to sociality [πρὸς ἀλλήλους κοινωνία]; thus, depending on particular conditions, justice articulates itself differently.'[16] We see in both of these citations how law and even justice are described in terms of their use and in particular how this use contributes to the utility of the community.

The notions of use and utility need to be further amplified, especially given that epicureanism is often understood as a hedonistic doctrine that identifies pleasure as the end of life – whereby it is often contrasted to Stoicism that emphasizes duty.[17] A closer scrutiny of the epicurean texts, however, contradicts this hedonistic interpretation precisely by emphasising the importance of use and utility that are so important for Epicurus's conception of the law.[18] Besides the law, the calculation of utility in epicureanism is understood as a defining feature of human activity and it is inseparable from pleasure. This is intimated in the *Principal Doctrines*. According to article 5, 'it is impossible to live a life of pleasure without being prudent [φρονίμως], and without conducing oneself ethically and justly' – and, Epicurus immediately adds, vice versa. This idea remains nonetheless undeveloped in the *Principal Doctrines*. From the few surviving texts by Epicurus, the greatest assistance on this connection between use and rationality as calculation of utility or prudence is offered by the letter to Menoeceus.

Let me quote a long passage from Epicurus's letter to Menoeceus to extract some insights that will be useful for our purposes of understanding the epicurean conception of the law:

> When we say, then, that pleasure is the end of action, we
> do not mean the pleasure of the prodigal or the pleasures

of sensuality. ... It is sober reasoning that calculates the causes of every judgment to do or avoid doing something good or harmful, and banishing those beliefs through which the greatest tumults take possession of the soul. *Of all this the principle and the greatest good is phronesis.* Wherefore phronesis is more significant even than philosophy; *from it spring all the other virtues*, for it teaches that we cannot lead a life of pleasure which is not also a life of usefulness, the good, and justice; nor lead a life of usefulness, the good, and justice, which is not also a life of pleasure. For the virtues have grown together with a pleasant life, and a pleasant life is inseparable from them.[19]

This is not simply a passage that blatantly contradicts the interpretation of epicureanism as hedonism. Additionally, the emphasis on phronesis, or what I also call above the calculation of utility, introduces a number of ideas that are crucial to Spinoza's epicureanism.

The first point to note is the startling predicate to pleasure that Epicurus provides, namely 'sober reasoning'. The word for reasoning here is *logismos*, not logos. If logos is what has come to be understood as Reason, *logismos* in the masculine or *to logistikon* in the neuter is instrumental reasoning – as, for instance, Aristotle makes clear in the opening of Book VI of the *Nicomachean Ethics*.

The life of pleasure requires this kind of instrumental thinking that concentrates on means and ends.

A distinctive feature of this instrumental reasoning is that it posits the inseparability of mind and body – it is, as Epicurus says, the absence of pain in the body and of anxiety in the soul.[20] This is the same point raised in article 33 of the *Principal Doctrines* cited above, according to which justice aims to prevent harm. This instrumental reasoning is prominent in all the epicureans of the seventeenth century. For instance, Spinoza puts it as follows in the *Ethics*: 'From the guidance of reason, we pursue [*ex rationis ductu sequemur*] the greater of two goods or the lesser of two evils'.[21] Spinoza immediately explains that this calculative or instrumental reasoning is not confined to the present but also includes the future in its considerations.[22] In any case, the point I am making is that this *logismos* is not abstract or theoretical reasoning but rather a practical kind of reasoning that entrains ends and considers action.

When Epicurus writes that this practical reasoning is more significant than philosophy, he is pointing to a reversal of Aristotle's position. According to Book VI of the *Nicomachean Ethics*, theoretical reason leads to wisdom and virtue more than practical reason. When discussing the priority of theoretical over practical reason in the *Nicomachean Ethics*, Heidegger notes that this is the starting point of metaphysics and onto-theology.[23] We see Epicurus here evading that move. For him, the primary kind of knowledge is practical and it is articulated in the form of judgments that are calculations about pleasure – that is, calculations that combine ratiocination with considerations about the body.

Epicurus designates this practical, instrumental judgment as phronesis. This is the standard Greek name for this practical knowledge that he describes here. What is unusual in Epicurus is that he makes phronesis the precondition of both the good and of virtue. Such a move is indicative of his materialism – of the fact that knowledge is not abstract but rather articulated through its effects and how it impacts on the corporeal order of things. It is the fact that – to use a contemporary formulation – knowledge is power. The suggestion that the good and virtue require phronesis is a bold one. Phronesis is a judgment that arises by assessing – or, calculating – one's given circumstances. Because it is a response to materiality, phronesis can never aspire to a thorough formalisation.

Materiality is contingent and hence unthematisable. Any calculation in relation to materiality is faced with its ineluctable unpredictability. Spinoza is fully cognisant of this point and he embraces its positive potential. As I argue elsewhere, the notion of error is constitutive of his understanding of politics and of history. The seeming deficiency of phronesis – the fact that it has no steadfast rules to prove its validity or that it has to think 'without banisters' – is turned into a positive heuristic principle by Spinoza.[24]

Neither positivism nor decisionism

I have dwelled on this passage from the letter to Menoeceus because it brings to the fore a key idea that is critical for Spinoza's definition of the law, namely, that the law is to be understood in terms of its use, which consists in how it facilitates the people's calculation of their utility or exercise of phronesis.

It is noteworthy that Giorgio Agamben in *The Highest Poverty* identifies a tradition that interrogates the law in terms of its use. This is the tradition of communal use in the Franciscan tradition. There is a key difference, however, from the epicurean tradition that I have designated as the source of Spinoza's conception of legality. For the epicureans, use is definitional of the law. For Agamben, by contrast, the Franciscan conception of use delineates an extra-legal space. For instance, he writes that 'the juridical argumentation is here [that is, in the context of referring to use] bent on opening a space outside the law.'[25] Whereas use pertains to jurisprudence through its exclusion from the law, according to Agamben, use pertains to jurisprudence because it is internal to the law by indicating the limits of legality, according to epicureanism and Spinoza.[26]

Despite this contrast, Agamben's starting principle that 'Western philosophy lacks even the most elementary principles' of what he terms 'a theory of use' is nonetheless sound.[27] We can demonstrate this by comparing two dominant ways in which the law has been conceived in the Western tradition to contrast them briefly with the epicurean conception of the law. First, we can identify legal positivism. I do not want to be distracted here by the various views expressed within this school of jurisprudence, starting with John Austin in the nineteenth century before being further developed by Hans Kelsen

in Austria and H.L.A. Hart in England in the following century. I just want to point out one key feature of this tradition, namely, that law needs to be understood as a system that is closed. Thus, Hart in his *The Concept of Law* (1961), which is a sustained attempt to define the law, rejects any view that conflates legal with moral norms, or that does not draw a clear line of separation from social factors.[28] Such a conception of the law as a closed system is incompatible with any definition of the law in terms of living, as in Spinoza's definition in chapter 4 of the *Theological Political Treatise*.

Second, one of the major critics of legal positivism— or more precisely, Kelsen's legal positivism—in the twentieth century was Carl Schmitt, whose influence in political philosophy has been powerful, especially in the last couple of decades. Unlike the positivists, Schmitt holds that the system of law can never be self-sufficient. Thus, he famously defines the sovereign as the one who decides on the exception. The law, according to Schmitt, lacks legitimacy in itself. Instead, the law requires the presence of a sovereign who has the capacity to transcend the law within specific circumstances of emergency.[29] Contra Schmitt, the epicurean conception of law as use rejects any notion of transcendence and it is decidedly anti-authoritarian requiring no recourse to a strong notion of sovereignty.

I have noted legal positivism and decisionism because they seem to form the antinomy upon which current political philosophy thinks the law, namely either as a closed system or as something that requires a strong personal political authority, given the impossibility of codifying every aspect of life. This antinomy is not so much mediated as entirely evaded by the epicurean definition of the law in terms of its use and utility. If the law is a logic of living, then the law is positioned prior to any codification, irrespective of whether that codification is understood as complete or incomplete.

If the epicurean conception of the law avoids the conflict between positivism and decisionism, then why has it not been taken up more vigorously in the theories of jurisprudence? What has it never been *explicitly* articulated? This is a speculative question, and as such it may have several answers, including the historical development of theories of the law, which excludes the epicurean theory. Nonetheless, there is an additional insight that is pertinent and significant, namely, the radical implication of an understanding of law in terms of use and utility contained in article 38 of the *Principal Doctrines*: 'the laws are just so long as they contribute to the utility of those living in a political community [τῶν συμπολιτευομένων], and when they cease to be expedient they are consequently not just.'[30] The implication here is clear: the legitimacy of the law does not rely on its statutes, nor on a political authority, but rather on the utility of the law for the community. In other words, so long as the law is not useful, it is no longer valid.

The same implication is contained in the definition of the law as having a certain logic of living that is directed toward a certain end. This end is the good and prosperity of the community. According to Spinoza, following the epicurean tradition, the law is invalidated as soon as this end disappears. Let me provide a couple of examples of this point.

In chapter 12 of the *Theological Political Treatise*, Spinoza returns to the divine law to examine in what sense we can say that it is sacred. Consistent with the definition of the law in chapter 4, Spinoza asserts that the sacredness of the divine law consists in its use. One of the illustrations of his point is the Tablets Moses carried when he descended from Mount Sinai the first time only to find the Hebrews venerating the golden calf. According to Spinoza, the Tablets were sacred only to the extent that 'on them was inscribed the Covenant under which the Jews had bound themselves to obey God.' But as soon as they started venerating the golden calf, they chose not to use the 'covenant [*pactum*]', whereby the tablets became useless and thus 'merely stones' (147/161). Use is more important than both revelation and a purported completeness of statute in defining the law. The law requires an end that is to be found within the lived experience of those it affects.

If we turn to chapter 20, Spinoza defends the position that everyone should be allowed to judge freely about matters pertaining to the running of the state as well as to express these judgments, but without acting to oppose the sovereign. He notes, at the same time, that 'nothing is more unbearable [*nihil magis impatienter*]' (226/244) than when people know what they are judging to be true and when they notice that the sovereign ignores this and consistently acts in such a way as to further his self-interest or harm the utility of the polity. For this reason, Spinoza adds, in a democracy people retain 'the authority to abrogate [*auctoritatem ... abrogandi*]' (228/245). This kind of authority is the opposite of the sovereign prerogative to decide on the exception. Whereas the sovereign decision reinforces a personal authority that transcends the law, the authority to abrogate is the assertion of the uselessness of certain laws and hence of their relevance to a polity only insofar as they are useful.

What is the use of use?

Let me conclude with a few brief remarks that consider the importance of the epicurean conception of the law according to its use that Spinoza employs in the definition of the law in chapter 4 of the *Theological Political Treatise*. How can such a theory be useful today?

An initial observation concerns how provocative Spinoza's predicate of the law as a *ratio vivendi* appears in a biopolitical era in which the main business of government is to manage life – as opposed to the classical sovereign power that has the right to exercise capital punishment.[31] On the one hand, Spinoza's definition suggests that there is no pure life as such. Living is always imbued with a certain *ratio* – with a certain logic and a determined system of rules. No one can be a 'bare life' that is excluded from legality. On the other hand, this does not need to lead to a despair about how biopower completely controls our lives. To the contrary, it becomes the basis for examining the way that power is exercised because it allows for the repeal of any laws or regulations that are no longer contributing to our utility.

A second point to note is that scholars have noted the function of use in jurisprudence, even if this has not been explicitly thematized. For instance, this is the case in the way that property has been defined in the colonial project. One of the key concepts that justified colonisation was the legal principle of *terra nullius*. The idea was that uncultivated lands, that is, lands that are in 'disuse', are not legally owned and hence they can be claimed by colonial power.[32] As Brenna Bhandar argues, the concept of use was mobilized by colonial authorities to create legal definitions of property that were both racially tinted and justifications of the appropriation of native land.[33] This shows the danger of a principle of use: it can be moulded in such a way as to suit established power – it can be a weapon in the service of 'the right of the strongest'.

At the same time, as Bhandar further argues in *Colo-*

nial *Lives of Property*, the 'fundamental paradox' of use is that many indigenous land claims also rely on the concept of use.[34] For a native title claim to succeed in a court of law, native people need to demonstrate that they used and continue to make use of their land. The notion of use may be adapted from its native conception to that of the jurisdiction of the court that is designed to defend ownership and the use of land in settler society, but in any case the key term is 'use.' The most famous example of this in Australia is the Mabo ruling that upheld the claim of native title.[35] Significant work has also been done to challenge colonial understandings of the use of land. For instance, Bruce Pascoe's *Dark Emu* shows that, far from being 'uncultivated', Australian aboriginal peoples had sedentary communities that had developed sophisticated systems of agriculture.[36] Again, the challenge to colonialism here consists in employing the concept of use.

A third implication arises at this point. It is possible to mobilise this idea of use as law-defining to determine a number of political concepts that are inseparable from legality. In my book *Sovereignty and its Other*, I define sovereignty, for instance, through the way in which constituted power uses justifications of violence against its 'others', that is, against anyone who is not part of that constituted power.[37] I argue that neither a decisionist conception of sovereignty in terms of the exception to the norm, nor a positivist definition in terms of legal norms, is sufficient to demonstrate the ways in which sovereign power is exercised and how its effects are registered.

Let me be clear: I am not simply advocating that we need to redefine *post factum* law and cognate concepts in terms of use. Rather, I am suggesting that, despite the fact that there has been no *explicit* articulation of the law in terms of use in jurisprudence – as I noted above – *in fact* the law has operated *implicitly* with such a sense of use. The law has been *used* with an eye to use, usefulness and utility, as the examples from the colonial definitions of property or of the sovereign justification of violence demonstrate. Thus, what I am suggesting is a revision that departs from the material use of the law – its 'undercurrent' use as Althusser might have said – instead of its explicitly stated definition or determination. This will lead to a materialist way of understanding the law. Spinoza and the epicureans can be useful allies in such a project.

Dimitris Vardoulakis is Deputy Chair of Philosophy at Western Sydney University, and author of Sovereignty and its Other: Toward the Dejustification of Violence *(2013)*, Freedom from the Free Will: On Kafka's Laughter *(2016)*, Stasis Before the State: Nine Theses on Agonistic Democracy *(2018), and* Spinoza, the Epicurean: Authority and Utility in Materialism *(forthcoming in 2020).*

Notes

1. All references to Spinoza's *Theological Political Treatise* are to the translation by Samuel Shirley (Indianapolis: Hackett, 2001) cited parenthetically by page number. I have often altered the translation. For the Latin, I have used the *Opera*, ed. Carl Gebhardt (Heidelberg: Carl Winters Universitätsbuchhandlung, 1924). The *Tractatus Theologico-Politicus* is contained in Volume 3. All page references to this edition follow after the English edition. I have used Edwin Curley's translation of the *Ethics* published by Princeton University Press as part of *The Collected Works of Spinoza*, volume 1, ed. and trans. Edwin Curley (Princeton: Princeton U. P., 1985), again often changing the translations.

2. Very little has been written on Spinoza's epicureanism, despite the fact that Spinoza explicitly avows his allegiance to it in Letter 56. For an exception, see Warren Montag, 'Lucretius Hebraizant: Spinoza's: Reading of Ecclesiastes', *European Journal of Philosophy*, 20.1 (2012), 109–29. I have tried to address this lacuna in various writings, but I cannot rehearse here all the arguments. See Dimitris Vardoulakis, *Spinoza, the Epicurean: Authority and Utility in Materialism* (forthcoming in 2020); Vardoulakis, 'Why is Spinoza Epicurean?', *Epoche* (forthcoming in 2019); and Vardoulakis, 'Freedom as Overcoming the Fear of Death: Epicureanism in the Subtitle of Spinoza's *Theological Political Treatise*', *Parrhesia* (forthcoming in 2019).

3. For law as non-commensurable with legitimacy in Spinoza, see Dimitris Vardoulakis, 'Authority and the Law: The Primacy of Justification over Legitimacy in Spinoza', in, *Spinoza's Authority Volume II: Resistance and Power in The Political Treatises*, eds. Kiarina Kordela and Dimitris Vardoulakis (London: Bloomsbury, 2018), 45–66. For teleology, see Filippo del Lucchesse, 'The Mother of All Prejudices: Teleology and Normativity in Spinoza', *Parrhesia* (forthcoming in 2019).

4. It is perhaps the polysemy of 'ratio' that forces all translators to render the expression 'ratio vivendi' in various different ways throughout the *Theological Political Treatise*. I will not trace here all the uses of *ratio vivendi* in the *Treatise* or its translations, not because this would be an arduous or tedious exercise, but rather because the most crucial and most ambiguous use is in chapter 4 – and it is crucial because it is used as the predicate of the law that is, in its turn, linked to authority by virtue of the fact that they both refer to obedience.

5. The edited volume by Beth Lord, *Spinoza's Philosophy of Ratio* (Edinburgh: Edinburgh University Press, 2018) has contributed a lot in identifying the first and second meanings of *ratio* that I identify above, but the third meaning is strangely repressed.

6. Spinoza, *Theological-Political Treatise*, ed. and trans. Edwin Curley, in *The Collected Works of Spinoza*, volume 2 (Princeton: Princeton University Press, 2016), 127.

7. Spinoza, *Theological-Political Treatise*, ed. Jonathan Israel, trans. Michael Silverthorne and Jonathan Israel (Cambridge: Cambridge University Press, 2007), 58.

8. As I outline in detail in *Authority and Utility*, the relation between monism and practical judgment, or phronesis, is a key characteristic of epicureanism and is a recurring theme in Spinoza. I cannot take up this issue in all its complexity here.

9. It is important to not confuse what Spinoza calls utility in the *Theological Political Treatise* and in the *Ethics*, especially Part IV, with various versions of utilitarianism. There are two reasons for this. First, there is a historical reason. The epicurean materialists in modernity hesitate to translate *phronesis*, the epicurean term for practical judgment, as *prudentia*, so as to not be confused with the Stoic and Christian uses of the term. Thus they resort to the term utility instead. Alison Brown has provided significant background to this in *The Return of Lucretius to Renaissance Florence* (Cambridge, MA: Harvard University Press, 2010). Second, the utilitarians, unlike the epicureans, tend to understand utility as something that ought to be calculated correctly and they attempt to construct algorithmic methods to do so. This is not the case in the epicurean tradition that focuses instead on the effects of the calculation of utility irrespective of whether that calculation itself is right or wrong. The only work on this topic that I am aware of is Jean-Marie Guyau's *La Morale d'Épicure et ses rapports avec les doctrines contemporaines* (Paris: Librairie Germer Baillière, 1878). I discuss both of these issues in *Spinoza, the Epicurean*.

10. This precedence of justification is described in detail in my book *Sovereignty and its Other: Toward the Dejustification of Violence* (New York: Fordham University Press, 2013). I return to this point later to show that it is a point where Spinoza's theory of the law differs both from decisionism and legal positivism.

11. There is a long literature examining Spinoza's idea of the mutual utility of the humans. For an astute account, see Hasana Sharp, *Spinoza and the Politics of Renaturalization* (Chicago: University of Chicago Press, 2011), chapter 3.

12. Ivan Sergé, *Spinoza: The Ethics of an Outlaw*, trans. David Broder (London: Bloomsbury, 2017).

13. See also Julia Annas, *The Morality of Happiness* (Oxford: Oxford University Press, 1993).

14. Diogenes Laertius, 'Epicurus', *Lives of Eminent Philosophers*, trans. R.D. Hicks (Cambridge, MA: Harvard University Press, 1931), X.150–153.

15. Diogenes Laertius, 'Epicurus', X.150.

16. Diogenes Laertius, 'Epicurus', X.151.

17. The contrast becomes something of a commonplace. See, e.g., G.W.F. Hegel, 'The Philosophy of the Epicureans', *Lectures on the History of Philosophy*, trans. E. S. Haldane and Frances H. Simson (London: Kegan Paul, 1895), vol. 2, 276–311.

18. See here Jean-Marie Guyau, *La Morale d'Épicure et ses rapports avec les doctrines contemporaines* (Paris: Librairie Germer Baillière, 1878). For a translation of the chapter on Spinoza, as well as an introduction to Guyau's work, see Guyau, 'Spinoza: A Synthesis of Epicureanism and Stoicism', trans. Frederico Testa, *Parrhesia* (forthcoming in 2019).

19. Diogenes Laertius, 'Epicurus', X.131–32 (emphasis added).

20. It is well-known that Spinoza also ascribes to the unity of body and mind. The best exposition of the Spinozan position is Chantal Jaquet, *Affects, Actions and Passions in Spinoza: The Unity of Body and Mind*, trans. Tatiana Reznichenko (Edinburgh, Edinburgh University Press, 2017) – which does not acknowledge the epicurean provenance of this position.

21. Spinoza, *Ethics IV*, 1985, p.65

22. *Ibid*, p.66

23. Martin Heidegger, *Plato's Sophist*, trans. Richard Rojcewicz and Andre Schuwer (Bloomington: Indiana University Press, 1997).

24. For a detailed analysis, see Dimitris Vardoulakis, 'The Figure of Moses: The Origins of Authority in Spinoza', *Textual Practice* 33.5 (2019), 771–85.

25. Giorgio Agamben, *The Highest Poverty: Monastic Life and Form-of-Life*, trans. Adam Kosko (Stanford: Stanford University Press, 2011), 125.

26. For a critique of Agamben's conception of something that is outside the law, see Vardoulakis, *Freedom from the Free Will: On Kafka's Laughter* (Albany, NY: SUNY, 2016), where I discuss a similar argument in Agamben's reading of Kafka's 'Before the Law.' For a detailed argument about the rejection of an 'outside' to the law in Spinoza, see Vardoulakis, 'Authority and the Law: The Primacy of Justification over Legitimacy in Spinoza', in *Spinoza's Authority Volume II: Resistance and Power in The Political Treatises*, eds. Kiarina Kordela and Dimitris Vardoulakis (London: Bloomsbury, 2018), 45–66.

27. Agamben, *Highest Poverty*, xiii.

28. H.L.A. Hart, *The Concept of Law* (Oxford: Oxford University Press, 1961).

29. See Carl Schmitt, *Political Theology: Four Chapters on the Concept of Sovereignty*, trans. George D. Schwab (Cambridge, MA: MIT, 1985).

30. Diogenes Laertius, 'Epicurus', X.153.

31. See Michel Foucault's last lecture in *Society Must be Defended: Lectures at the Collège de France 1975-1976*, trans. David Macey (New York: Picador, 2003).

32. For a concise account of the history of this legal term, see Andrew Fitzmaurice, 'The Genealogy of *Terra Nullius*', *Australian Historical Studies* 129 (2007), 1–15.

33. Brenna Bhandar, *Colonial Lives of Property: Law, Land, and Racial Regimes of Ownership* (Durham: Duke U. P., 2018).

34. Bhandar, *Colonial Lives of Property*, 65.

35. For a Spinozan account of the Mabo case, see Moira Gatens and Genevieve Lloyd, *Collective Imaginings: Spinoza, Past and Present* (London: Routledge, 1999), chapter 6.

36. Bruce Pascoe, *Dark Emu: Aboriginal Australia and the Birth of Agriculture* (Broome: Magabala Books, 2014).

37. Dimitris Vardoulakis, *Sovereignty and its Other: Toward the Dejustification of Violence* (New York: Fordham University Press, 2013).

The philosopher's bass drum

Adorno's jazz and the politics of rhythm

Maya Kronfeld

[Music] itself must act upon time, not lose itself to it; must stem itself against the empty flood.

Theodor W. Adorno[1]

Music is our witness, and our ally. The 'beat' is the confession which recognises, changes, and conquers time.

Then, history becomes a garment we can wear, and share, and not a cloak in which to hide; and time becomes a friend.

James Baldwin[2]

The philosophical significance of rhythm in the United States has been undermined from both sides of what Adorno and Horkheimer called the 'dialectic of enlightenment'.[3] When rhythm has not been falsely exalted, promising a fetishised, racialised 'return' to the body, it has been devalued through the tainted associations of rhythmic synchronisation with fascist regimes and the demand for compliance. In this article, I engage these issues as they inflect the politics of musical form. Adorno's notorious critique of jazz – developed across a wide range of essays spanning three decades (1933-1962) – has been rightly disparaged, but his concept of the politics of metric regularity has not been repudiated.[4] In what follows, I provide an analysis of how metric regularity works for Adorno as a concept – its limitations and presuppositions. Adorno opens up new critical thought about rhythm by taking seriously the problem of the bass drum in jazz and its historical and structural relation to the military march. However, he gets seriously wrong the different implications of marching rhythm for African-American (and therefore American) history, failing to understand its radical difference from the dangers of European fascism for its victims.

In the following article I use the bass drum to cast into metonymic focus the larger question of the ways in which being philosophically and politically attuned to the discourses of German fascism and Nazi race theory both enables perception of racism and artistic form in the United States, and distorts it.[5] Adorno's famous misapprehension of jazz music ironically gets *right*, in this sense, I argue, the philosophical salience of rhythm and its bearing on collective agency – a musical lesson which jazz musicians know all too well, but which has yet to be internalised in contemporary philosophy, despite the rejection of Adorno's views on the subject.

Transnational rhythmic forms in the black diaspora (including the United States) and the interracial experiences that these forms enable, at least as in-principle possibilities, continually contest the 'the divisions between life and thought' that have been taken for granted by majoritarian philosophy in the West.[6] From this perspective, the segregation of intellect from *feel* (a technical term among musicians to indicate those normatively *right* aesthetic choices that nevertheless emerge in excess of pre-determined rules[7]) is not tenable given the polyrhythmic background that must be presupposed in order for any piece of diasporic music, including and especially in the United States, to be intelligible.

In this way, the music referred to as 'jazz' calls into question Adorno's account, at the same time that the more nuanced aspects of his analysis can lead, I argue, to a new account of rhythm – and perhaps to a form of philosophy that, like the music itself, undoes majoritarian clichés about time and collective agency. For example, rather than taking for granted syncopation as *rhythm manqué*, I show that Adorno's notion of syncopation makes explicit the bias and distortion that results from the presupposition that 'straight time' is primary. And yet the construct of 'syncopation' – defined by Ted Reed as 'when a temporary displacement of the regular metrical accent occurs, causing the emphasis to shift from a strong accent to a weak accent'[8] – remains indispensable, both for the transmission of drummer wisdom and for the philosophies made possible by black American music. In this way, the concept of syncopation, like the individual beats that it encompasses within its scope, operates fluidly – even if its rigidification needs to be guarded against. As tenor saxophonist and cultural historian Howard Wiley suggests, the construct of syncopation *itself* is perpetually in the process of being freed by its practitioners, although, by the same token, this generates the ever-present danger and possibility that it can be 'taken back' at any time.[9]

Adorno's critique of rhythmic syncopation, in spite of his conclusions, indirectly calls for a critical reevaluation of syncopation as musicological nomenclature – by laying bare precisely those forms of polyrhythmic (and historical) interracial experience in the United States that are 'in excess' of the concept of syncopation. This is just one way in which theorisations of rhythm that have come from jazz practitioners themselves not only persistently obviate logical impasses that are proper to the dialectic of enlightenment diagnosed by Adorno and Horkheimer, but also offer a critical commentary on the dialectic's binary terms. The analysis I present below concurs in this respect with important recent work by, for example, Fumi Okiji, who in her aptly named *Jazz as Critique*, shows how Adorno's very unwillingness to acknowledge black rhythmic form as radical art can be used to sharpen the critical potential always known by jazz practitioners to inhere in the music.[10]

'Blues March'

Adorno argues, infamously, in 'On Jazz' (1936) that 'the basic rhythm of the continuo and the bass drums is completely in sync with march rhythm, and … jazz could be transformed effortlessly into a march.'[11] Later in the same paragraph, Adorno's makes his notorious assertion: 'jazz can be easily adapted for use by fascism.' This assertion follows from two sets of considerations in Adorno's reasoning: his formal understanding of jazz's internal

rhythmic structure and his historical observations that 'not only the saxophone has been borrowed from the military orchestra; the entire arrangement of the jazz orchestra … is identical to that of a military band.'[12] Adorno's critical engagement with jazz's European, march-like components reflects, in this respect, a form of listening that is attentive to the art form's musical make up, especially as it was conceived by the jazz innovators themselves, even if he was wrong to limit the scope of what that engagement with hegemonic forms meant or could mean. On the one hand, then, a distinction needs to be drawn between what walking in march step meant in the context of European fascism (in keeping with the principle of *Gleichschaltung*, the standardisation of political, economic and social institutions), and what the resignification of the march and marching meant and might continue to mean in the context of the transatlantic history by which jazz became international. On the other hand, however, it is precisely that transatlantic history which already mutually implicates the two forms of marching.

Adorno's formal-historical hypothesis about the relationship between jazz and marching music is oddly truthful: the structural affinity with marching music that jazz musicians sometimes preserved (and ironised) within the music is borne out by jazz's actual historical development in the United States and across the Atlantic. Indeed, as Ben Sidran observes, the marching band is often associated with 'the rise of music as a *profession* in black America'.[13] The famed 15th Infantry Regiment of the New York National Guard, led by the ragtime conductor Lieutenant James 'Jim' Reese Europe, who fought in World War I and also toured widely in Europe, is just one among many salient examples in the history of African American soldiers as members of hugely influential military bands, going back to the Civil War. Indeed, during World War I, 'most of the black combat regiments contained their own bands, some led by professional musicians.' As Chad L. Williams writes in his study of African American Soldiers in the World War I era: 'African American musicians played a significant role in the fetishisation of blackness that emerged during the [first world] war and flourished during the postwar period. Black regimental bands took France by storm and became almost singularly responsible for the international spread of jazz during the war and its immediate aftermath.'[14] Linking this history with the question of musical interpretation,

Sidran claims, somewhat schematically, that 'the black circus, early marching, and minstrel bands were an organised acceptance of Western forms, whereas the blues idiom and tradition can be seen as a rejection, or at least a reevaluation, of Western forms.' And yet actual musical-historical moments seem always to contest or jumble the neat divisions produced by such a binary paradigm.[15]

One of the most iconic jazz tunes of the late 1950s, 'Blues March', is a signature tune written by saxophonist Benny Golson for the Art Blakey band in 1958. In its title, as well as in its musical content, 'Blues March' displays on its surface, to an exaggerated effect, these two apparently conflicting traditions of blues idiom and 'Western' form. But one ought to be wary of idealising such a self-conscious display of hybridisation. In an interview, Benny Golson recalled:

> [When I wrote] 'Blues March,' I knew it couldn't be the kind of march you hear from military bands ... It had to be a funky, Grambling College-type thing. It's a blues, but just a little different. I figured it was a novelty and would never last, just something to get us over, maybe. I took it in and we rehearsed it. I told Art to pretend he was with the American Legion band, and he did. Until this day, nobody has played 'Blues March' the way Art Blakey did, and I've played it with some of the best jazz drummers in the world.[16]

Or, as Blakey himself, in a separate interview, remembered:

> The two most popular numbers that we play are 'Blues March' by Benny Golson and 'Moanin'' by Bobby Timmons. We started playing them both in 1958, and we still have to play them every night. When we first played them, we laughed at them. We laughed at them because they're so simple. And then they became our biggest hits.[17]

Even though these compositions are band originals, Golson and Blakey's accounts concur: 'we laughed at them' almost as a part of 'playing them.' Interesting, and probably revealing of the relation of jazz improvisation to commercial forms, *even* when the forms have been furnished by the improvisers themselves, is the fact that the laughter directed at the tune itself is not self-directed laughter.[18] In missing this laughter – which I am taking as a metonymy for a critical posture that is embedded within the musical structure itself, not merely as an ancillary response – Adorno misses the ways in which the music itself parodies the white expectations held for it.

This is related to the important question of what musical forms Adorno actually had in mind by 'jazz', and, indeed, whether jazz is even an appropriate designation for what are, arguably, strictly commercial forms – the knockoff, rather than the music itself.[19] But to ask this question of Adorno's text alone is to miss the entire critical philosophy of naming that is always embedded in the music that speaks an unutterable history, in a country where one cannot hope to even begin to tell the truth using extant majoritarian language. As James Baldwin observed in 1962, 'We live in a country in which words are mostly used to cover the sleeper, not to wake him up.'[20]

If European jazz was initially Adorno's primary point of reference, American music became the basis for the same conclusions after he emigrated to the U.S. in 1938, and it continued to inform his views for the next quarter of a century. And yet the special salience, for Adorno, of the 'march' (which, on other accounts, might just be one among jazz's many heterogeneous inherited musical idioms) must be directly linked to his understanding of the culture of Nazi Germany – the original context in which Adorno sarcastically bid jazz 'farewell'. Richard Grunberger offers the following description of 'cumulative subjection to martially disciplined sight of goose-stepping SA columns':

> ... the thump of march-rhythms and songs resembled brain-washing ... the associations set up by the rhythm of the march are transmitted to the whole of the body and defection from the marching column appears tantamount to the loss of content of one's previous existence.[21]

Keeping in mind power's need to preserve adherence to the rhythm of the march explains the set of Nazi regulations for jazz orchestras, including the edict that 'so-called jazz compositions may contain at most 10 percent syncopation.'[22] But as I show below, the paradoxical projected idea of '100% syncopation' as an untenable limit exposes in some way the incoherence at the heart of the concept of syncopation, or rhythmic 'dissonance' itself. In light of these and further materials, Michael Golston makes reference to one fascist preoccupation by asking, 'Can one alternately shape or disfigure a body or a state or a nation by exposing it to rhythm?' The Nazi ban on 'Negerjazz'[23] occurred in October of the same year, 1933, in which 'Farewell to Jazz' was written and in which Hitler rose to power in Germany. Later, in 'On Jazz' (1936), Adorno suggests that 'march-like' jazz escaped

the Nazi ban and continued to be heard on the radio after the ban was issued.[24] Indeed, the symbolic work that jazz was made to perform in the racist contexts of the United States and, differently, of Nazi Germany is crucial to an understanding of Adorno's analysis.[25] Golston offers several relevant examples from Nazi Germany. As he writes: 'a "scientific" apparatus for justifying the segregation of ethnic groups based on genetically determined racial rhythms is thus firmly in place by the early 1930s.'[26] Severus Ziegler, the manager of the Weimar theatre, had this to say, for example, in relation to his 'degenerate music' exhibition: 'We do not reject dissonance per se, or the enrichment of rhythm, but dissonance as a principle, and the irruption of alien rhythm.'[27] Goebbels was more decisive: 'Now I speak quite openly on the question of whether German radio should broadcast so-called jazz music. If by jazz we mean music that is based on rhythm and entirely ignores or even shows contempt for melody … then we can only reply to the question entirely in the negative.'[28]

The idea that non-white rhythms issue from distinct bodily forms is as fringed with racial violence in the United States as it was in Germany. This did not es-cape Adorno. And yet, in just these historical contexts, rhythmic periodicity intersects the biological body in important ways. Is moving in rhythm not a real strategy for pain relief, when it comes to backbreaking work? Or, consider a commonplace of jazz pedagogy today, which Adorno would have despised – the idea that rhythmic periodicity is as natural as one's heartbeat. There is thus an urgent need to disentangle, at least partially, rhythmic movement from the shards of fascist and American racist 'immediacy'. Adorno's concerns about the march elements of jazz rhythm touch, in their very specificity, on the most general philosophical and political stakes of metric regularity, or rhythmic periodicity. Those very stakes, however, require us to resist his total equation between keeping a beat and compliance with power. Indeed, this need for alternative theorisation is precisely why musicians have used the term 'groove' (among others) as a placeholder for non-compliant, and yet rigorously structured rhythm. If adhering to traditional forms is a way of repeatedly citing the past, then the problem of repetition is compounded when what is cited is already rhythm, already periodic.

In fact, there are multiple registers of iteration at

play in Adorno's philosophical analysis of metre, which together make the question of rhythm so salient. First, there are the spaces between one beat and another in a musical performance; these distances can be reiterated through time, yielding the temporal dimension of a groove.[29] Second, the rhythmic form as a historical entity can *itself* be iterated through time – that is, the mode of repetition itself becomes a musical idiom, gets inhabited, replayed, alluded to, transformed in subsequent performances. This second form of repetition, we might say, by being overtly social, allegorises the first. To test out Adorno's thesis concerning the march is to ask under what conditions the metric rule that governs a first musical bar carries through *beyond* the final bar, bringing also future performances into compliance. The question is, in this sense, whether the march form, like the individual beats that constitute it, lays the framework for future innovation and subversion – iterations with change. In this specific sense, musical time and historical time are as one in the moments of Adorno's account that I discuss here. But this raises the question of whether metric regularity, the hegemony of the 'beat', is *always* an instance of borrowed time, or whether the rubric of the 'groove' is instead one that provides an alternative time in which to live (and act) – a 'garment', as James Baldwin suggested, worn collectively in order to make history more bearable

The threat, for Adorno in the shadow of fascism, is evidently one of an ever-present return to metric regularity. Is the hegemony of the 'beat' always being partially carried *out* by being carried on? Adorno's attentiveness to the political stakes of rhythmic form invites, therefore, a larger question about what happens to rhythmic forms (or rhythmic displacements) as they *themselves* travel over time. On the one hand, of course, commentators have often identified jazz with primitivism, with an irrational 'feeling' and a racialised idea of sexual licentiousness; on the other hand, they have appealed to European or nationalist norms (and continue to do so) in order to secure jazz's status as America's 'classical music'.[30] In this context, I would argue that Adorno's critical engagement with jazz's European and march-like elements reflected a form of listening that was in fact attentive to the histories encoded in jazz as a form, even if he was deeply wrong to limit the scope of what such an engagement with hegemonic forms meant or could mean. Suggestive in this context is the statement attributed to legendary drummer and educator Alan Dawson: 'The difference between jazz and other music is like the difference between marching and dancing.'[31]

'Jazz is not what it "is"'

Adorno's analysis renews with pointed rhythmic inflection the question of how to distinguish between gestures of contestation and gestures of compliance, a risky negotiation similar to what Fred Moten characterises as 'the relation between fugitivity and the musical moment, between escape and the frame.'[32] In a strange and grouchy footnote in which Adorno imagines filming some jitterbug dancers, he confesses a somewhat obsessive fantasy about being able to distinguish *empirically* between the two gestural forms of protest and submission:

> It would be worthwhile to approach this problem experimentally by taking motion pictures of jitterbugs in action and later examining them in terms of gestural psychology. Such an experiment could also yield valuable results with regard to the question of how musical standards and 'deviations' in popular music are apperceived. If one would take sound tracks simultaneously with the motion pictures one could find out, i.e., how far the jitterbugs react gesturally to the syncopations they pretend to be crazy about and how far they respond simply to the ground beats. If the latter is the case it would furnish another index for the fictitiousness of this whole type of frenzy.[33]

Which is the dance scene's reigning rhythmic order: the deviant 'syncopations' or the hammered-out 'ground beats'? Adorno is fantasising about a schema that could chart precise correlations between the dancer's anatomical components and the music's metrical components; he wants to test whether the music's 'true' rhythmic subversions are really audible to the dancers, and if so, to what extent these so-called subversions are registered by the bodies that respond to them. Adorno wants to test, in other words, the audibility of true rhythmic difference and its inhabitation of the body.

The jitterbug example raises a problem of expression in that the dancer represents, at best, radical receptivity, the scintillating insect in the light, to literalise the jitterbug metaphor. At worst, the dancer is only the 'actor of his own enthusiasm', as Adorno puts it in 'On Popular Music'.[34] If music represents a special susceptibility to a rhythmic framework, it brings into relief the extent to which rhythmic expression may be sited outside the subject. On Adorno's account, then, the dancer is in a bind: the accentuation of new spaces in musical time only serves to underscore what Adorno calls the 'ground beats'. It is not clear how rhythmic behaviour – that which must seek collective validation, or in extreme cases functions as an 'agent of occupation'[35] – could ever be understood as non-predetermined behaviour on such an account. The rhythmic gesture is neither one's own, nor does it offer a meaningful form of collectivity. The possibility of lyrical expression in jazz is cast in a parodic light by the uncertainty about rhythmic gestures: to whom do they really belong? What Adorno does not consider is the ways in which the parodic element in the scene is generated by the slippage between a musical form and its white appropriation; between a dance and a figment in the white imagination – in ways that are invisible to his analysis, but never to the musicians themselves. Efforts to address Adorno's error in interpreting this dance scene (or in seeking a rubric of interpretation for it) have focused on the fact that he 'conflates a mass dance craze with collective conformity'.[36] But what this correction misses is the gaping conflation at the heart of a 'mass dance craze' that cannot distinguish between a black American art form with interracial possibilities, on the one hand, and its instantaneous white appropriation, on the other – or, the imbrication of both modes in the art form itself and its conditions of legibility.

The jitterbug dance scene may be a strange point of entry into Adorno's ongoing perception of jazz. But he will argue over and over again in his essays that jazz only reinforces, in its rhythmic articulations, the very mainstream cultural forces that it purports to subvert. In this sense, Adorno's complaints about 'jazz' are, ironically, exactly in line with those complaints about the term made by the innovators of jazz themselves. A question that is often raised at the outset of any discussion of Adorno and jazz is: what musical forms did Adorno have in mind by 'jazz' and did the music he hear really correspond to that label? But this question ignores the fact that the label 'jazz' itself is inextricably (and indexically) linked to the white markets that have threatened to appropriate black American music from its inception; and it turns a blind eye to the extent to which this has been a central concern of the music itself, both in the implicit and the explicit poetics of musicians. The music has from

the beginning problematised its own relation to white expectations. Oddly enough, then, when Adorno writes 'Jazz is not what it "is"', this expression of non-identity is not in the least enigmatic or paradoxical;[37] rather, such a formulation would be completely in line with a tradition of innovators from Duke Ellington to Miles Davis, through Max Roach and Abbey Lincoln, who have clearly and programmatically contested the term 'jazz', citing it as an obviously damaging label or more specifically as a label that has never once captured what it purports to capture.[38] Indeed, in the context of the United States and its tainted epistemologies, the word 'jazz' would just be one of many majoritarian terms whose sense distorts its reference. The term 'jazz', on this account, would have the distinction of meaning exactly the opposite of that to which it refers. It is a term marking an erasure. This debate has been renewed in the last few years by the New Orleans-born trumpet player, Nicholas Payton, who writes in favor of the music being renamed 'Black American Music': 'Jazz', as he puts it, 'is an oppressive colonialist slave term and I want no parts of it. If Jazz wasn't a slave, why did Ornette try to free it?'[39]

'Free jazz' – a reference to the innovations of Ornette Coleman – may represent something very much like the kind of true 'interference' that Adorno might have imagined for jazz. And yet the clarification that Payton and others routinely make is that 'free jazz' does not represent an effort to break with 'tradition' so much as to break with the co-optation of that tradition. Indeed, considering that Ornette Coleman's first major intervention appeared in 1958 (with his first album, *Something Else*), the very same year that 'Blues March' appears on Art Blakey's *Moanin'*, 'free jazz' has to be understood, first of all, as an early form of contestation and dialogue within the music itself, and therefore as simultaneous and synonymous with its development (rather than as the last phase in some kind of evolutionary trajectory). On Payton's definition, 'Jazz is the White caricaturisation of Black American music'.[40] In other words, jazz is an appropriate term for an actual phenomenon of (linguistic and cultural) displacement; at the same time and for that reason, the term 'jazz' itself calls for an alternative designation that would define the music not in relation to white markets. It is not the term's (often-cited) hopelessly contested and multi-valent etymology (almost like an etymological *métissage*) that provokes the problem of

39

jazz's 'identity', as is sometimes lamented, but rather the fixity/solidity of its reference.

In all of Adorno's essays on jazz, the potentially subversive but ultimately un-free musical parameter of rhythm is always foregrounded. In his 'Farewell to Jazz' (ironically, his first jazz essay), he exclaims: 'The virtuoso sax or clarinet, or even percussion, who made his audacious leaps in between the marked beats of the measure … *he*, at least, should have been exempted from industrialisation. His realm was considered to be the realm of freedom.'[41] The question of to what extent a rhythmic (or grooving) subject can be an individual, even as he or she by definition seeks a form of collective acceptance, is one of the *good* questions that Adorno leaves us with. But in 'On Jazz' Adorno links such 'audacious' rhythmic dissidence with the figure of the 'eccentric', whose ambivalent relationship to the underlying rhythmic schema, and hence to the collective, finally results only in an erotic 'virtuosity of adaptation'.[42] The notion of immediacy implied here plays a complex role: immediate expression is longed for, while simultaneously being flouted by what is *apprehended* immediately. 'The sex appeal of jazz is a command: obey, and then you will be allowed to take part. And the dreamthought, as contradictory as reality, in which it is dreamt: I will only be potent once I have allowed myself to be castrated.'[43] The Freudian subtext here clearly requires further investigation. But this much is clear: for Adorno, the march has an erotics of submission that converges, somewhat paradoxically, with the erotics of audacious expression. He thinks this happens when what he calls the 'jazz subject' tests out the limited range of his rhythmic intelligibility. To return to the 1933 essay, the 'farewell' of the essay's title is ironic in that jazz is not bidden farewell to because it is under censorship but rather because of the conditions of its acceptance.[44] At the same time, what the march means for Adorno cannot be reduced to its perceived residual military character; there has to be an account of what regular, regulated time means as both the agent and the object of directed behaviour (although it is true that such a discussion applies to popular music generally, and not to jazz alone).

Whatever can be made of jazz's march-like aesthetics continues to permeate Adorno's account when he observes that 'rhythmic emancipation is restricted to the sustained quarter notes of the bass drum.'[45] Continu-

ing to elaborate upon the role played by that element of the drum kit, Adorno now problematises its referent: 'The bass drum, whose previous purpose was the representation of the dance-like primal feelings of colonial peoples, now regulates the march step of local formations.'[46] Indeed, the bass drum, with its traditional role in the military band, is the instrument through which commands are given.[47] For Adorno, the directive character of the bass drum, executed 'on and on', is never lost.[48]

This attention to the bass drum is not coincidental; certainly in the second half of the twentieth century, with disco and now electronic dance music, the relation of the bass drum (on all four beats) to commercialisation has been intensified.[49] In Adorno's critique of the bass drum's four articulated beats, it is as if there has been an evacuation of the space of 'implied' time; the rhythmic schema becomes over-explicit. What could counter such a form of rhythmic articulation?

As a matter of fact, what is often regarded as jazz's first modernist moment, what Amiri Baraka calls 'the anti-assimilationist sound of bebop' in the 1940s, correlates precisely with the drummer's release from his four-beat obligations with regard to the bass drum. As Robert O'Meally writes: 'What evolved in turn was an aesthetic of speed and displacement – ostentatious virtuosity dedicated to reorienting perception even as it rocked the house. Every instrument became immediately more mobile, everything *moved*. Drummers Kenny Clarke and Max Roach no longer thumped the bass drum four beats per bar, as some other drummers had done.'[50] On the standard historiographical account, the bebop era, with its increasingly fast tempos, was the moment when jazz musicians turned their back on their audiences. It was 'a form of jazz that was created as a revolt against the restrictions on creative freedom that were typical of the big bands of the swing era.'[51] Thus, a dichotomy between 'serious' intellectual activity, on the one hand, and dance-based entertainment, on the other, appears to answer Adorno's critique of a rhythmic and aesthetic subservience to mass taste. And yet, a 1992 interview with Barry Harris and Billy Higgins, who came of age during the bebop era, suggests that the possibility of a co-occurrence between 'popular' and 'serious' music may have been overlooked by jazz's defenders and detractors alike:

> Barry Harris: Everybody in the block would sing Charlie Parker's solos ... Can you imagine a music so sophisticated, and people dancing to sophisticated music? People not dancing to one tempo. You had to know how to dance to about three, four or five different tempos.
>
> Billy Higgins: In fact, you had to dance to the fast tempo and *cut* the time. You could dance to the ballad, and you'd *double* the time! People were really hip, I mean people were hip. Like he's saying, not *musicians* knew the song, *people* knew the songs. *They* knew.[52]

Higgins' and Harris' emphasis on the *dances* ('not concerts') where one went to hear Charlie Parker provocatively counteracts the erasure of black spaces for the enjoyment of art in the conventional historiography of jazz's 'popular culture'. In this sense, their account seriously questions the necessity of equating dance as such with mass culture and commercialisation. And yet the perceived mark of 'sophistication' in the music is Adornian in that the translation from musical metre to bodily movement is not a matter of automatic procedure but rather must be constructed by the listener herself. Indeed, just as 'bebop dance' (still heard as a kind of oxymoron[53]) is not determined by its Swing era inheritance, the complex story of jazz's birth in New Orleans is one which centres around the marching or brass so-called 'second-line band', which however can hardly be identified with the military marching band from which it emerged, either in terms of its musical content or its

social function. In relation to these politics and aesthetics of motion, one is reminded of a Hegelian lesson that Adorno draws upon in 'The Relationship of Philosophy and Music':

> [The fact] that what is first and original is not coterminous with the truth is something that can be said of no sphere of life with greater justification than of that art whose most sublime works virtually legitimate themselves by the fact that their truth does not emerge until the last measure ... For music, the nullity of the beginning becomes the motor of its own form.[54]

The same could be said of the 'first measures' from which jazz drew its physical and symbolic material. However, as Robert Adlington demonstrates, Adorno's analysis is also shot through with a vehement critique of an idea of rhythmic totality that can be found in Hegel. In a special section of Hegel's *Aesthetics,* entitled 'Time, Bar [*takt*], Rhythm', Hegel seems to defend metric regularity against the 'unregulated running riot' in undifferentiated time, which

> contradicts the unity of the self ... and the self can find itself again and be satisfied in this diversified definiteness of duration only if single *quanta* are brought into one unity .... In this respect the bar has the same function as regularity in architecture where, for example, columns of the same height and thickness are placed alongside one another at equal intervals, or a row of windows of a specific size is regulated by the principle of equality. Here too a fixed definiteness and a wholly uniform repetition of it is present. In this uniformity self-consciousness finds itself again as a unity. [55]

Hegel even discusses 'syncopation' as a correlate of poetic enjambment. Rhythmic syncopation, by 'emphasising some specific beats and subordinating others', actually 'animates this abstract rule' of metric regularity.[56] This last point is one that Adorno makes differently when he talks about syncopation (and other modes of 'interference') as a force that 'shakes' the underlying schema in a fashion that does not contest its hegemony but rather enforces it. The subject articulating himself through the rhythmic totality is only further deformed or distorted by the process of articulation. It is as if such ecstatic 'shaking' – in some way the sign of rhythmic expression itself – does not trouble or modify something, but rather re-presents something in the mode of exclamation. In a later essay, 'Music, Language and Composition'

(1956), Adorno writes: 'It is difficult to exaggerate the rage against the musical element: prisoners shaking the bars of their cells or people robbed of language driven by the memory of speech.'[57] But the idea that interference 'animates' or somehow gives life to the rule suffuses both his account of syncopation and his account of melodic vibrato in the jazz essays.

The implicit analogy between such rhythmic and melodic elements is novel and generates some figural relationships that are worth exploring. Vibrato 'causes a tone which is rigid and objective to tremble as if on its own',[58] an effect Adorno links – as in the 'On Jazz' essay – to impotent sexuality. Its 'whimpering' sound-motion is not permitted 'to interrupt the fixedness of basic sound pattern', just as syncopation is not permitted to interrupt the basic metre:

> The jazz-sound itself … is determined not through one specific conspicuous instrument, but functionally: it is determined by the possibility of letting the rigid vibrate, or more generally by the opportunity to produce interferences between the rigid and the excessive. The vibrato itself is an interference in the precise physical sense, and the physical model is well suited for representing the historical and social phenomenon of jazz.[59]

In contrast to but also in juxtaposition with the beat, the figure of vibrato is understood as a form of rhythmic oscillation whose periodicity waxes and wanes. Taking the point of view of the listener/consumer as opposed to the performer, Adorno writes: 'The schema can still be heard, even through the most digressive breaks in the arrangement. He who is reproducing the music is permitted to tug at the chains of his boredom, and even to clatter them, but he cannot break them',[60] where breaking them would probably mean renouncing the pleasure principle which is the correlate of boredom as a social phenomenon. Vibrato is 'inserted into the rigid sound', just as syncopation is 'inserted into the basic metre'.[61]

In his essay 'On Popular Music' (1941), Adorno writes that blue notes,[62] which he also calls 'worried notes, dirty tones, in other words false notes', are 'apperceived as exciting stimuli only because they are connected by the ear to the right note.'[63] He continues: 'This however is only an extreme instance of what happens less conspicuously in all individualisation in popular music. Any harmonic boldness, any chord which does not fall strictly within the simplest harmonic scheme demands *being perceived as false* … that is, as a stimulus which carries with it the unambiguous prescription to substitute for it the right detail, or rather the naked scheme.'[64] The listener is implicated in the regulative scheme that appropriates even the performance's 'fugitive' moments into what *might* have been said under a normative framework which the listener imaginatively completes. Indeed, by means of this counterfactual logic, the normative thing *is* eventually said, after all. But what produces the 'falseness' of the tone as intentional object? Is Adorno's notion of 'false' here produced by perception – or by designation? The same analysis applies to the 'false bar' or *Scheintakt* which is his privileged example in 'Farewell to Jazz': 'The false bars [or pseudo-measures], which essentially constituted the supposed rhythmic charm of jazz, have their essence precisely in the fact that rhythmically free, improvisational constructions complement each other in such a way that, taken together, they fit back into the unshaken schema after all.'[65] There is a startling analogy between the harmonic and the rhythm domain. On Adorno's understanding: the blue note, like the pseudo-measure – *especially in the hands of white commercialism* – only reinforces the rule that is being 'bent'. For Adorno, 'coming back in on the one', *especially* after having completed a circuitous journey, is a way of folding fugitivity back into the governing structure. However, such a metaphorics of interpretation also exposes the lack of a polyrhythmic framework as a glaring philosophical absence.

In a much later recapitulation of his earlier views on jazz, Adorno writes somewhat viciously: 'It is not as though scurrilous businessmen have corrupted the voice of nature by attacking it from without; jazz takes care of this all by itself.'[66] However, I do not believe that this statement could stop at an indictment of jazz specifically, but rather reveals the paradoxical nature of what Adorno calls, in the 'Philosophy and Music' essay, the 'dual nature' of music's 'linguistic character'. On the one hand, an idiom or inherited musical language becomes 'second nature' to the subject, a 'more or less stable system, whose individual moments have a meaning that is at once independent of and open to the subject'. On the other hand, and incommensurable with the previous aspect, 'the legacy of the pre-rational, magical, and mimetic also survives in the aspect of music that resembles language'.[67]

Beyond Syncopation

In his 1932 essay 'On the Social Situation of Music', Adorno summarises the claim which he would repeatedly make with regard to rhythm in jazz, in a series of statements spanning from 1933 to 1962: 'Metrically the eight-bar structure dominates, making use of syncopation and the interpolation of false beats only as ornaments.'[68] As we have seen, this is not one particular observation but a definite line of analysis that permeates all the jazz essays in which the musical parameter of rhythm is always foregrounded. Adorno identifies rhythm as the one potentially progressive element in jazz music, but somehow the radical potential of rhythm cannot be realised or cannot be enacted in a manner that could be understood as a form of freedom. 'If someone had wanted to take the syncopation and rhythmically improvisational impulses to their logical conclusion', he writes, 'then the old symmetry would have broken apart.'[69] And yet there is a way in which syncopation is made out, paradoxically, to be a principle whose logical conclusion is not available to it from the very beginning. Indeed, as he polemically puts it, syncopation itself is 'beaten down by [the beat]'.[70] This arresting formulation disrupts the possibility of conceiving the 'beat' as a free-standing musical element; it is rather a grammatical subject subordinated violently to its object.[71] Rather than syncopation functioning as 'interference' or intervention into the standardised scheme, rhythmic agency and the transitive capacity to 'strike' is accorded to the beat and not to the syncopation.[72] In the same way, the vibrato is not so much a citation or modification of the root note as itself subjected to that root note.

Adorno's account of syncopation has what may be regarded as a sequel in the influential work of musicologist David Temperley, who, taking examples from rock and soul music, argues that 'syncopated rhythms often seem to reinforce the metre of a song rather than conflicting with it.'[73] Temperley offers a model according to which a syncopated melody can be expressed as a 'surface structure' whose underlying 'deep structure representation' is inferred by the hearer. The deep structure is 'similar [to the surface melody], except that the syncopations have been "normalised".'[74] Yet, I would argue that the 'deep structure' versions of songs yielded by this analysis (for

example, those of Marvin Gaye) are hopelessly squared and rhythmically disfigured. To construe Marvin Gaye's melody as syncopation, as Temperley does, is to presuppose an underlying 'straight' version in which Gaye's melody comes in directly on the downbeat. The idea that a non-syncopated mental representation (for instance, one in which Gaye phrases his melody squarely on the downbeat) functions as the implied basis of the music's intelligibility, or even as an 'idealisation' of the music (which would be a weaker claim), is highly problematic:[75] Any musician who has played Marvin Gaye's music will tell you that the way he weaves his melody through the spaces between the beats is the rule, not the exception; furthermore, crucially, if he *had* landed on the downbeat, this too would have been syncopation. Notably, Temperley does not consider the possibility that any rhythmic schema inconsistent with European 'strong beats' could constitute such a 'deep structure'. This suggests that the framework of 'syncopation' might be wholly inappropriate for characterising the music in question, even though it is routinely cited as *the* essential feature of black American music.

The framework of polyrhythm, as elaborated by master drummer, educator and theorist C.K. Ladzekpo, implicitly anticipates, and deflects, the same misconceptions that Adorno's deployment of 'syncopation' crystallizes: *the main beat scheme cannot be separated from the secondary beat scheme.*[76] My point in citing Ladzekpo here is not to collapse the differences between rhythmic subversion in black American music (jazz) and in African music, but rather to point out the limitations for thought that are posed by staying within a white musicological discourse. Polyrhythmic frameworks show that the so-called 'strong beats' depend on syncopation for *their* articulation. This suggests that the 'secondary' beat or syncopation does not merely call into question the 'main beat' but could be used as the grounds for contesting any claim on the part of the 'ground beat' to have an identity independent of that contestation. Unlike the white, dominant power structure, the 'strong beats' that Marvin Gaye's melody dances around are not holding onto the fantasy that their identity is independent of that contestation.

Standard definitions of syncopation all rely on a concept of a measure divisible into a normative hierarchy of accented beats, yielding what Adorno means by the 'good part of the measure [*vom guten Takteil*]'; a hierarchy which syncopations (the stressing of 'off-beats') upend. But the notion of 'weak' and 'strong beats' derives from a theoretical framework, initially prescriptive and not descriptive, which began to develop in late eighteenth-century Europe, apparently adapted from theories of prosody in poetry.[77] In no way does the notion of metre itself imply such a hierarchy. And if syncopation is also (in the domain of grammar) the contraction of a word by omission of one or more syllables or letters in the middle, then syncopation will indeed always be understood as an 'interruption' of something antecedently given – or an ellipsis, a maiming of something whole. The resulting view is that what is 'off-beat' has what is 'on-beat' as its ground, and that it is only intelligible by reference to that ground (which, for some reason, it avoids). If syncopation, as Adorno claims, is inefficacious for disrupting the workings of power, then those workings operate as much in the realm of rhythmic nomenclature as in the realm of musical time proper.

While the 'referent' of syncopation is normative march time, the polarity of march-syncopation (norm-deviation) eclipses those rhythmic elements of jazz that have their origin elsewhere, elements which are brought into contact with the march but which themselves do *not* refer to the march. As Sidran reminds us, 'the rhythmic feeling of the earliest marching bands had its "swing" or "syncopation" not from the alteration of Western time signatures but from the imposition of African ... rhythms on these signatures.'[78] Indeed, the West African and black diasporic framework of polyrhythm (for example, a 12-beat rhythmic period in which the overlay of patterns can simultaneously be felt in 3 and in 4 time) is one which makes systematic ambiguity a vital feature. But whereas gestalt psychology would orient the viewer towards a set of mutually exclusive interpretations, the aspiration of the polyrhythmic listener and player-in-training is always projected towards experiencing more aspects of the ambiguity simultaneously. As one jazz drummer, Charli Persip, explains, in Paul Berliner's landmark study *Thinking in Jazz,*

> See, the triplet feeling in rhythm, 'dah-dah-dah, dah-dah-dah,' makes you relax ... It makes you hold back; you can't rush triplets. But the duple part of the rhythm is like marches, 'one and two and' or 'one and two and three and four and.' That kind of division of time makes you move ahead, forge ahead, march – 'boom, boom, boom,

boom.' That's the push of the rhythm. And that's why it is so nice when you combine those two feelings. Then you get a complete rhythm that marches and still relaxes.[79]

The aesthetics of swing (the key rhythmic principle that Adorno does not discuss) do not revolve around a modification of 'straight' rhythm but rather rely on a relationship between two distinct polarities. Sidran's and Persip's accounts of creolisation describe an integration between West African and European rhythmic schemes, but it is important to note that, on another level, the model of polyrhythm *itself* is West African, and hence the framework in which the integration itself can productively take place is not itself hybridised. Persip's recourse to polyrhythm here is not about the capitalist West raiding native cultures to refresh its own stale expression – rather, polyrhythm furnishes the *meta*-language of Persip's example. For Adorno, 'the burgeoning joy brought on by triple rhythms inserted into a four-beat metre ... seem to loosen all the bonds of upbringing and custom [*Zucht und Sitte*]'.[80] 'Swung' time need not primarily operate on or modify straight time, as some kind of pre-existing norm encoded or violently imposed somewhere in its history. Rather, swing can be thought of as the assertion of a polyrhythmic framework under which alone the very negotiation in question becomes possible. Against its assimilation into the framework of syncopation, the background polyrhythmic framework of this music is subject neither to the 'empty flood' of time, nor to a pre-scripted matrix of permissible accents. Indeed, those who choose to come back in on the downbeat may be reconciling themselves with history in any number of ways.[81]

Maya Kronfeld has recently completed a PhD in Comparative Literature at the University of California, Berkeley. She has collaborated with some of the most innovative drummers on the contemporary scene, and is piano faculty at the Stanford Jazz Workshop.

Notes

1. Theodor W. Adorno, 'On Some Relationships between Music and Painting', trans. Susan Gillespie, *The Musical Quarterly* 79:1 (1995), 66.
2. James Baldwin, 'Of the Sorrow Songs: The Cross of Redemption' [1979], in *The Cross of Redemption: Uncollected Writings*, ed. Randall Kenan (New York: Pantheon Books, 2010), 124. For more on Baldwin and the centrality of black Atlantic music for

the theorisation of 'distinct conceptions of time that have a special political and philosophical significance', see Paul Gilroy, *The Black Atlantic: Modernity and Double Consciousness* (London and New York: Verso, 1993), 203.

3. Max Horkheimer and Theodor W. Adorno, *Dialectic of Enlightenment* [1944], ed. Gunzelin Schmid Noerr, trans. Edmund Jephcott (Palo Alto: Stanford University Press, 2002).

4. Critiques include Nick Nesbitt, 'Sounding Autonomy: Adorno, Coltrane and Jazz', *Telos* 116 (Summer 1999), 81–98; Ulrich Schonherr, 'Adorno and Jazz: Reflections on a Failed Encounter', *Telos* 87 (March 1991), 85–96; Theodore A. Gracyk, 'Adorno, Jazz, and the Aesthetics of Popular Music', *Musical Quarterly*, 76:4 (Winter 1992), 526–42. See a response to Gracyk in Fumi Okiji, *Jazz as Critique: Adorno and Black Expression Revisited* (Stanford: Stanford University Press, 2018), 19–20. For attempts to grapple with the specific problematics of rhythm in Adorno's discussions of jazz, see Robert Witkin, 'Why Did Adorno "Hate" Jazz?', *Sociological Theory* 18:1 (March 2000), 145–70; J. Bradford Robinson, 'The Jazz Essays of Theodor Adorno: Some Thoughts on Jazz Reception in Weimar Germany', *Popular Music* 13:1 (1994), 1–25; Lee B. Brown, 'Adorno's Critique of Popular Culture: The Case of Jazz Music', *Journal of Aesthetic Education* 26:1 (Spring 1992), 17–31.

5. The difficulty of this comparative task, which I merely gesture at here via the metonymy of the bass drum, is powerfully and cautiously argued in the section 'Children of Israel or Children of the Pharaohs' in Paul Gilroy, *The Black Atlantic*, 205–212. With Fredric Jameson, Gilroy elaborates the link between the dialectic of enlightenment and racial terror, glossing the dialectic as 'that scientific domination of nature and the self, which constitutes the infernal machine of western civilisation … this experience of fear in all its radicality, which cuts across class and gender to the point of touching the bourgeois in the very isolation of his town houses or sumptuous apartments, is surely the very "moment of truth" of ghetto life itself, as the Jews and so many other ethnic groups have had to live it: the helplessness of the village community before the perpetual and unpredictable imminence of the lynching or the pogrom, the race riot.' Fredric Jameson, 'History and Class Consciousness as an Unfinished Project', *Rethinking Marxism* 1:1 (Spring 1988), 70; quoted in Gilroy, *The Black Atlantic*, 206.

6. See Robert Kaufman, 'Red Kant, or The Persistence of the Third *Critique* in Adorno and Jameson', *Critical Inquiry* 26:4 (Summer, 2000), 709: 'The Frankfurt school holds that Kantian antinomies, while not to be regarded as immutable, at the very least reflect accurately the divisions between life and thought (and the divisions present inside each) under actually-existing capitalism and "really-existing socialism" both.'

7. Hannah Ginsborg offers a reading of Kant's Third *Critique* according to which 'imagination can be "lawful", or "conform to rules", yet without being governed by any rule or concept in particular.' See Hannah Ginsborg, 'Lawfulness without a Law: Kant on the Free Play of Imagination and Understanding', in *The Normativity of Nature: Essays on Kant's Critique of Judgement* (Oxford: Oxford University Press, 2015), 55. Those (like me) who grapple with the Kantian notion of aesthetic judgment can gain much elucidation from the way jazz musicians theorise their own practice: At Smalls Jazz Club in New York City I recently overheard a musician describing what happens when jazz improvisation is successful: 'it's not predictable, and yet that sh*t is right.' A philosophically nuanced position in which one must play *correctly* what could never be formulaically prescribed – this is exactly what I argue must be recognised in the domain of *rhythm*.

8. I trust drummers to define rhythmic concepts in the context of their practical application. Rather than quoting musicologists on syncopation, I therefore quote here from a classic drumming exercise book, beloved by jazz drummers: Ted Reed's *Progressive Steps to Syncopation for the Modern Drummer* (Clearwater, Florida: Ted Reed, 1958): 'Syncopation occurs when a temporary displacement of the regular metrical accent occurs, causing the emphasis to shift from a strong accent to a weak accent.' (33). The rest of the book consists in drum exercises, not definitions.

9. Personal conversation with the author, 15 May 2019. For a major musical and ethnographic intervention in the historiography of swing, based on research at the Louisiana State Penitentiary at Angola, see Howard Wiley & The Angola Project, *12 Gates to the City*, 2010, compact disc. See also Daniel E. Atkinson, '"Feets Don't Fail Me Now": Navigating an Unpaved, Rocky Road to, through and from the Last Slave Plantation', in *Civic Labours: Scholar Activism and Working-Class Studies*, eds. Dennis A. Deslippe, Eric Fure-Slocum, and John W. McKerley (Chicago: University of Illinois Press, 2016).

10. Okiji, *Jazz as Critique*. My account is thus in line with scholars and jazz musicians who have in recent years written of their own affinities with a version of Adorno on jazz that sheds light on what Okiji describes as 'the contradiction of music being both *of* society and set *apart* from it', while simultaneously heeding Okiji's call for a 'more penetrating, and more difficult, conversation with Adorno' than was 'afford[ed] by the early attacks on his jazz writing.' Ibid., 19, 35.

11. Adorno, *Essays on Music*, 485.

12. Ibid.

13. Ben Sidran, *Black Talk* (Cambridge, MA: Da Capo Press, 1983), 23.

14. Chad L. Williams, *Torchbearers of Democracy: African American Soldiers in the World War I Era* (Chapel Hill: University of North Carolina Press, 2010), 165.

15. For an account of James 'Jimmy' Europe directing his men to strike up 'La Marseillaise' to French soldiers who are subsequently unable to recognise their own national anthem in its 'syncopated' version, see also Chad L. Williams, *Torchbearers of Democracy*, 165–166. See also Paul Gilroy's discussion of Reese, and his regiment's drum major Noble Sissle's own account of the effect of 'syncopation' on the French: 'It is significant that the military was the most important means through which attractive and exciting aspects of black American culture were first introduced into the heart of Europe.' Gilroy, *Against Race*, 290.

16. Alan Goldsher, *Hard Bop Academy: The Sidemen of Art Blakey and the Jazz Messengers* (Wisconsin: Hal Leonard Corporation, 2002), 56.

17. John S. Wilson, 'Blakey Proud of New Faces in His Latest Messengers' [February 23, 1983], in *The New York Times Guide*

to the Arts of the 20th Century (Chicago: Fitzroy Dearborn, 2002), 2679.

18. The 'Stalinist March' section in the Fourth Movement of Shostakovich's Fifth Symphony comes to mind. The problem of interpretation generated by 'Blues March' is not so novel, but rather, as Richard Taruskin writes about Shostakovich's Fifth, the problem of a 'richly coded utterance, but one whose meaning can never be wholly encompassed or definitively paraphrased'- except that it requires 'two categories of … study: one dealing with the creation of art under conditions of censorship or persecution; the other … with the question of irony.' Richard Taruskin, 'Public Lies and Unspeakable Truth: Interpreting Shostakovich's Fifth Symphony', in Shostakovich Studies, ed. David Fanning (Cambridge: Cambridge University Press, 1995) 29–30. I would like to thank drummer and percussionist Savannah Harris for sharing this comparison.

19. Doing this kind of clarifying work on Adorno's behalf is deeply problematic, precisely because, as Robert Witkin points out, 'Adorno resorts to a number of generalised and negative characterisations of jazz as music, rather than offering, as in the case of the classical composers, analyses of specific works.' On the limits of defending Adorno by appealing to the distinctness of 'real jazz' as opposed to popular music, see Robert Witkin, Adorno and Music (London and New York: Routledge, 1998), 170–175; Okiji 4.

20. James Baldwin, The Cross of Redemption: Uncollected Writings (New York: Pantheon, 2010), 36.

21. Richard Grunberger, The 12-Year Reich: A Social History of Nazi Germany, 1933–1945 (New York: Da Capo Press, 1995), 76.

22. Michael Golston, "'Im Anfang War Der Rhythmus": Rhythmic Incubations in Discourses of Mind, Body and Race from 1850–1944', Stanford Electronic Humanities Review 5, supplemental: Cultural and Technological Incubations of Fascism (1996), last updated 17 December, 1996, http://www.stanford.edu/group/SHR/5-supp/text/golston.html

23. See Richard Leppert's commentary in Adorno, Essays on Music, 359.

24. Adorno, Essays on Music, 485.

25. See Clarence Lusane's historical research on the assault on jazz in Nazi Germany, which was undoubtedly motivated by anti-blackness, while at the same time 'the ideological attacks on jazz were a necessary correlate in the attempt to build the racial state, and in turn in racialising Jews.…On moral, political, and racial grounds, jazz and its black and Jewish practitioners would find themselves at war with the incoming regime. … Unlike any other cultural expression of the period, jazz was viewed by the Nazis as both black and Jewish.' Clarence Lusane, "'Nigger Music Must Disappear": Jazz and the Disruption of Cultural Purity', in Hitler's Black Victims: The Historical Experience of Blacks, Africans and African Americans During the Nazi Era (New York: Routledge, 2003), 184–186.

26. Golston, "'Im Anfang War Der Rhythmus"'.

27. Richard Grunberger, The 12-Year Reich, 410. See also the discussion in Golston, "'Im Anfang War Der Rhythmus"'.

28. S. Frederick Starr, Red and Hot: The Fate of Jazz in the Soviet Union, 1917-1980 (New York: Oxford University Press, 1983),

174. See also the discussion in Lusane, Hitler's Black Victims, 86.

29. Pieces that alternate between different forms of musical time can also be considered 'regular' in so far as there is a mutually agreed upon relationship between (or pulse underlying) each of the related metres; even in these cases one measure contains within it the 'rule' for the next measure in the form of a plan to be realised jointly.

30. A term which Adorno himself derides as 'informed barbarism'. See Essays on Music, 135.

31. The Drummer's Complete Vocabulary as Taught by Alan Dawson: Book & 2CDS (Van Nuys, Los Angeles: Alfred Publishing, 1997), ix.

32. Fred Moten, 'TASTE DISSONANCE FLAVOR ESCAPE: Preface for a solo by Miles Davis', Women & Performance: A Journal of Feminist Theory 17:2 (July 2007), 241.

33. Adorno, Essays on Music, 467.

34. Ibid..

35. Golston, "'Im Anfang War Der Rhythmus"'

36. Richard Leppert, Commentary in Adorno, Essays on Music, 345.

37. Adorno, Essays on Music, 472.

38. See the article by Max Roach, 'What Jazz Means to Me': 'Let us first eliminate the term "jazz" … What "jazz" means to me is the worst kind of working conditions, the worst in cultural prejudice … the term "jazz" has come to mean the abuse and exploitation of black musicians; it has come to mean cultural prejudice and condescension.' The Black Scholar (Summer, 1972), 3–4. I thank drummer Allison Miller for calling this to my attention. An indispensable resource that details the critique of the term 'jazz' by the jazz greats themselves is Arthur Taylor's Notes and Tones: Musician to Musician Interviews (New York: Da Capo Press, 1993).

39. Nicholas Payton, 'An Open Letter to my Dissenters on Why Jazz Isn't Cool Anymore' (2 December, 2011), quoted in Thomas Zablinger, 'Jazz', in The Palgrave Encyclopedia of Imperialism and Anti-Imperialism, ed. Immanuel Ness and Zak Cope (Basingstoke: Palgrave Macmillan, 2016), 502.

40. Nicholas Payton, 'On the European Influence in Black American Music', last modified 2 August, 2012, https://nicholaspayton.wordpress.com/2012/08/02/on-the-european-influence-in-black-american-music/

41. Adorno, Essays on Music, 497.

42. Ibid., 489.

43. Ibid., 491.

44. For a conflicting interpretation, see Michael H. Kater, who argues that Adorno was opportunistic in 'applauding' the Nazi censorship. 'Forbidden Fruit? Jazz in the Third Reich', The American Historical Review 94:1 (February, 1989), 14. For a rebuttal, see Richard Leppert, in Adorno, Essays on Music, 14.

45. Adorno, Essays on Music, 430

46. Ibid..

47. 'Bass drum', New Grove Dictionary of Music, Grove Music Online, ed. Dean Root, http://oxfordmusiconline.com

48. Adorno, Essays on Music, 497.

49. One can be sure that Adorno would have been alarmed by the now-standard metronomisation of recorded music (where virtually all of popular music is recorded to a metronome or 'click

track', a massive break in twentieth-century recording practices). Live drummers now imitate and incorporate the aesthetics of hip-hop computerised drum programming, in part in order to remain 'danceable' by contemporary standards and therefore be able to compete with DJs.

50. *The Jazz Cadence of American Culture* (New York, Columbia University Press: 1998), 461.

51. Kenneth G. Robinson, '"Everyone's Welcome" at the Ozark Club, Great Falls, Montana's African American Nightclub', *Montana the Magazine of Western History* 62:2 (Summer 2012), 52.

52. 'JazzStories: Barry Harris and Billy Higgins – The Majesty of Tap', *Jazz at Lincoln Centre*, last modified December 2011, https://beta.prx.org/stories/42053

53. This oxymoronic effect is finally starting to be undone. Recent work by Christopher J. Wells actively explodes the binary opposition according to which bebop as modernist sensibility would have had to preclude dancing: 'When asked about bebop's "undanceable" nature, dancer and folklorist Mura Dehn replied, "It was very, very danceable – it was magnificent. It was not done by white people. It was mostly done by black people, and it was done in spurts"'. Wells' refreshing counter-history corroborates Higgins and Harris. Here is Wells: 'As a practice, bebop dance exposes the separation of the terms "dancing" and "listening" as a false dichotomy.' Christopher J. Wells, 'You Can't Dance to It', *Daedalus* 148:2 (Spring 2019), 44, 47.

54. Adorno, *Essays on Music*, 142.

55. G.W.F. Hegel, *Aesthetics: Lectures on Fine Art*, trans. T.M. Knox, vol. 1 (Oxford: Clarendon Press, 1975), 914–5. See discussion in Robert Adlington, 'Musical Temporality: Perspectives from Adorno and De Man', *Repercussions* (Spring 1997), 9.

56. Hegel, *Aesthetics*, 913.

57. Adorno, *Essays on Music*, 120–121.

58. Ibid., 472.

59. Ibid., 471.

60. Ibid., 480.

61. Ibid., 480.

62. Blue notes are errant notes, vibrations and other dissonant possibilities found within the musical scale that characterise the blues as a form or feel, especially at but not limited to the third and seventh degrees of the scale. Blue notes are sometimes thought of as being in excess, for example, of the western musicological distinction between a major third and a minor third, but their conception should not be limited to that categorial failure of fit. For an explication of 'blue notes' that ties blue tonality to the power of 'naming', a 'central function of the blues', see Angela Y. Davis, *Blues Legacies and Black Feminism* (New York: Pantheon Books), 33. For 'blue notes' as 'harmonic syncopation', see Nicholas Payton, 'Dissertation on Bebop and Hiphop', accessed 1 May 2016, https://nicholaspayton.wordpress.com/2011/08/16/dissertation-on-bebop-and-hiphop/.

63. See Richard Leppert on Adorno's misunderstanding of the *Scheintakt* in Adorno, *Essays on Music*, 492fn1. My appeal to the basic fact of polyrhythm as governing rhythmic epistemology goes beyond this correction.

64. Adorno, *Essays on Music*, 446.

65. Ibid., 498.

66. Theodor W. Adorno, 'Jazz: Perennial Fashion' in *Prisms*, trans. Samuel Weber and Shierry Weber (Cambridge: MIT Press, 1981), 121.

67. Adorno, *Essays on Music*, 145.

68. Ibid., 430.

69. Ibid., 481.

70. Ibid., 492.

71. While engaging with Adorno, Fred Moten makes clear the epistemological import of 'the rupturally rhythmic, asynchronous suspension better known as syncopation' by linking it to 'the holding off, as it were, of any simple and immediate experience of the object and its story.' Fred Moten, *Black and Blur* (Durham: Duke University Press, 2017).

72. Okiji emphasises that the erasure of syncopation as radical critique is linked to a failure to acknowledge swing feel as 'a musical manifestation of specific conditions of black modern being.' For Okiji, Adorno 'is right to note that syncopation does nothing to overturn the underlying pulse. What he fails to realise is that jazz emerges from a subject constituted by the holding of contradictory positions.' In Okiji's work, the critical elaboration of syncopation goes hand in hand with a deep reading of Du Bois' 'grand concept' of double consciousness (a reading not confined to 'cultural hybridity'). A reading of syncopation necessitates and is necessitated by a re–reading of double consciousness.

73. David Temperley, 'Syncopation in Rock: A Perceptual Perspective', *Popular Music* 18:1 (1999), 26.

74. Ibid., 27–8.

75. The downbeat is sometimes interpreted as the first beat of a musical measure; this interpretation does not begin to address the myriad structural dimensions of the downbeat as a concept and feeling.

76. C.K. Ladzekpo, Foundation Course in African Dance Drumming, accessed 23 August 2016, http://www.richardhodges.com/ladzekpo/Foundation.html

77. William E. Caplin, 'Theories of Musical Rhythm in the Eighteenth and Nineteenth Centuries', *The Cambridge History of Western Music Theory* ed. Thomas Christensen (Cambridge: Cambridge University Press, 2002), 659.

78. Sidran, *Black Talk*, 48.

79. Paul Berliner, *Thinking in Jazz* (Chicago, University of Chicago Press: 1994), 153.

80. Adorno, *Essays on Music*, 497.

81. Early versions of this article were presented at the 'Improvisation Weekend: Why Do We Improvise?' at the UC Berkeley Department of Music on 17 March 2013, and at the conference on 'Marxism, Musicology and the Frankfurt School' at University College Dublin, Ireland, on 2 July 2014. I am grateful to Nicole Grimes, Max Paddison, Richard Leppert and Shierry Weber for their feedback. I am also grateful to Judith Butler, Robert Kaufman, Bluma Goldstein, Tobin Chodos and Paul Grimstad for their detailed engagements with this project. I also thank Nicholas Payton, Howard Wiley, Raul Perales, Valerie Troutt, among many other musicians and practicing cultural historians whom I consulted. Finally, I thank Ruthie Price, Allison Miller, Savannah Harris, Nikki Glaspie, Tommie Bradford, Thomas Pridgen, Justin Brown, Amichai Kronfeld, and my other treasured drummer collaborators for keeping me honest.

47

The radical intellectual legacy of Saba Mahmood

Ratna Kapur

But what I have come to ask of myself, and would like to ask the reader, as well, is: Do my political visions ever run up against the responsibility that I incur for the destruction of life forms so that 'unenlightened' women may be taught to live more freely? Do I even fully comprehend the forms of life that I want so passionately to remake? Would an intimate knowledge of lifeworlds that are distinct from mine ever question my own certainty about what I prescribe as a superior way of life for others?[1]

Saba Mahmood's work marks a turning point in critical thought and has become part of the canon across a range of disciplines including Islamic studies, postcolonial and feminist theory as well as cultural anthropology. In opening space for thinking beyond the limits of the liberal imaginary, Saba's scholarship encouraged a radical reframing of intellectual thought. It was an invitation to become more aware of the parochialism of our own positions and the hubris with which even avowedly critical and progressive scholars operate. It pushed back against the presumed self-sufficiency of western liberal knowledge, exposing it as divisive, exclusionary and implicated in the harms, injuries and tragedies that we see unfolding across the globe, not only in authoritarian regimes but also liberal democracies.

It not possible to do full justice to Saba's oeuvre in this short contribution. I will therefore highlight two features of her work that have been radical and transformative. My insights are offered both in celebration of her work and as a lament over the loss of an eminent intellectual and dear friend. First, I highlight her work on the veiled subject and its challenge to liberal individualism, drawing largely on her path breaking first book, *Politics of Piety: The Islamic Revival and the Feminist Subject* (2005).[2] Second, I present her analysis of secularism which culminated in her last book, *Religious Difference in a Secular Age: A Minority Report* (2016).[3] I dwell at greater length on the latter text, given that discussion of it was cut off prematurely by Saba's death. My discussion homes in on how these texts have unmasked the exclusionary and retrogressive features of the liberal imaginary, while also taking us beyond it.

The radical veiled subject

Politics of Piety unsettled the Eurocentrism of cultural anthropology, political theory and feminist politics. The book provides an ethnographic analysis of the practice of veiling amongst the Muslim women's revival or *da'wa* – a conservative mosque movement in Cairo in the 1990s. Saba analyses the role of piety as an ethical practice in spiritual pursuit reflected in part by the practitioner's personal choice and active desire to veil. It is a practice that permeates every aspect of the adherent's life and includes women who are highly literate and socially mobile. They are actively engaged in the process of self-making in and through the ethical parameters of Islam. Saba offers a critique of notions of agency based on western conceptions of rationality and liberal conceptions of freedom that necessarily require an 'Other' to flourish. She traces how these concepts have been aggressively asserted in the post-9/11 era, where feminists have joined liberal democratic governments in their excoriations of Islamic practices, including the practice of veiling. She provides a powerful rebuttal of this position by dissecting and disrupting the lines between the religious and the secular. She foregrounds the lifeworlds of non-liberal 'Others' in non-Western societies that are foreclosed by positions that view veiling exclusively as a tradition that invariably subordinates and from which women *must* be rescued. In the process, she demolishes the assumption that the non-Western 'Other' simply acts out of deference to tradition or an antiquated cultural code by default or lack of choice.

Politics of Piety offers an incisive critique of agency as aligned with either liberal autonomy or resistance. The critique argues against the rescue or saviour mentality that informs human rights, especially feminist endeavours, and encourages greater reflection on the imperialist tendencies and righteousness nestled in such pursuits. In this text, as in much of Saba's scholarship, there is a renegotiation of the feminist political project, to ensure that it does not remain static, become dogmatic or morph into a salvific force that broaches no challenge or interrogation. Saba practiced the very ethics that she witnessed in her subjects and was willing to pose enormously challenging questions:

> What do we mean when we as feminists say that gender equality is the central principle of our analysis and politics? How does my being enmeshed within the thick texture of my informants' lives affect my openness to this question? Are we willing to countenance the sometimes violent task of remaking sensibilities, life worlds, and attachments so that women like those I worked with may be taught to value the principle of freedom?[4]

In *Politics of Piety,* feminists in the global north and south are singled out as invariably adhering to a specific form of liberal agency, one that is sexualised, unveiled and rational / without the trappings of tradition. Saba's analysis reveals how the issue of the veil cannot be reduced to being for or against the practice; or as operating along a gender equality/tolerance divide. These binaries miss the challenge posed by the subjectivity of the veiled woman and her *decision* to wear the veil as an ethical practice as well as a tool of emancipation. The practice of wearing the veil not only transcends the liberal framing of life along a public and private divide, it also cannot be understood within a politics of 'resistance to relations

of domination, and the concomitant naturalisation of freedom as a social ideal.'[5] The practice of veiling is not understood within the terms of subordination or oppression, but as an ethical practice that reflects another way of being and living in the world. In interpreting ethical subject formation in relation to the pietistic Muslim woman through Foucault's analysis of the technologies of the self, Saba brought into crisis the 'unfettered' liberal autonomous subject to which Western feminism has attached itself.

The book exposes the patronising and imperialist approach of feminists and liberal intellectuals towards Muslim women especially in the post-9/11 era that witnessed the resurgence of old colonial tropes about the 'Other' and claims about the civilizational superiority of the West. Saba points to the need to bring humility to our global quest to liberate women. She pointedly asks,

> [D]oes a commitment to the ideal of equality in our own lives endow us with the capacity to know that this ideal captures what is or should be fulfilling for everyone else? If it does not, as is surely the case, then I think we need to rethink, with far more humility than we are accustomed to, what feminist politics really means.[6]

The turn to the ethical subject is a turn that compels the progressive scholar to take seriously another's worldview. It pushes us to interrogate how our own interventions can inflict harm and result in epistemological erasures. It is an argument that has enormous appeal to those scholars who are either seeking, familiar with, live alongside or within alternative lifeworlds. It is a politics that proposes a space from which to challenge cultural relativists, religious nationalists of the Hindutva, Islamist or Buddhist Singhalese variety, and other orthodox positions, while also remaining critical of liberalism as the default positon for progressive and feminist politics in these despairing times.

The Janus-face of secularism

Saba's work on agency and the religious subject cannot be separated from her second major contribution – analysing the relationship between secularism and religion at a structural level and its devastating impact on religious minorities. In her book *Religious Difference in a Secular Age*, Saba traced the many contradictions in secular governance and how it is implicated in solidifying religious difference and division.

In bringing religion 'out of the closet' Saba does not seek to reinforce subordinating or retrograde practices, nor does she accept that the evacuation of religion from liberal thought is an accomplished fact. She engages critically with the concept of secularism, tracing the work that it does in liberal democratic and authoritarian spaces, and its impact on minority rights in both contexts. She argues that while at a formal level the minority is projected as an equal citizen in law, this claim neglects the power inequalities that have produced the very category of the minority through the privileging of majoritarian norms. These norms remain obscured from view by political secularism's claims to neutrality.

Secularism is largely conceived of as a progressive end goal marking the transition of society from the irrational dark ages of religious domination and belief into the period of rational thought and modernity. It is purportedly achieved through the separation of religion from the state and the neutral role of the state in matters of religion. This teleological narrative and minimalist formulation presents secularism as an end goal that will ultimately resolve religious conflict. Building on critical scholarship that has challenged this classical account of secularism, Saba puts into crisis the received wisdom about secularism as a social and political ideal, by setting out its genealogy and demonstrating how it has in fact exacerbated religious conflict.[7]

Drawing on the work of Talal Asad, Saba sketches the discursive operations of political secularism that produce and naturalise the public and private domains, and through which the modern secular state reorganises religious life. In establishing these domains, secularism determines and regulates the content and shape of religion and its concomitant practices. Far from separating religion from the state, Saba demonstrates how secularism is implicated in producing religious difference and religious inequalities. It claims to relegate religion to the private sphere while at the same time regulating any number of aspects of socio-religious life, thereby falsifying the public/private distinction. In other words, it both regulates and constructs religion as a space free from state intervention, which requires that it be called upon to adjudicate the line between the public and private. This also means that when courts are called upon to determine whether a particular practice is an essential part of religious belief or a practice that can be regulated through the public order exceptions to religious freedom, 'secular' judges are engaged in nothing short of theological reasoning.

Saba demonstrates how religious liberty and minority rights took shape in the nineteenth century and within the context of the nation-state and global political inequality. She traces the Protestant origins of the distinction between religion and secularism and how this distinction is framed, sustained and maintained by the modern secular state. The analysis makes evident how religious majoritarianism is implicated in secularism, so that religious difference cannot be understood or settled simply by 'the heavy hand of the law.'[8] The resolution of sectarian or religious conflict cannot be pursued through a better model of secularism or through more secularism, given how secularism is itself implicated in producing the conflict.

In *Religious Difference,* Saba compares how the right to freedom of religion, which is a key component of secularism, functions in secular democracies in Europe as well as in Egypt to regulate and contain the rights of religious minorities through a majoritarian lens. This comparative analysis may at first glance seem counterintuitive. The open recognition of Islam as the official religion of Middle Eastern states, including Egypt, and as integral to national identity, seems to be illustrative of their lack of commitment to secularism, which demands state neutrality. This lack is further evidenced in the conjoining of religion and citizenship through the existence of separate family laws as opposed to a shared civil code delinked from religious affiliation.[9] These features are also present in a range of Asian countries which are also hence presumed to be non-secular.

However, Saba persuasively demonstrates how religion also remains a predominant feature in the separation model of secularism based on State neutrality, where Christianity is central to the identity of Euro-Atlantic states. She illustrates how this fact is at times openly acknowledged by intellectuals, politicians and even the judiciary.[10] She singles out the case of *Lautsi v Italy* decided by the European Court of Human Rights in 2011, which upheld the right of Italian public schools to display the crucifix in the classroom.[11] The Court held that Christianity in Europe is linked to the Enlightenment values of liberty and freedom of the person. While liberal demo-

cracies are more reluctant to acknowledge the presence of religion in secularism, Christianity remains integral to the national identity of some European states. The Court ultimately upheld the right to display the crucifix in public schools, stating:

> It can therefore be contended that in the present-day social reality the crucifix should be regarded not only as a symbol of the historical and cultural development, and therefore identity of our people, but also as a symbol of a value system: liberty, equality, human dignity and religious toleration, and accordingly also of the secular nature of the state.[12]

As becomes evident, the religious majoritarianism informing secularism is obscured through the ruse of neutrality and its histories cast as universal. Saba captures this seamless equation of secularism and Christianity in a quote from Jürgen Habermas:

> Egalitarian universalism, from which sprang the ideals of freedom and social solidarity, of an autonomous conduct of life and emancipation, of the individual morality of conscience, human rights and democracy, is the direct heir to the Judaic ethic of justice and the Christian ethic of love. This legacy, substantially unchanged, has been the object of continual critical appropriation and reinterpretation. To this day, there is no alternative to it. And in light of the current challenges of a postnational constellation, we continue to draw on the substance of this heritage. Everything else is just idle postmodern talk.[13]

As Saba remarks this statement attributes the entire development of secularism and democratic governance to a Judeo-Christian ethics of justice and love. It not only reinforces and reproduces a historically inaccurate narrative, but also draws attention to how Christian norms, values and sensibilities are instantiated into narratives about European identity and become part of common sense thinking about secularism.[14] An account that simply speaks to the deficiencies of secularism in non-Western contexts does not grasp how secularism structures the practices of religious belief and practices in the western, liberal democratic world. Saba's analysis reveals how the precarious positions of minorities in liberal and authoritarian contexts is continuously produced and sustained.[15] Instead of offering a solution to the problem of religious tensions and demolishing religious hierarchies through the pursuit of equality, secularism is implicated in creating them. Saba argues that modern secular governance has played a prominent role in transforming pre-existing religious differences, producing communal strife, and making religion salient to both the minority and majority communities.[16] In this narrative, neutrality is unmasked and the modern state exposed as being deeply involved in managing and regulating religious life including by adjudicating on matters of religious doctrine and practice. The continued presence of religion in the public arena is not a sign of incomplete secularisation, but part of the structural paradoxes of the secular project that has helped to shape relations between the minority and majority.[17]

Recuperating radicality from the despair of progressive politics

In exploring alternative subjectivities with reference to the veil as well as exposing the integral relationship between secularism and religion, Saba opened herself to excoriating critiques from the progressive left and feminists. With regard to the veil, the critiques centred on Saba's ostensible negation of Muslim women's desire to be free from traditional practices. Similarly, her work on secularism has been challenged as undermining the possibility of an exit for those caught in the web of religious fundamentalism. Yet in interrogating and reframing questions of secularism, religion and equality, Saba did not seek to demolish these concepts. Her position is more nuanced and thoughtful than these critiques suggest.[18] Saba's arguments are informed by a desire to recuperate radicality from a progressive politics that remains lodged in despair and hopelessness. Her insights are designed to sharpen our intellectual tools in order to push back against Islamophobia as well as the limits of western liberal thought, without slipping into the position of a cultural relativist.

With regard to the veil, she demonstrates how a logic that insists on disrobing the Muslim woman perpetuates a colonial fantasy that this single, essential act of unveiling will ensure her liberation from patriarchy and the oppressive practices of her culture. Penalising her failure to do so severely constricts and distorts the eman-

cipatory principle of gender equality by equating it with the right of women to wear what they want in public – *except* when it is a veil. These strategies fail to appreciate how the meaning of the veil, for some Muslim women, cannot simply be inscribed within secular assumptions about choice and freedom. For committed practitioners of piety, 'the veil' is not simply what they opt to wear – a garment that can be donned or removed as required – but rather signifies a mode of being, an elision of self-conception, interiority and identity.

Similarly, while some of her critics expressed the fear that her analysis of secularism could play into the hands of religious fundamentalists to advance their anti-western, anti-secular agendas, Saba's analysis reveals how right-wing and conservative forces have proven adept at being able to advance their ideological agendas in and through liberal values, including the discourse of secularism and its constituent elements, equality and tolerance. These political processes speak to the urgent need to retrieve and counter these encroachments through a focused critique. Saba's work can encourage thinking in a more productive and radical direction, including the exploration, recovery or seizing of heterodox and esoteric components within different philosophical traditions that have been marginalised or obscured in the hegemonic claims of religious fundamentalists.

The critiques of Saba's work in these areas speak to a deep reluctance on the part of the left, including critical and feminist scholars, to engage the terrain of religion. In fact, such critiques invariably and reflexively fall back on uninterrogated understandings of secularism and liberal individualism as a political counter to religious and right-wing agendas. Such reluctance cannot countenance new conceptions of freedom or alternative lifeworlds that have the slightest traces of 'religion'. And yet the questioning of secularism, equality and agency does not imply support for the rhetoric of cultural relativists, or ideologues of various persuasions. In fact, the analysis seeks to recuperate a radical political agenda, by occupying the semantic and political 'nonliberal' space that has too easily been ceded to reactionary forces and orthodoxies by progressive, leftist and feminist forces out of fear that it may mark them as 'religious' or unsecular. Indeed, it opens the possibility that has eluded postcolonial scholars to ground their positions outside of the violent legacies of the Enlightenment rather than to seek solutions from within them.[19]

In questioning assumptions about religion and politics in liberal thought and feminism, Saba dared to explore spaces that were deemed off limits in left politics or taboo in feminist advocacy. In the process, she turned the gaze back on progressive politics and encouraged engagement in a politics of 'self-parochialization' reflected in the opening quote of this piece.[20] Quite specifically this process involves surrendering our conceits, engaging with another's worldview and demonstrating a willingness 'to learn things that we did not already know before we undertook the engagement.'[21]

Ratna Kapur is Professor of International Law at Queen Mary University of London. She is the author of several books including, most recently, Gender, Alterity and Human Rights: Freedom in a Fishbowl *(2018).*

Notes

1. Saba Mahmood, 'Feminist Theory, Agency, and the Liberatory Subject: Some Reflections on the Islamic Revival in Egypt', *Temenos: Nordic Journal of Comparative Religion* 42:1 (2006), 61.

2. Saba Mahmood, *Politics of Piety: The Islamic Revival and the Feminist Subject* (Princeton: Princeton University Press, 2005).

3. Saba Mahmood, *Religious Difference in a Secular Age: A Minority Report* (Princeton: Princeton University Press, 2016).

4. Mahmood, 'Liberatory Subject', 62.

5. Ibid., 39.

6. Ibid., 62.

7. For other accounts see Hussein Ali Agrama, *Questioning Secularism: Islam, Sovereignty and the Rule of Law in Modern Egypt* (Chicago: Chicago University Press, 2012); Talal Asad, *Formations of the Secular: Christianity, Islam, Modernity* (Stanford: Stanford University Press, 2003); Mayanthi Fernando, *The Republic Unsettled: Muslim French and the Contradictions of Secularism* (Durham: Duke University Press, 2014); Tracy Fessenden, *Culture and Redemption: Religion, the Secular, and American Literature* (Princeton, NJ: Princeton University Press, 2006); Joan Wallach Scott, *The Politics of the Veil* (Princeton, NJ: Princeton University Press, 2007); Charles Taylor, *A Secular Age* (Cambridge, MA: Belknap Press, 2007); Ratna Kapur and Brenda Cossman, *Secularism's Last Sigh? Hindutva and the (Mis)Rule of Law* (Oxford: Oxford University Press, 2001). See also Saba Mahmood and Peter Danchin eds., 'The Politics of Religious Freedom,' *South Atlantic Quarterly* 113:1 (2014), and the 'Teaching Law and Religion Case Study Archive', curated by Winnifred Sullivan and Elizabeth Shakman Hurd, available at https://sites.northwestern.edu/lawreligion/ The site builds on the earlier joint research project 'Politics of Religious Freedom' with Saba Mahmood and Peter Danchin.

8. Talal Asad, Wendy Brown, Judith Butler and Saba Mahmood, *Is Critique Secular? Blasphemy, Injury, and Free Speech* (Berkeley: University of California Press, 2009). Mahmood argues that the moral injury experienced by Muslims in the Danish cartoon controversy was not addressed in the debates. Such an injury cannot be expressed in terms of rights and is hence incommensurable with a rights discourse. As she argues, the rights of minorities are framed, judged and litigated within the larger context of the rights of the majority. This framing remains incapable of fully grasping the nature of the injury or even the deeper epistemological challenge being presented by the 'Other'.

9. Saba Mahmood, *Religious Difference in a Secular Age: A Minority Report* (Princeton: Princeton University Press, 2015), 149–180.

10. See Mahmood's critique of Taylor, *A Secular Age*, which describes secularism as a unique achievement of 'Latin Christiandom', which is itself portrayed as homogeneous and with little acknowledgement of its encounters with its 'Others': Saba Mahmood, 'Can Secularism Be Other-Wise?', in *Varieties of Secularism in a Secular Age*, eds. Michael Warner, Jonathan Vanantwerpen and Craig Calhoun (Cambridge, MA: Harvard University Press, 2010), 282–299.

11. Joseph Weiler represented *pro bono* 18 European states who challenged the lower chamber's ruling upholding the ban on crucifixes in Italian public classrooms. Weiler argued that the lower chamber disregarded the religious dimension to Europe's history and that '[I]t is not the case that the cross is only a national symbol as some people would hold. That is nonsense. The cross is a national symbol and a religious symbol ... It is both and it is understandable'. George Weigel, *The Cube and the Cathedral: Europe, America and Politics Without God* (New York: Basic Books, 2006), 19. See also Joseph Weiler, *Un'Europa Cristiana: Un Saggio Esplorativo* [Christian Europe: An Exploratory Essay] (Milano: Biblioteca Universale Rizzoli, 2003).

12. *Lautsi and Others v. Italy*, 18 March 2011, http://hudoc.echr.coe.int/sites/eng.pages/search.aspx?i=001-104040, para 15.

13. Mahmood, *Religious Difference*, 8.

14. Ibid., 8.

15. Ibid., 6.

16. Ibid.

17. Ibid., 2.

18. See for example Rachel Rinaldo, 'The Islamic Revival and Women's Political Subjectivity in Indonesia,' *Women's Studies International Forum* 33 (2010), 422–431, on how a focus on the ethical subject can run the risk of overemphasising the role of individual agency in decision-making; Elizabeth M. Bucar, 'Dianomy: Understanding Religious Women's Moral Agency as Creative Conformity,' *Journal of the American Academy of Religion* 78: 3 (2010), 662–686, on how the concept of 'dianomy' focuses on both the discursive and performative environment of religious women and better captures the model of agency being exercised.

19. Thus it challenges Chakrabarty's resignation that the postcolonial thinker must inevitably come to terms with this bind. Dipesh Chakrabarty, *Provincializing Europe: Postcolonial Thought and Historical Difference* (Princeton: Princeton University Press, 2000).

20. Webb Keane, 'Saba Mahmood and the Paradoxes of Self-Parochialization', available at https://www.publicbooks.org/saba-mahmood-and-the-paradoxes-of-self-parochialization/

21. Mahmood, *Politics of Piety*, 37.

Calls, Invitations, Summons
'Gender' in the aftermath of *Politics of Piety*

Sîan Melvill Hawthorne

Da'wa, Saba Mahmood tells us, is 'a Quranic concept associated primarily with God's call to the prophets and to humanity to believe in the "true religion", Islam'. It 'literally means "call, invitation, appeal, or summons"'.[1] Whilst cognisant of the uncompromising specificity of the demand it places on those to whom the call is addressed, I want in this short response to take up the concept as a *spur* to ask what Mahmood's work may summon, invite, call us to *do* in the aftermath of *Politics of Piety*. What praxis does it incite?

Beyond the myriad of responses generated by *Politics of Piety* – some appalled at its apparent cultural relativism, adamant in their refusal to countenance the idea that critique may arrive one fine day from beyond the pale (or veil) of a globalised if not universalised white secular liberalism,[2] others more attuned or ambivalent[3] – what I do not want to do here is to rehearse the well-worn line that poses piety as an alternative model for thinking through agency against the limitations posed by the liberal frame of resistance or collusion. Rather, my intent is to gesture, in general terms, to the metatheoretical implications for feminist praxis and conceptuality of Mahmood's call to see beyond the frameworks of secular liberalism and the commitments these engender and constrain. More specifically I want to suggest that we should attend to the historicality of 'gender'[4] and its constitution within the logics of secular modernity which are also and always colonial and racist. Thus my focus here is on the extent to which, following in the wake of Mahmood's provocative invitation to recognise the ethnocentric limits of 'the feminist subject' within secular liberal thought, we might begin the work of examining the assumptions that underwrite 'gender' as a historical, political, and thus provincial category.

The subtext of such a metatheoretical argument pushes me to extend the critique Mahmood ranges against the impoverished concept of agency that proceeds from a liberal sensibility, in order to ask whether we may need to subject 'gender' to an assessment of its parochial origins such that its various political articulations can be shown to be as embedded in the constraining imaginary of liberalism as 'agency' may be. And further, and by implication, to question whether 'gender' is translatable, by which I mean to ask, is it universalisable and if so, in whose terms?

Of course, in a brief response such as this, it is not possible to undertake what would be a necessarily lengthy and detailed cataloguing of the ways in which 'gender' is tied to the liberal imaginary of secular modernity. Rather, my intention here is to indicate the broader epistemological problematic and opportunity that feminism is left with in the wake of Mahmood's invitation to attend to the mediation of conceptual and political histories in the construction of foundational premises. This concern with the role of conceptual mediation across different social milieux runs through Mahmood's text, stated from the outset as a question:

> If we recognize that the desire for freedom from, or subversion of, norms is not an innate desire that motivates all beings at all times, but is also profoundly mediated by cultural and historical conditions, then the question arises: how do we analyze operations of power that construct different kinds of bodies, knowledges, and subjectivities whose trajectories do not follow the entelechy of liberatory politics?[5]

Given the process by which 'gender' emerges as a category constitutive of secular modernity and its ostensible alignment with liberatory politics via feminism may it not also need to be subjected to an assessment of that which mediates it and which it mediates?

Translations

What if 'gender' *is* untranslatable?[6] The issue of (un)translatability, of the movement of a concept from here to there, of the meanings that travel and those which do not, of the histories that remain in place and those which are displaced, is one that Mahmood's work also addresses. Is 'gender' translatable? What is it that such a question asks? Is it a question of correspondence? A gesture towards the relationship between a universalised genus and a range of differentiated species? If we pose 'gender' in such terms we might suggest that it is the genus – all cultures have a means of categorising humans into one, two or several genders – in relationship to which the various different cultures or societies structure some variant or other of what is recognisable as a gender system. But what does such a circularity reference? What precisely is this original genus that engenders these variations which nonetheless all share something in common? In what does this commonality lie and whence? What is it that we – and who this 'we' is, is the question – think we see when we look out into the world and see the genus translated into species? Is there translation without coloniality?

Although Mahmood only briefly raises the question of (conceptual) translation and its connection to assumptions of universalisability,[7] particularly the ways in which concepts' histories may be marked by a certain intractability if not incommensurability that restricts their transversal mobility, it seems that such a question underlies her call to understand agency otherwise, to extend its lexical range beyond that which has been imagined within secular liberalism. That is, she summons us to see how translation out of the set of liberal commitments to autonomy, liberty, choice, and so on, into a social and political context with a different set of priorities and concepts of a subject who acts intentionally, inevitably constrains, distorts and conceals. Thus, the persistence of assertions of similitude masks a will to universalise which is always a colonial move. As Butler notes, in a passage that Mahmood cites approvingly,

no assertion of universality takes place apart from a cultural norm, and, given the array of contesting norms that constitute the international field, no assertion can be made without at once requiring a cultural translation. Without translation, the very concept of universality cannot cross the linguistic borders it claims, in principle, to be able to cross. Or we might put it another way: without translation, the only way the assertion of universality can cross a border is through colonial and expansionist logic.[8]

So, when 'gender' as produced within (white) liberal feminist thought travels, what does it reference? What political and ideological commitments and histories does it connect to and imply? What histories are neglected or forgotten? Might we need to begin (again) to speak of the 'coloniality of gender'[9] in order to speak of it at all?

Genealogies

By way of seeing how 'gender' may be caught up in a history that limits its capacity to account for social arrangements beyond the purview of its provincial origins, the parallel case of 'religion' can prove instructive. In the last twenty-five years, scholars have drawn attention to how the *taxon* 'religion' is closely tied to the (opaque) ethnocentric creation of public/private, secular/religious, religion/state dichotomies that underpin and sustain the project of European modernity and the nation-state, and are further inevitably embedded in forms of colonialist governmentality, both of which render the continuing use of 'religion' as a category of knowledge or descriptor for anything other than western Protestant Christianity deeply suspect.[10] Scholars have pointed to the ways in which Religious Studies has traded in a series of rhetorical techniques (for example, claims to the uniqueness, universality, irreducibility, etc. of the datum 'religion'), that obscures the manufactured nature of its central category, and moreover demonstrates the myriad ways in which this work of manufacture, and indeed translation, is to a large degree implicated in, supportive of, and served by colonial conceptuality and its universalising logic.

What this scholarship has established, further, is how the contemporary common-sense notion of religion's universality obscures the history of its production and its subsequent violent inscription qua translation on to cultural practices, traditions and conceptual schemas quite alien to the specificity of its European provenance. The translation of non-western traditions and worldviews as 'religions' interpellated them into a highly provincialised debate that not only restricted their possible modes of articulation and signification but also predetermined their reception and dissemination. Thus to use the term 'religion' to refer to non-European lifeways is to subject them to a conceptual regime that always already implies their inferiority and mistakenly assumes a shared referentiality, that of the agonistic dichotomisation of the religious and the secular realms characteristic of post-Enlightenment European history. Europe's struggles to overcome 'religion' were struggles to overcome a particular form of Christianity but at the same time Christianity was the primogenitive model for those traditions we now understand as religious.

If the genealogy I point to here has by now been well rehearsed within Religious Studies, a parallel effort in white feminism[11] regarding the history of 'gender' as a critical category tied to secular liberal and colonial modernity (and the line between these two is paper thin), such that the conceptual scope of 'gender' is tempered, has yet to be undertaken in any systematic manner. Whilst this is not the place to undertake such work,[12] what we might simply note here is what such a task may involve. It would involve tracing the various strands of thought, histories, politics and practices that have informed and produced 'gender' as a category of analysis and critique, as a site of identity, a process of meaning-making (and imposition) and political organising. In tracking this history what would be shown is how these strands enact racial and colonial politics and exclusions even in their most benevolent figurations. It would imply attending to 'gender's' production in several intersecting contexts, namely secular modernity's segregation of women from the bourgeois public sphere alongside the rise of the nation state and the heteronormative nuclear family; Enlightenment discourses of sovereignty and their relationship to the 'self', that is, the 'man of reason'; the legislative connection forged between ownership of property and the basis of citizenry; the liberal emphasis on 'equality, liberty and community' as the markers of toleration and inclusion and which serve as the organising itinerary of early and contemporary feminist thought; European colonialisms, where 'gender', like 'religion', was wielded as a civilising tool and a point of contrast to the European metropole; and the rise of race 'science' and the slave trade. Each of these contexts should, I would argue, be read not only as the history of the conceptual emergence of 'gender', but also as those in which the conceptualisation of 'gender', whether as a sign of negativity or positivity, operated as a technology of anti-blackness inasmuch as racist anxieties and imaginaries underwrote not only theorisations of both the content and form of 'gender', but also enabled the prioritisation of a privileged, deracinated gender imaginary which was and is able to neglect race and coloniality as central to its construction.

This neglect enables the persistent universalisation of 'gender' as a tool in the pursuit of emancipation – providing both its form and content (all the while compliant with the chimeric quality of liberal governmentality),[13] and enabling the assumption that 'gender' has some privileged, thus necessarily segregated, role to play in the dismantling of patriarchy. There are at least five dominant tendencies that, I have argued,[14] signal the neglect of the racist and colonialist underpinnings of 'gender,' which play out in contemporary white feminism, and which point to the necessity for reconfiguration of its priorities, institutional practices and structures, and organising categories. Briefly, these are: (1) the tendency to employ an ethnocentric model of 'gender' parading as universal but which is informed by predominantly western liberal feminist assumptions and political agendas, and which at the same time selectively appropriates non-western traditions and practices in its service; (2) a propensity to conflate feminist, black, womanist, post- and decolonial feminist interests and experiences as similar if not the same, and to treat misogyny, colonialism, slavery and racism as analogous forms of oppression; (3) relatedly, the habit of predominantly addressing questions of race, ethnicity and colonial histories when considering non-white populations and practices such that whiteness disappears as a significant frame for all and any sociality it nonetheless structures and informs; (4) the adoption and distortion of 'intersectionality' as a mode of transactional analysis that presupposes an unqualified, unmarked subject to whom identity markers accrue and which are interchangeable or brought into play at different times and in different contexts. Such a move fails to reference its origins in Black feminist thought and thus to understand intersectionality as both an analytic

and lived experience of oppression and inequality within matrices of power that persistently cross-cut, one which indicts white feminism as one such matrix; (5) the tendency to attribute to 'religion' and religious allegiance the status of cause of oppression rather than source of solidarity and nourishment, if not emancipatory insight.

To insist on the similitude of oppression across a spectrum of difference whilst prioritising gender as the tie that binds, is to indulge in a form of discursive imperialism that not only weakens the intellectual credibility and political force of feminist work, but also obscures the embeddedness of much feminist thought in white privilege and its persistent, if apparently unwitting, collaboration with racist and colonialist practices of exclusion and universalisation, all in the name of freedom, equality and sisterhood. Moreover, it suggests that an invisibly etiolated feminism is adequate to the task of thinking and writing about, or better listening to, hearing and centring material and persons wholly or partially different historically, philosophically or geographically.[15] Gayatri Spivak's assessment of a broader problem for white feminism, echoing Mahmood's own critique, is pertinent here when she draws attention to how it glosses a significant problem when it attempts to embrace 'multiculturalist or postcolonial marginality' in the articulation of its mission: 'that a concern with women *and* men who have not written in the *same* cultural inscription (a working hypothesis that works well in colonial situations) cannot be mobilised *in the same way* as the investigation of gendering in one's own'.[16] The lesson here is that the conceptual terrain – the categories, histories, methods, and assumptions – of white feminism's conceptualisation of 'gender' and its indebtedness and allegiance to secular liberalism is so ethnocentrically specific that its extension beyond that specificity to co-opt the values, practices and histories of others in the service of its political itineraries should be approached very warily.

Mahmood shows well how such a dynamic operates with regard to the vexed question of women's agency. Demands for women's autonomy and voice, and recognition of even their *religious* agency have animated much feminist scholarship. More often than not – and this is where Mahmood's challenge to 'the feminist subject' and the subject of feminism rings so true – feminist engagement with notions of agency and voice has rubbed against 'traditionalist' understandings of women's piety where women are then framed as either passive and compliant, or resistant and rebellious. Consonant with the secularising imaginary of the liberalist political structures of western states, agency is thus advanced as an appropriate response and form of resistance to the assumed or mandated passivity of the religious woman. Failure to exert agency as resistance or to exercise one's voice autonomously is routinely read as a failure of the willing subject, a sign of the improperly formed political subject and of her retrogressive subjugation to patriarchal structures of power. But to impose such a frame is silencing and imperialist. Saba Mahmood thus warns against the feminist scholarly co-optation of women's agency in support of 'the goals of progressive politics' because it obscures those 'dimensions of human action whose ethical and political status does not map onto the logic of repression and resistance'.[17]

Calls

What has made it possible for white feminism to fail to see race and postcoloniality as the place from which configurations of centre and periphery must be rethought and even overturned? Part of the answer lies in the collective failure of white feminism to attend to the ethnocentrism of the field's history such that 'gender' is prioritised as the site of origination for critique (because it is assumed in the liberal feminist tradition to be the site of origination for the self), rather than the historical facticity of colonialisms, racisms, enslavement and their afterlives. 'Gender' rendered as a singularly central formation is claimed as both the place of enunciation and as providing the content and analytic framing for that enunciation. It appears to be unimplicated in colonial and racist value codings and the theorisations of embodiment, agency, voice and place, etc. that these assume and invite. These colonial and racist histories have formed the present, for all of us, however differentiated our relations to those histories might be and it thus remains a place from which the necessity or even possibility of the translation of 'gender' and its foregrounding must be tested.

The Indian feminist Uma Narayan, addressing the agonistic encounters between western and non-western feminists, has argued that 'Working together to develop a rich feminist account of this [colonial] history that di-

vides and connects us might well provide Western and Third-World feminists [with] some difficult but interesting common ground, and be a project that is crucial and central to any truly "international" feminist politics'. Narayan here implies that 'western' efforts of self-definition are also therefore profoundly 'political responses to this history'.[18]

Might we not then read the prioritisation of 'gender' within feminist thought as precisely embedded in the neo-imperialist politics of secular liberalism that of necessity invokes a temporally and spatially differential – hierarchical – relation to a series of Others? Must we not try to see how this differential relationship is then (mis)represented as analogous to many forms of marginality, where 'gender' is nonetheless a first amongst equals? Is this not a collusion with the structures of coloniality and racism that insist on, indeed require, the simultaneous homogeneity and non-universalisability of the apparent periphery? When we fail to account for and to the colonial and racist history that is in fact *the* place of common ground for all feminists, is white feminism in particular not indulging in a project of self-definition that repeats the colonial appropriation of the other in order to accrue social and intellectual capital? If we were to take seriously the vexed specificity of white colonial and racist conceptuality as a significant part of the making of 'gender' as a site of critique, might it be that 'gender' will no longer be the site where all the usual intersections 'intersect'?

The most pressing question which I think Mahmood, albeit obliquely, invites us to pursue, is why it is that white feminism has not started from the place of the other with whom it asserts political and intellectual solidarity, from the 'history that divides and connects us', and from the forms of sociality, belonging and responsibility that are other to its imaginary. Mahmood's call, the *da'wa*, with which we began, all the more poignant in the aftermath of her death, invites us to begin again with a work of translation, that now may fracture the certainties of the secular liberal monopolisation of 'freedom': '[W]e can no longer arrogantly assume that secular forms of life and secularism's progressive formulations necessarily exhaust ways of living meaningfully and richly in this world.'[19] The call is to move beyond the constrained commitments of the secular, liberal modern, recall its long history of withholding the promise of freedom, and seek those ways of living meaningfully that are not captured by its paradoxes. Responding to such a call is, must become, a feminist praxis.

Sîan Hawthorne is Senior Lecturer in Philosophy and Religion at SOAS University of London. Her research interests lie in the areas of religion and gender, intellectual history in the study of religions and its intersections with post- and decolonial thought.

Notes

1. Saba Mahmood, *Politics of Piety: The Islamic Revival and the Feminist Subject* (Princeton: Princeton University Press, 2005), 57.

2. Stathis Gourgouris, 'Detranscendentalizing the Secular', *Public Culture* 20:3 (2008), 437–45, and 'Antisecularist Failures: A Counterresponse to Saba Mahmood', *Public Culture* 20:3 (2008), 453–9; Sindre Bangstad, 'Saba Mahmood and Anthropological Feminism After Virtue', *Theory, Culture & Society* 28:3 (2011), 28–54.

3. Sarah Bracke and Nadia Fadil, '"Is the Headscarf Oppressive or Emancipatory?" Field Notes from the Multicultural Debate', *Religion and Gender* 2:1 (2012), 36–56; Quỳnh N. Phạm, 'Enduring Bonds: Politics and Life Outside Freedom as Autonomy', *Alternatives: Global, Local, Political* 38:1 (February 2013), 29–48; Peter Van der Veer, 'Embodiment, Materiality, and Power: A Review Essay', *Comparative Studies in Society and History* 50:3 (2008), 809–18.

4. I mark gender in this way to signal its conceptual function in feminist discourse, and thus am not referencing whatever materiality it may be assumed to describe.

5. Mahmood, *Politics of Piety*, 14.

6. I paraphrase here a question posed by Jacques Derrida with respect to 'religion' and it is the kind of questioning that he inaugurates with this query that I wish to pursue. See Jacques Derrida, *Acts of Religion*, ed. Gil Anidjar (New York and London: Routledge, 2002), 67. Derrida here asks 'And what if *religio* remained untranslatable?' in order to assess the operations of what he names as 'globalatinization' (*mondialatinization*).

7. See Mahmood, *Politics of Piety*, 16, 39, 163, 190.

8. Judith Butler, Ernesto Laclau and Slavoj Zizek, *Contingency, Hegemony, Universality: Contemporary Dialogues on the Left* (London: Verso, 2000), 35; Mahmood, *Politics of Piety*, 163, n. 9.

9. María Lugones, 'Toward a Decolonial Feminism,' *Hypatia* 25:4 (Fall 2010), 742–759.

10. See for example Daniel Dubuisson, *The Western Construction of Religion: Myths, Knowledge, and Ideology*, trans. William Sayers (Baltimore: Johns Hopkins University Press, 2003); Timothy Fitzgerald, *Discourse on Civility and Barbarity: A Critical History of Religion and Related Categories* (Oxford: Oxford University Press, 2007); Richard King, *Orientalism and Religion* (London and New York: Routledge, 1999); Tomoko Masuzawa, *The Invention of World Religions, or, How European Universalism was Preserved in the Language of Pluralism* (Chicago: University of Chicago Press, 2005). Despite important differences, these scholars share an interest in the rhetorical, discursive or geo-political operationalisation of the category 'religion' and indeed the constituting roles of coloniality and secularity in its figuration.

11. I use the term 'white feminism' not to indicate feminists who happen to be racialised as white, but rather those whose feminist approaches, politics and priorities are embedded in an epistemological framework where whiteness operates as an invisibilised, unmarked and unnamed normative ground and where non-whiteness, in contrast, is marked as specific, (hyper)visible, non-universalisable and marginal.

12. See Sîan Melvill Hawthorne, *Religion, Gender and Race: A Polemic* (London: Bloomsbury, forthcoming 2021).

13. Here I mean what Butler names, after Foucault, the 'ambivalence' at 'the heart of agency,' that is, the paradox of subjectivity within liberal thought: subjectification is both dependent on discursive formations which are not chosen but which nonetheless inaugurate, enable and sustain agentive subjectivity. The promise held out in the liberal imaginary with respect to freedom and autonomy is thus simultaneously constraining and enabling and is what Mahmood diagnoses as one of the problematics involved in representing agency in the constrictive oscillation between repression or resistance. See Judith Butler, *The Psychic Life of Power: Theories in Subjection* (Stanford: Stanford University Press, 1997), 18.

14. For various examples of these tendencies in the field of religion and gender, and white feminism more generally, see Sîan Melvill Hawthorne, 'Displacements: Religion, Gender, and the Catachrestic Demand of Postcoloniality', *Journal of Religion and Gender* 3:2 (2013), 168–187; 'Entangled Subjects: Feminism, Religion, and the Obligation to Alterity', in *The Sage Handbook of Feminist Theory*, ed. Mary Evans et al., (Thousand Oaks: Sage, 2014), 114–130; and 'Inhospitable Landscapes: Disciplinary Territories and the Feminist "Paradigm Shift"', *Journal of the British Association for the Study of Religions* 19 (2018), 36–55.

15. Here I would suggest that this difference is itself marked ambiguously because all lives are marked by the universalising impulse of secular liberalism in colonial modernity and its globalising frame. Mahmood's point of course is that compliance with this impulse is neither inevitable nor seamless, that we may choose to see those moments and sites where its totalising affects are neither referenced nor wholly effective.

16. Gayatri Chakravorty Spivak, *A Critique of Postcolonial Reason: Toward a History of the Vanishing Present* (Cambridge, MA: Harvard University Press, 1999), 176; author's emphasis.

17. Mahmood, *Politics of Piety*, 14.

18. Uma Narayan, *Dislocating Cultures: Identities, Traditions and Third World Feminism* (London and New York: Routledge, 1997), 80.

19. Mahmood, *Politics of Piety*, xi-xii.

Thinking critically with Saba Mahmood

Pınar Kemerli

Saba Mahmood made immensely important contributions to the critical understanding of secular power and its operations, without which the field would be significantly impoverished. Tragically cut short by her untimely death, her scholarship offers especially powerful insights into the critical turn in secularism studies: first and foremost that secularism is a modality of governance involved in the persistent regulation of religion and religious subjectivities in order to advance the prerogatives of the nation-state. More specifically, Mahmood conceptualises secularism as an expression of 'the modern state's sovereign power to reorganise substantive features of religious life, stipulating what religion ought to be, assigning its proper content, and disseminating concomitant subjectivities, ethical frameworks and quotidian practices.'[1] In her books, she meticulously traces the operations of secularism in their rich anthropological complexity in modern Egyptian society and dissects the dilemmas thereby generated specifically with respect to issues of agency, religious freedom and minority rights.[2]

Mahmood was central to the group of scholars that built upon Talal Asad's work and questioned the conventional understanding of secularism as the separation between religious and political spheres, and state neutrality towards religion.[3] The new body of scholarship, which we might call critical secularism studies, merged theoretical analysis of secularism as a political arrangement with empirically-grounded research into the effects of this arrangement. Rejecting simplistic narratives of separation, these critical approaches instead trace the complex permeations of the religious and the secular in modern political governance. Secularism is here portrayed as an exercise of sovereign power which entails the 'fashioning of religion as an object of continual management and intervention, and the shaping of religious life and sensibilities to fit the presuppositions and ongoing requirements of liberal governance.'[4] The question of how to separate religion from politics thus becomes a particularly salient issue and specific attention is directed to the tensions and paradoxes generated by the negotiations of this question within particular nation-states.

Mahmood's contribution to our understanding of secularism has provided a framework for a generation of scholars concerned with the role of secularism in the Middle East and North Africa (MENA) region. It was partly in response to the inspiration provided by Mahmood that I myself began to study another Muslim majority country, modern Turkey, to ask how the critical framework she developed might help us better understand the complexities of Turkish secularism. In the following reflections on the intellectual and political legacies of Saba Mahmood's work, I would like, then, to examine how her insights invite us to reconsider some of our basic assumptions about secularism in Turkey and the problems that its operations generate for the exercise of some religious freedoms.

In many ways, Turkey is an appropriate context in which to apply Mahmood's critical insights. In modernist accounts in particular, modern Turkish history is depicted as an exemplary instance of institutional and cultural secularisation.[5] Foregrounding the radical secularisation programme that the emergent republic pursued in its first few decades, scholars emphasise the dramatic speed of the modernisation of the legal system, the institutional structure and social norms which the new republic had inherited from the Ottoman era, praising the civic conception of nationalism thereby established as a 'radical rupture with the Islamic past'.[6] Emulating the example of the French republic, Turkey's founders significantly empowered the state to harness religion to advance the political purposes of the new regime. For instance, immediately after the abolishing of the Ottoman caliphate in 1924, Turkey established a governmental institution called the Directorate of Religious Affairs (Diyanet İşleri Başkanlığı) to control and regulate religion and religious practices.[7] The Directorate remains one of the largest and most powerful state institutions in Turkey to this day and oversees all issues concerning Islamic doctrine and worship including the training of religious personnel. Given this strictly regulative organisational structure, scholars such as Ahmet Kuru define the Turkish model of secularism as 'assertive'. In this model, Kuru writes, 'the state excludes religion from the public sphere and plays an assertive role as the agent of a social engineering project that confines religion to the private domain.'[8] Against this background of assertive secularisation, the successive electoral victories of Turkey's moderately Islamist Justice and Development Party (Adalet ve Kalkınma Partisi/AKP) in the last few decades are depicted as the transformation or 'backsliding' of Turkey's aggressively secular project. An increasing accommodation of religion alongside the civic revival of religious expression is thus characterised as indicative of a transition from an authoritarian to a more (neo)liberal form of secular rule.[9]

Yet the insights from Mahmood's work would urge us to question – I think quite correctly – this commonly provided story of the evolution of Turkish secularism. Indeed, this portrayal does not hold up well in the face of critical scrutiny. A diverse body of literature has recently shown that Turkish secular modernisation involved not as aggressive a 'rupture' with the Islamic past as was often suggested. Scholars have instead demonstrated the pervasive nature of religion's incorporation within the institutions and norms of Turkish nationalism and statecraft since the early days of the republic.[10] The claim that the republican state's dominant impulse has been hostility towards religion has also come to be disputed. While it is true that the Turkish state has persistently sought to control and regulate religion, this secular project did not always take the form of repression or elimination. As revisionist scholarship has shown, Turkey has in fact pursued a consistently pragmatic approach in this regard, accommodating religious values and institutions deemed necessary for the protection of state interests while attacking others found to be dangerous for state sovereignty and security. For instance, to combat the increasing appeal of communism among Turkey's youth, the junta government established after the 1980 coup adopted a cultural program known as the Turkish-Islamic synthesis. The program integrated Islamic values of obedience and sacrifice within national education while continuing to uphold the controversial headscarf ban in public offices and education.[11]

Such pragmatism, which has long marked the exercise of secular power in Turkey, raises doubts also about the portrayal of the recent transformations in secular governance as a sharp transition from an authoritarian past. As Mahmood's work persistently reminds us, 'the religious' remains a 'constitutive feature' of secular governance throughout its operations while the particular shape and intensity of its imbrication with 'the secular' may vary depending on particular historical conditions and necessities.[12] Thus, while it is true that AKP rule involved a more accommodating approach to religion within public life, it has continued the modern Turkish state's founding policy that religious sensibilities need to be carefully shaped and controlled to preserve state interests. The most dramatic recent expression of this continuity has perhaps been the colossal crackdown on the Gülen movement – an influential transnational socio-religious movement also known as Hizmet (Service) under the leadership of the US-based cleric Fethullah Gülen – whom AKP blamed for the failed coup attempt of 2016.[13]

The imbrication of Turkish sovereign interests with the exercise of secular power is further evinced in the operations of the military. As Mahmood's critical insights would suggest, it is here, in one of the 'most secular' of Turkish institutions, that the interplay between the religious and the secular emerges in its full complexity. The utilisation of Islamic values of obedience and warfare in the Turkish military has been a central pillar of the social and political power of an institution that has simultaneously projected itself as the staunchest defender of the secular regime in that country. Not only does this turn to religion in national defence stand for a salient representation of Turkish secularism's pragmatism when it comes to the roles religion should play in public life, but as we shall see it also poignantly shows how such pragmatism may nonetheless generate challenges for the state's very control of religious imagination and claims to religious freedom.

Turkey has imposed compulsory male conscription since 1927. Since its implementation, the institution has operated as a force of socio-political modernisation. Especially in the early decades of the republic, conscription served the important pedagogical function of educating the young men of the new nation in the ideals and norms of nationalism and citizenship. To this day, military service continues to serve this civic nationalist purpose and is widely revered as a sacred institution of Turkish nationalism. But in addition to civic-nationalism, the Turkish state educates conscripted civilians in a particular version of Islam during their service.[14] The interpretation produced and disseminated through the conscripts' education involves a highly militarised reading of religious doctrine, emphasising unconditional obedience to the state. A textbook entitled *Askere Din Kitabı – The Book on Religion for the Soldier* – is at the centre of this enterprise. Prepared by the Directorate as early as 1925, the book has since then been through seven editions, the last being published in 2002. Making frequent references to sacred texts and resources such as the Quran and *hadith* (sayings attributed to the Prophet Muhammad) alongside anecdotes from early Islamic and Turkic histories, the book presents the Turkish army as a sacred institution and calls on 'Muslim Turks' to faithfully obey the commands of their government and commanders. The primary aim is to present military service as a requirement not only of citizenship but also of Islamic faith and thereby strengthen citizens' resolve and enthusiasm for soldiering.[15] The book also idealises self-sacrifice and frequently invokes Islamic idioms of martyrdom, thereby presenting the national army as an avenue through which to achieve this 'blessing'.[16]

Importantly, the military's emphasis on the religious value of soldiering and national defence is reproduced in civilian education. As Sam Kaplan has shown, especially in the aftermath of the 1980s coup, there has been a gradual increase in the mobilisation of Islamic values of martial valour and self-sacrifice in revised school curricula.[17] The historical context of this development is of course crucial. This is the period that marks not only the junta government's embrace of the Turkish-Islamic synthesis but also the onset of the Kurdish liberation struggle in Turkey's southeast. Quickly escalating into guerrilla warfare, the conflict between the state and Kurdish insurgents has claimed thousands of lives, transforming military service into a highly dangerous undertaking. Under pressure to meet the rising requirements of military mobilisation and at pains to justify the loss of civilian lives, the state thus intensified its military recourse to religious values, thereby demonstrating secular power's attempt to generate the kinds of religious sensibilities that would help citizens respond to the difficult demands politics sometimes places on them.

How then should we interpret this systematic integration of the religious within national and pedagogical institutions and discourses of the state – especially in a country like Turkey that has been criticised for the rigidity of its secular impositions across most of its modern history? Are these moments of 'aberration from secularism'[18] or woefully incomplete approximations of it? Mahmood provides us with a different framework with which to tackle such questions. Rather than approaching these instances as signs of incomplete secularisation or 'third-world exceptionalisms', Mahmood argues that we should see them as 'diagnostic' of what she refers to as 'the dual impetus internal to political secularism – namely the modern state's disavowal of religion in its political calculus *and* its simultaneous reliance on religious categories to structure and regulate social life, thereby linking the private and public domains that the secular state aims to keep apart.'[19] According to Mahmood, this duality is an inescapable character of secular power despite generating most of its contradictions. A secular state like Turkey therefore could simultaneously uphold *and* violate norms and requirements of secularism – including the doctrine of the separation of the religious and the secular – so long as such violations ultimately serve the interests of the nation-state. Likening such transgressions of secularism to sovereign exceptions in the Schmittian sense, Talal Asad further points out the pervasive nature of such secular exceptionalism.[20] Put differently, like many other nation-states across the globe, by deciding what counts as religion and what its proper exercise should look like, Turkey could invoke the priority of its sovereign rights in this instance and every time it transgresses secular norms. While such sovereign transgressions may strike against secular expectations, critical approaches to secularism thus tell us that they ultimately are 'actualisations of potentialities within secularism, and are thereby integral to its very foundations.'[21]

Importantly, however, as Saba Mahmood points out, a significant consequence of these constitutive entanglements of secularism and sovereignty is that the question of how to separate religion from politics becomes a constant point of 'legal and political contestation' in modern liberal democracies.[22] In her final book *Religious Difference in a Secular Age* in particular, Mahmood explores the effects these constant renegotiations have on religious freedoms, emphasising how precarious their exercise may actually become in secular nation states despite ostensible commitments to their protection. Once again, this insight proves useful and appropriate in understanding Turkey's secular regime. The case of a Muslim conscientious objector (CO), Muhammed Serdar Delice, who sought to legally dispute the state's disavowal of the religious legitimacy of his objection to service illustrates how a particular claim to religious freedom in the context of military conscription has recently become the topic of legal and political controversy in Turkey.

While conscientious objection to conscription is considered a legitimate exercise of the right to freedom of thought, conscience, religion and belief by international institutions including the United Nations and the European Convention on Human Rights (ECHR), Turkey does not recognise this right. In the absence of laws regulating their refusal, COs are imprisoned for crimes that do not correspond to their actions, including desertion, persistent disobedience and alienating the public from the institution of military service. They may be imprisoned for periods of up to two years if found guilty of any of these charges. Given that conscription is a mandatory citizenship duty, COs are condemned also to a life of illegality even after their release. The European Court of Human Rights describes the subsequent living conditions of released COs as 'civil death', resulting in 'an inability to vote, marry, legally register a child, work, or get a passport.'[23]

But despite these difficulties awaiting COs, Turkey has had a small and persistent CO movement since the late 1980s. Unlike the trajectory followed by many other CO struggles in the world,[24] Turkish activism emerged as a secular anarchist movement gradually evolving to include other ideological commitments including religious objectors. In addition to a small number of Jehovah's Witnesses, Muslim objectors began to appear in the mid-2000s. Given the deep-seated Islamic valuation of military service in Turkey, which, as we have seen, the modern state itself cultivated, the appearance of an Islamically grounded opposition to the draft was in many ways surprising and marginal. Yet it also reflected the transformations occurring in Turkey's dissident public sphere partially as a result of the increasing accommodation of religious expression in public life under AKP rule. Delice was thus among the earliest Muslim COs to ground their objection to service in Islamic reason and join the antiwar movement in 2010.

Delice's public declaration of his refusal initiated the vicious legal circle that awaits all COs in Turkey. He was arrested multiple times for other crimes and served short-term sentences during which he experienced harassment and mistreatment.[25] When he found out that a military court had sentenced him in absentia to ten months in prison for desertion, he carried his case to an appellate court in 2012. The routine procedure in conscientious objection cases is to disavow the domestic relevance of this internationally recognised right, but, in Delice's case, the appeal court made a surprising exception, and took the decisions of the European Court of Human Rights (ECtHR) as the basis for evaluating domestic conscientious objection cases.[26] Because the ECtHR categorises conscientious objection under Article 9 of the ECHR, which concerns the freedom of thought, conscience and religion, this was a very positive development for the Turkish COs. However despite this important acknowledgement, the Turkish court upheld a narrow interpretation of Article 9 and argued that its provisions would apply only to those COs who are members of religions that categorically reject military service.[27] Comparing Delice's claims to those of Jehovah's Witnesses, the court argued that the latter 'reject military service, because they are part of this group or institution which fundamentally rejects military service.'[28] But in the case of Delice, who identifies as Muslim, this group requirement was not fulfilled. 'As a belief system', the court claimed, 'Islam does not reject the use of weaponry, the wearing of uniform, and other provisions entailed in compulsory military service.'[29] According to the court, in other words, Delice's claim to an Islamic conscientious objection was religiously inauthentic as Islam does not reject military service or violence.

Insisting that his claim to CO status is based on his religious convictions, Delice opposed the court's reasoning and asked a local mufti to be heard as an expert witness on the matter of the permissibility of conscientious objection in Islamic doctrine and conduct. (In Islamic law, a Mufti is a jurist expert on the Sharia.) His goal was to counter the court's theological interpretation that his refusal to serve was incompatible with Islam. But the court rejected this request on the grounds that only 'scientific' testimonies could be considered accountable evidence and that a mufti's testimony could not be considered scientific. 'The religious sphere', the court argued, 'is intrinsically related to beliefs and is dogmatic, [and] hence any view expressed from this field cannot be based on science and includes subjective elements.'[30] The glaring contradiction in the court's reasoning is hard to miss. While claiming that religious assessments cannot be considered determinative in legal proceedings given the intrinsic subjectivity of the religious sphere, the court nonetheless grounded its judgment of the validity of Delice's conscientious objection on its own theological assessment of the irredeemably militarist character of Islam.[31] That is, despite affirming theology to be inadmissible in the courtroom, the judges asserted as authoritative their own theological opinion as to the inauthenticity of Delice's religious convictions.

The court's position was thus a striking representation of Mahmood's observation about the extent to which modern state institutions are 'embroiled in substantive issues of religious doctrine and practice' despite the commitment to separating the religious from the political in legal calculations.[32] As we have seen, complex questions about the interpretation of conscientious objection and militarism in Islamic law and conduct were transformed into legal and political questions in Delice's case, with important consequences for whether Muslim COs could claim religious exemption from military service as some Christian citizens have. Moreover, Mahmood suggested that a further consequence of this politicisation of religious issues could be the intensification of inequalities among religions and their accommodation by the state. In line with such a suggestion, the Turkish court's claim that religious exemptions from service may be granted to Jehovah's Witnesses while denying the same religious freedom to Turkey's Muslims shows how secular governance and law itself can come to determine the religious freedom claims made within a nation state, thereby possibly generating distinctions and tensions in interfaith relations. Given Islam's majoritarian status in the Turkish context examined here, the opinion of the court in the Delice case did not lead to major social tension between Muslim and Jehovah's Witnesses COs. But as Mahmood's analysis of the strained interfaith relations between Muslims and Coptic Christians in Egypt has shown, the secular state's persistent intervention in religious issues and subsequent allocation of religious privileges and accommodations are necessarily prone to intensifying existing tensions and generating new ones.

Thanks to the critical turn in secularism studies as a result of the work of Saba Mahmood, amongst others, we now have a richer and more complex repertoire of concepts and insights with which to analyse the aforementioned paradoxes of secular power. As I have tried to show here, by utilizing Mahmood's insights in my analysis of Turkish secularism and its problems, I find the renegotiation of existing assumptions about secular power's relationship to sovereignty and law to be one of the most important legacies of Saba Mahmood's work. Her thinking will undoubtedly continue to shape our explorations of the paradoxes and inequalities that the operations of secularism generate. But perhaps more importantly, it may also inspire us to think about what we can actually do about them.

Pınar Kemerli is Clinical Assistant Professor in Global Liberal Studies at New York University.

Notes

1. Saba Mahmood, *Religious Difference in a Secular Age: A Minority Report* (Princeton: Princeton University Press, 2015), 3.

2. Saba Mahmood, *Politics of Piety: The Islamic Revival and the Feminist Subject* (Princeton: Princeton University Press, 2004); Mahmood, *Religious Difference*.

3. See Talal Asad, *Genealogies of Religion* (Baltimore: The Johns Hopkins University Press, 1993); Talal Asad, *Formations of the Secular: Christianity, Islam, Modernity* (Stanford: Stanford University Press, 2003); Hussein Ali Agrama, *Questioning Secularism: Islam, Sovereignty, and the Rule of Law in Modern Egypt* (Chicago: University of Chicago Press, 2012); Charles Hirschkind, *The Ethical Soundscape: Cassette Sermons and Islamic Counterpublics* (New York: Columbia University Press, 2006); Elizabeth Shakman-Hurd, *The Politics of Secularism in International Relations* (Princeton: Princeton University Press, 2007); Winnifred Sullivan, *The Impossibility of Religious Freedom* (Princeton: Princeton University Press, 2005); Humeira Iqtidar, *Secularizing Islamists* (Chicago: University of Chicago Press, 2014).

4. Agrama, *Questioning Secularism*, 24.

5. See, for example, Bernard Lewis, *The Emergence of Modern Turkey* (London: Oxford University Press, 1961); Halil Inalcik, *From Empire to Republic: Essays on Ottoman and Turkish Social History* (Istanbul: Isis Press, 1995); Niyazi Berkes, *The Development of Secularism in Turkey* (Montreal: McGill University Press, 1964).

6. Binnaz Toprak, 'Secularism and Islam: The Building of Modern Turkey', *Macalester International* 14 (2005), 32.

7. Andrew Davison, 'Turkey, a "Secular" State? The Challenge of Description', *South Atlantic Quarterly* 102 (2003), 333–50; Markus Dressler, 'Making Religion through Secularist Legal Discourse: The Case of Turkish Alevism', in *Secularism and Religion-Making*, ed. Markus Dressler and Arvind-Pal S. Mandair (Oxford: Oxford University Press, 2011), 187–209.

8. Ahmet Kuru, 'Passive and Assertive Secularism: Historical Conditions, Ideological Struggles, and State Policies toward Religion', *World Politics* 59:4 (2007), 582.

9. See Jenny White, *Muslim Nationalism and the New Turks* (Princeton: Princeton University Press, 2013); Jeremy Walton, *Muslim Civil Society and the Politics of Religious Freedom in Turkey* (Oxford: Oxford University Press, 2017).

10. Soner Cagaptay, *Islam, Secularism, and Nationalism in Modern Turkey: Who Is a Turk?* (London: Routledge, 2006); Barış Ünlü, *Türklük Sözleşmesi* [The Turkishness Contract] (Istanbul: Dipnot, 2018); Mesut Yeğen, 'Turkish Nationalism and the Kurdish Question', *Ethnic and Racial Studies* 30 (2007), 119–51; Aslı Iğsız, *Humanism in Ruins: Entangled Legacies of the Greek-Turkish Population Exchange* (California: Stanford University Press, 2018).

11. Sam Kaplan, *The Pedagogical State: Education and the Politics of National Culture in Post-1980 Turkey* (Stanford: Stanford University Press, 2006); Sam Kaplan, 'Din-u Devlet All Over Again? The Politics of Military Secularism and Religious Militarism in Turkey Following the 1980 Coup', *International Journal of Middle East Studies* 34:1 (2002), 113–27; Pınar Kemerli, 'Religious Militarism and Islamist Conscientious Objection in Turkey',

International Journal of Middle East Studies 47:2 (2015), 281–301; Serdar Şen, *Silahli Kuvvetler ve Modernizm* [Social Engineering of the Armed Forces] (Istanbul: Sarmal Yayinevi, 1996); Bozkurt Güvenc and Şaylan Tekeli,*Türk-İslam Sentezi* [Turkish-Islamic Synthesis] (Istanbul: Sarmal Yayinevi, 1991).

12. Mahmood, *Religious Difference*, 22.

13. 'Turkey's Failed Coup Attempt: All You Need to Know', *Al Jazeera*, 15 July 2017; Amberin Zaman, 'Ankara Rounds up More "Gulenist" Military Pilots', *Al-Monitor*, 30 January 2019.

14. Şen, *Silahli Kuvvetler ve Modernizm* [The Armed Forces and Modernism]; Sinem Gurbey, 'Islam, Nation-State, and the Military: A Discussion of Secularism in Turkey', *Comparative Studies of South Asia, Africa and the Middle East* 29:3 (2009), 371–80; Kemerli, 'Religious Militarism'.

15. Ahmet Hamdi Akseki, *Askere Din Kitabı* [The Book on Religion for the Soldier] (Istanbul: Diyanet İşleri Yayınları, 1977), 29–30.

16. Akseki, *Askere* [The Book on Religion for the Soldier], 300.

17. Kaplan, 'Din-u Devlet All Over Again?'; Kaplan, *The Pedagogical State*.

18. Agrama, *Questioning Secularism*, 8.

19. Mahmood, *Religious Difference*, 25.

20. Talal Asad, 'Trying to Understand French Secularism', in *Political Theologies: Public Religions in a Post-Secular World*, ed. Hent de Vries and Lawrence Eugene Sullivan (New York: Fordham University Press, 2006), 494–526.

21. Agrama, *Questioning Secularism*, 8.

22. Mahmood, *Religious Difference*, 4.

23. Hülya Üçpınar, 'The Criminality of Conscientious Objection in Turkey and Its Consequences', in *Conscientious Objection: Resisting Militarized Society*, ed. Özgür Heval Çınar and Coşkun Üsterc (New York: Zed Books, 2009), 242–56.

24. See Charles C. Moskos and John Whiteclay Chambers, eds., *The New Conscientious Objection: From Sacred to Secular Resistance* (New York: Oxford University Press, 1993).

25. In the following discussion of Delice's case, I draw upon interviews I conducted with him as well as legal and newspaper coverage of his case. For a more detailed analysis of his court case, see my 'Refusing to Become Pious Soldiers', in *Contested Spaces in Contemporary Turkey*, ed. Fatma Muge Gocek (London: I.B. Tauris, 2018), 367–94.

26. War Resisters' International, 'Turkey: Military Courts Recognise Right to Conscientious Objection', *War Resisters' International* (2012).

27. Mine Yıldırım, 'TURKEY: Selective Progress on Conscientious Objection', *Forum 18 News Service*, May 2012.

28. Ekin Karaca, 'Mahkeme Delice'yi Degil Ama Vicdani Reddi Tanidi' [The Court Recognised Conscientious Objection but not Delice], *Bianet*, March 2012.

29. Karaca, 'Mahkeme Delice'yi Degil Ama Vicdani Reddi Tanidi' [The Court Recognized Conscientious Objection but not Delice].

30. Yıldırım, 'Selective progress'.

31. See Winnifred Sullivan's analysis of the tensions faced by secular law while reflecting on issues of religion freedom in *The Impossibility of Religious Freedom*.

32. Mahmood, *Religious Difference*, 2.

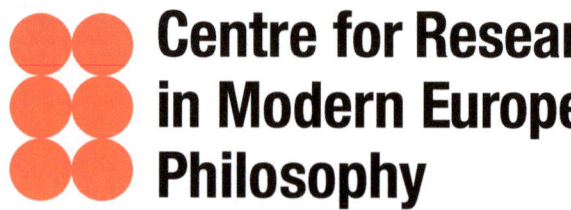

Centre for Research in Modern European Philosophy

EVENTS

Friday 4 October
17.30–19.00
Weber and Workers
Mario Tronti
Followed by a book launch for the English translation of Tronti's *Workers and Capital* (1966; Verso 2019)

Thursday 17 October
17.30–19.00
Natural History, Transcendental Logic and Race
Stella Sandford

Friday 1 November
11.00–18.00
Workshop on
Authority, Depoliticization, Dehumanization
Speakers include
Natacha Israël
(University of Rennes),
Hager Weslati
(Kingston University)

Kingston University London

Details at **www.kingston.ac.uk/crmep**

edited by
PETER OSBORNE
ÉRIC ALLIEZ
ERIC-JOHN RUSSELL

Éric Alliez
Étienne Balibar
Tithi Bhattacharya
Boris Buden
Sara R. Farris
John Kraniauskas
Elena Louisa Lange
Maurizio Lazzarato
Antonio Negri
Peter Osborne
Eric-John Russell
Gayatri Chakravorty Spivak
Keston Sutherland

CRMEP BOOKS

Capitalism: concept, idea, image
Aspects of Marx's *Capital* today

Planetary Utopias

Angela Davis and Gayatri Chakravorty Spivak in conversation with Nikita Dhawan

This conversation was recorded on Sunday 24 June 2018 as part of the closing plenary of the symposium 'Planetary Utopias: Hope, Desire and Imaginaries in a Postcolonial World' (curated by Nikita Dhawan) in the 'Colonial Repercussions' event series at the Akademie der Künste, Berlin. It was transcribed by Anna Millan and has been revised for the current publication.

Nikita Dhawan: Let me begin by asking you about your understanding of the role of the intellectual in nurturing habits of thinking and imagination that would facilitate postimperial politics. You warn against tales of heroic individualism and the Messiah-model of leadership, which erases the contribution of collectives as agents of social change.

Angela Davis: We have the habit of assuming that 'leaders' must correspond to a masculinist notion of individualism – they must be heroic individuals. Interestingly, during the Ferguson protest in 2014, when some of the veteran Civil Rights leaders visited Ferguson, they weren't well-received because of the way they foregrounded assumptions about movements and leaders that emanated from their experiences in the Civil Rights Movement. Their position was that the Ferguson protesters lacked leadership, that they needed a single recognizable leader. 'You have no recognizable leader', the protesters were told. In fact, there was leadership and most of the people in leadership were women. To the veteran 'leaders', the idea of women in leadership was equivalent to no leadership. In the era of Black Lives Matter, not only are women assuming positions of leadership, young activists today are also exploring different leadership paradigms –for example, what it might mean to develop collective forms of leadership. In this we have little experience. Even those of us who have been involved in revolutionary activism for many years, were schooled in these notions of the heroic male leader. And so I am learning a great deal from the younger generations who are trying to imagine new forms of leadership – leadership that invites people to participate in unprecedented ways, unprecedented because they are invited to bring their whole selves into the movement. They are invited to come with their pain and their traumas. As revolutionary activists in the past, we were asked to leave everything behind except our revolutionary commitment. And so I think that this moment is very exciting, because we are witnessing new forms of leadership – collective leadership, empathetic leadership. In my presentation, I intentionally used the example of Lauren Olamina, the character in Octavia Butler's *Parable of the Sower* and her hyper-empathy syndrome. These new leadership approaches attempt to incorporate what is often referred to as self-care – I think we need a better word for that, because that has become so jargonistic – into the process of conceptualising and organising movements for radical change.

Gayatri Spivak: I would agree and I would also say that in the postcolonial world the real problem is what Frantz Fanon, in the third chapter of *The Wretched of the Earth*, wrote about using the English word 'leaders'. They can use the democratic structure to keep what Weber would call a neopatrimonial society going. Today because of this voting as body count, these are the leaders we know: Duterte, Erdoğan, Trump. This is now no longer exclusive to the Third World, for Europe is also turning to the right in that way. In our village schools[1] we try to discourage the tendency to breed 'leaders', in this special sense, who will then become agents of violence. This is what the students learn from the usually avaricious rural middle class. So they fall for that. I will say, for example, to someone, a nice kid who knows the answers and is constantly putting up his or her hand: 'Hey, you know, who is really smart knows how to be quiet. See, I know all the answers. I'm not saying anything. So, let you and me be quiet together and see if everybody can come up with what you say.' My teachers are also trained to discourage someone answering all the questions. It isn't that they are not being rewarded for being intelligent. They are being told what intelligence is. This is what Abiola Irele said in his book, *The African Scholar*. He asked me to introduce his final book just before his death, for which I feel extremely honoured. In that book he calls it followership, because good leaders follow in every sense of the word. An unexamined idea of leadership is all around. You really have to see what's coming out from all of the people who are doing something, rather than telling them, 'you ought to do this, movements are like this, we know'. This is what I've called feudality without feudalism. Feudality, loyalty. So I am with Angela, I totally am.

Nikita Dhawan: Another extremely instructive lesson that we have learnt from you is to adopt a critical posture towards the tools, concepts, vocabularies and organising practices that characterise landscapes of struggle. There is this wonderful, possibly apocryphal, quote that 'The last capitalist we hang shall be the one who sold us the rope.' What do we do with this double bind that the instruments we have to use to change unjust structures are inherited from these very structures?

Angela Davis: This is what we have and we have no other choice than to use them and to simultaneously question them. And so the process of developing critical habits, habits of self-questioning, is a process that never ends. And we are learning a great deal now especially, given the activism of transgender communities. We are learning a great deal about what it means to challenge categories that we have considered to be so normal that they aren't even worth questioning. But they actually constitute the arena, the ground of our thinking. Thus when we look at movements around transgender issues, movements against the violence directed against transgender women of colour, we realize that they constitute *the* sector of the population that is the target of more forms of violence – state, personal, individual, etc. – and more consistent violence than any other group. So we are learning how to challenge the binary structure of gender even though there is often a telling awkwardness, especially in instances where you are asked to introduce yourself with your preferred pronouns. And that awkwardness is good and productive because it makes us question that which we haven't previously known how to question. So I don't think anything is immune from that process, even the ways in which we are formulating this question about how to be critical regarding that which we consider most normal, that which otherwise is ideologically constructed. And I guess it's about education, about the kind of education that Gayatri was speaking about, as opposed to the education that simply wants to produce skilled subjects who are able to participate well in the machinery of global capitalism. The last thing I would say is that we have to really beware of these terms that are supposed to carry the entire weight of struggles for justice. Sara Ahmed was talking about the term diversity yesterday and I really hate that notion. I cannot stand the notion of diversity, because it means largely the effort to make the machine run more effectively with those who were previously excluded by the machine. Who wants to be assimilated into a racist institution, when the institution continues to maintain its racist structure? This is why we always have to be hyperconscious of our vocabularies. This is a practice that I want to carry to my grave.

Gayatri Spivak: Yes, it is legitimation by reversal. Before they were all bad and now they are all good. This is why I find 'Global South' to be a reverse racist term. I mean there are some real self-constructed native informants selling themselves from these places. But this issue of having only a tainted methodology with which to work, I find that to be completely ok. You work with what you can: an affirmative sabotage. When Audre Lorde said that you can't break down the master's house with the master's tools, she was extremely angry because of the treatment she had received at NYU. A thing like 'The subaltern cannot speak' – these are enraged declarations. Many take it as an excuse for avoiding homework. 'No, no, we don't have to read any of the master's tools. No, the house will not be broken down.' Lorde was not giving a formula for saving intellectual labour.

In that context I would say that the masters had the leisure of the theory class. They had all the leisure on our backs – and some of us also collaborating with our tongues hanging out, so let's not just do a finger-pointing – to develop these theories. And also, they had such a very long time in early capitalism that they could do this slowly, whereas many colonial places got the mode of exploitation without the mode of production, so they couldn't do it from inside. We should take those well-developed methods, make our former masters our servants as it were, put them on tap rather than on top, inhabit them well, turn them around. Don't accuse them, don't excuse them, use them for something which they were not made for.

I mean, I could give you such an Indian thing right now and you'd say 'Oh Gayatridi, Yoga!' Look what's happening in India. My religion is becoming genocidal, it's a theocracy, and every Global South elite person is selling alternative epistemologies. No Sir! (It's very good to do descriptive alternative epistemologies; I don't censor work.) But one more thing. You know how I teach English to my students in India. Of course, without English they are going to go to hell. There are no books in their houses. They shit in the woods. I mean, they don't know colonialism. They know the caste system, right? So they have not seen white people. When Ben Baer first went they thought Ben had a disease. Most of my students and their parents haven't seen trains, and at least one teacher has not been on a train. So I say to them, our alphabet is so extraordinarily beautiful. I mean, it's true. As Todorov told me so long ago, the structuralists almost died when they discovered it was from 500 BC, or whenever Pānini's date is. All beautifully structured. And I say to them, look, it's extraordinarily well-structured, but we don't even use these things. And the people who have made the books, they don't even realise that this is what the language is. They just screw it up. We love our mother tongue. It's our mother, it's a wonderful language. And I say, 'Hey, but why did English win, hey? Look at this map, this is the little place where we speak Bangla and everybody in this whole huge place is speaking English, why did they win? Because there are just 26 letters, man.' And they can just do anything with them. You put the E at the end and 'cut' becomes 'cute' and 'plan' becomes 'plane'. I am a teacher of English and I am going to deprive these kids? So, I say to them, 'look, in our vowels, we don't have a long A, but English has a long A. P-L-A-N is plan and P-L-A-N-E plane has a long A. We have just got OI and OU, they have an AI.' So I make them excited about this. ...

The English classes in my schools are for people who have no sense of English at all. When a Chinese guy said to me that you speak English well, because the British had their boots on your neck, I said 'Brother, you are right. And you are here because the WTO has its boots on your neck. But the thing is, we defeated the English by loving the language. So that's what I will tell you. There is no way that a language is just a criminal language. You turn it around.' Really it's these kids who have taught me this way of approaching the language. Taught this way, it is an extension of their mother tongue. I have argued with Wai Chee Dimock that that is how the great Arab translators of Greek classics translated, making the so-called 'foreign' language their own, rather than 'foreignising' them. Here, historically, the teacher can make elite and subaltern meet.

Nikita Dhawan: À propos contaminated structures and 'affirmative sabotage', I had this conversation with Angela in Frankfurt and I think we agreed to disagree about what to do with the state. So to Gayatri, my question is what is the relation of planetarity to the state? Angela, you propose that we need to reimagine and envision other ideas of justice and punishment as the state is heavily invested in the prison-industrial complex and through its monopoly on violence, reproduces social and political forms of violence. Angela, would you describe your position as anarchist, and your utopia as a post-state world, where the state withers away? Or can we hope for a state that is capable of representing the interests of vulnerable citizens, so that these subaltern citizens can make a claim on the state to serve them?

Angela Davis: It depends on how far into the future you are thinking about. Because certainly there are instances now where it is really important to compel the state to speak to the needs of people, and I am really excited about the fact that in the US people are demonstrating outside of detention centres all over the country. But I think ultimately the model of the bourgeois nation state, ensconced as it is in capitalism, will never do the work of guaranteeing justice. While we will have to deal with the state for the time being, we have to engage in the kind of organising and activism that teaches and encourages people to imagine something very different from this institution that only guarantees the rights of a very small minority of people. The nation state serves a world, as Gayatri was pointing out, where the overwhelming majority of the wealth is concentrated in a few hands – eight billionaires own more than half of the world's population.

Gayatri Spivak: Bill Gates owns 93 billion dollars.

Angela Davis: Yes, I mean, you can't even imagine that. Jeff Bezos of Amazon just bought Whole Foods. I mean, capitalism, maybe this is the beginning of another conversation … you know, this kind of acquisitive nature of capitalism that makes people want more and more and more. So, no, I don't think that we will be able to retain any aspect of that state.

Gayatri Spivak: Ok, I give support to this, but I am also a little bit different, because if I have a model, it's Rosa Luxemburg-style social democracy – so, not the usual, not even a Marxist party. They voted in the war credits for the First World War, right? Luckily Marx was dead by then. I consider Angela's position a very serious position that is not opposed to mine. We certainly do think of the ones who think that we must be able to envisage the uselessness of the state in the future as our allies. But in the meantime the state is both medicine and poison, because the so-called international civil society – as I have said before, the word 'civil society' simply means they went to civics class in school, they know that anything that's not government is civil society – has no social contract. They are self-selected moral entrepreneurs often based on corporate funding. History is larger than personal goodwill and Marxism is not about kneecapping. So, I am not questioning the good will of people who work within the NGO system. I know many good people, for example Mpho Ndebele, who are working totally within an NGO. She is using that bad instrument to good ends: affirmative sabotage. So, this is not personal. But I would say that if the state is ignored, then the fuzzy side of the state, nationalism, which is based on the world's wealth of languages, we won't be able to hold it at bay. Therefore what I very much suggest is a more regional version of the abstract structures of welfare that the state cannot use under the contemporary conjuncture. Now the state is managerial of global capital. Neoliberalism removes the barriers between global capital and state capital. And then the human rights people come and shame the state, thinking that the state is supposed to be bad anyway.

The subaltern are people who are, by Gramsci's definition, small social groups on the fringes of history. Our work is so much to insert the subaltern – so the 'subaltern' is potentially generalizable – into the circuit of citizenship. That's as far as they can go and they can work with that structure. As I say, the Angela Davises of the world with a view of the state as something that we must finally get rid of, they are our allies, they are not our opponents. But nonetheless, for the moment – and we are non-teleological even in the long run – the work with the subaltern is for citizenship. It's very hard because there has to be follow-up implementation, because the state ain't going to like the fact of citizenship being worked at in this way. How do I know this? You know, I haven't taken American citizenship after 58 years. I have a 58 year-old green card, basically because I like to vote in India, and also keep on teaching at those rural schools, visiting India as often as I can without compromising my work at Columbia, that has allowed me to participate in the voting action of hundreds of students over 54 years of teaching. Thus I can see how uneven, what a relief map citizenship is. And if that is so for me as a metropolitan world traveller, how much more for the subaltern people. Citizenship, as the world teaches us every day, is a resource we ought to protect persistently.

This is what has happened with subalternisation, with Occupy Wall Street, since the Reagan-Bush era in the Eighties – when all of the welfare structures of the New Deal, including, finally, the Glass-Steagall, keeping commercial banks and investment banks separate – were annulled and the crash of 2007 was built on the material text of family values: 'We love our home', the classic mistaking of Department I, producing further capital, for Department II, producing for individual consumption. It is not an accident that in buying a house, the individual releases the largest amount of financial instruments into the circuit of capital. This is the material description of ideology, mistaking the housing industry as a resource for family values.[2] Therefore it is this kind of involvement one needs to work with, strategising with the state as medicine that can become poison, to heal the polity repeatedly, always only partially. And that's why, just from the practical point of view, I follow Rosa Luxemburg, whom I admire greatly. What I say to the people who are my supervisors, my teachers, etc. is that I am your enemy in the context of the state because I am good, my parents are good, but two generations of goodness do not undo thousands of years of the denial of the right to intellectual labour which is what we have undergone. Now the state is somewhat ok with you because I am here, but what we are really trying to do is to see if the state is going to work for you without me. How can you materially come to the place where the state is your servant?

One of my supervisors was running for the Panchayat (rural local self-government unit) elections as a Communist Party Marxist candidate. He was not allowed even to put in his nomination because of Hindu nationalist violence. In that kind of context, I am not ready to give up on the state yet. But yes, regionalism rather than state competition. I am trying to think like China. I just did a thing that I called 'Imperatives to Reimagine the Silk Road', so that I could try to imagine myself outside of my US personship or my Indian personship, competitively nationalistic as they are. States in this effort are not bound inside their boxes fighting to see who is growing more. We must promote critical regionalism at the higher level. Regional groups such as ASEAN (Association of South East Asian Nations) and SAARC (South Asian Association for Regional Cooperation) should not be just economic. NATO, for example, should not have been so poorly conceived. I could go on forever, because this is about my actual practice. I could go on to stories about land reform, for example. Let me stop here.

Nikita Dhawan: In light of these considerations, what do you think about the possibilities of international organising and transnational solidarity in the contemporary world?

Angela Davis: I have to keep reminding myself that we are in Germany where it has been very difficult to generate a vibrant Palestine solidarity movement and support for BDS – am I right?[3] If we think about the solidarity work Palestinian activists did in 2014, when the Ferguson protest served as a catalyst for a very new movement, a black freedom movement, a movement for black lives, the Black Lives Matter movement, we realise how central Palestinians were to the production of a new historical moment for Black people in the US. Most of you probably know that Palestinian activists on the ground in Palestine were the very first to contact the Ferguson protesters through social media and not only offered solidarity but provided advice to the protesters as to how to deal with tear gas. Interestingly, they noticed, from visual images of the protests in Ferguson, that the tear gas canisters – made by Combined Tactical Systems in the US – were the same tear gas canisters which were used in occupied Palestine. This served as a catalyst for further researching the links between Israel and the US as they directly influence policing in black communities – the exchange of weapons, the training of small police departments such as Ferguson in the US in 'anti-terrorist' strategies. Moreover, Palestinian activists inaugurated the international solidarity for Black Lives Matter. I don't know whether the US contemporary black movement would exist as we know it had it not been for the solidarity extended by people in

Palestine. It should also be the case that Palestine solidarity is recognised as central to all social justice struggles during this period just as in a previous period, whatever involvements we had, we all took a stand against apartheid in South Africa. South African solidarity was indeed a measure of the importance of the work we were doing, whether it was around women's issues, education activism, anti-repression, etc. Palestine is the South Africa of our contemporary period.

Gayatri Spivak: Today, also think of the Rohingyas in this way. Please think of the Rohingyas in this way. They cannot show any solidarity because they are now so massively uneducated. They don't know the world exists, cannot think about South Africa or Palestine. I am of course a member of the BDS, but think of the Rohingyas. Nobody really thinks of them. Do something. Maria do Mar Castro Varela organised a wonderful conference on 26th of February in Berlin, so we add their name – Rohingyas – to the list. Today, with self-promoting promises of repatriation, what we have to keep in mind is that Myanmar will not give them citizenship. In India, citizenship is being withdrawn from Bengali Muslims, even, in one case, from a veteran of the Indian army.

Angela Davis: You are absolutely right and thank you so much, Gayatri, for constantly insisting on rendering visible the predicament of the Rohingyas. What people often don't realise also is Palestinian Americans were protesting in Ferguson. The Black Lives Matter movement is often perceived as an all-black movement. They assume that only black people were protesting the killing of Mike Brown in 2014. But there were Palestinians, there were Latinx people, there were Asian-Americans, it was multi-racial. But I want to use this opportunity to say something about the way in which the notion of 'anti-blackness' has travelled. I know this concept does do important work, but I'm very careful about the implications of this category that black people constitute the most important group that is subject to racism. Sometimes 'anti-blackness' is used as an implicit criticism of the category 'people of colour' and to point to 'anti-blackness' in communities of people of colour. Of course there is racism everywhere. And black people are not immune to either anti-black racism or racist-inspired ideological assaults against other people of colour. So it is important to be careful regarding assumptions that black people are always the primary targets of racism. Discussions of anti-blackness often centre on pain and injury, which although not unimportant, can create barriers to developing solidarity, to developing the kind of empathy we were talking about. And if, from where I stand, the importance of black people's histories in the Americas resides precisely in the fact that there has been an ongoing freedom struggle for many centuries, the centrality of black struggles is much more about freedom than it is about blackness.

Gayatri Spivak: I just have a question: what do you think about Afro-pessimism? I really want you to say something about that.

Angela Davis: Well, this was my way of speaking about Afro-pessimism.

Gayatri Spivak: Well, ok, I get a good mark. Good, good, I am with you 100 percent.

Angela Davis: You know, in many places in Europe I have noticed that these ideas are travelling so rapidly.

Gayatri Spivak: It started in France.

Angela Davis: Yes, in France, in the Netherlands. And I think it is linked to a kind of black nationalism that always appears to be the stance to which black movements defer. No matter how much we contest it, there seems to be a regular capitulation to nationalism – it keeps coming back. W.E.B. DuBois suggested that anti-imperialism was more effective than nationalism. One of the dangers of black nationalism is the way it does its ideological work of reinforcing the nation-state paradigm through many of us who nevertheless believe that we are contesting the state.

Gayatri Spivak: Yes, it is an object of resistance, Angela, that's why I said medicine and *poison*. You constantly train, you constantly have to be a Gramscian permanent persuader, in order to use that bloody structure, but no, it is capable of great harm. But I just don't think that the state has to be like that, for those of us who are working on the subaltern sections of the electorate ...

Nikita Dhawan: Angela, you stood as a Vice Presidential candidate, so somehow there must have been a plan...

Angela Davis: But I didn't think I was going to win. I had no intentions of winning. It was about disrupting the electoral process. It was about also demonstrating that electoral politics can't claim all of the terrain of politics. And it was about bringing issues into the electoral arena that otherwise would not have been addressed.

Nikita Dhawan: And what would you have done if you had won?

Angela Davis: That's not even a fair question though. I remember the years before I was acquitted – you know I was charged with three capital crimes and faced the death penalty three times – I remember saying during that period if I am ever acquitted I am going to run for Sheriff, the Sheriff of Marin County, which is the place where I was being held as a prisoner, but of course that was in jest. But I do think it is important to address electoral politics, although in a nuanced way. For some reason people assume that whenever you venture in that direction you have somehow betrayed your radical roots. I was arguing before the Trump election that people needed to vote, they needed to go to the polls and they needed to vote against Trump. And I made a statement at one point to the effect, I think, I said I am not so narcissistic as to say that I cannot bring myself to vote for Hillary Clinton. And then that travelled all over social media that I was, you know, betraying my radical roots just because I was going to vote for Hillary Clinton. And I spent the rest of the talk that I was doing explaining why Hillary Clinton would not be a good president. I think the point that I was making is that we need in the US, within the context of the state and electoral politics, to imagine, to build toward a very different kind of radical political party. We need a political party that represents the interests of the working class, that is feminist, that is anti-racist, that challenges heteropatriarchy, that does all of those things.

Gayatri Spivak: And here I am not with you.

Angela Davis: Okay. This is good, we disagree here.

Gayatri Spivak: I don't think a party is a good thing.

Angela Davis: I mean I think you are right. I think you are right. But I am talking about a party with a different kind of leadership, a different kind of structure, the discussions we were having before about feminist leadership can help us to imagine a formation that we are compelled to call a party formation, but that does not correspond to what we know as political parties.

Gayatri Spivak: Yes and you know I am making the same kind of arguments about the state, about what we know as the state. So, it's okay, I mean again…

Angela Davis: So, would you be with us?

Gayatri Spivak: For a party? No, and I will tell you why, because you are talking here in the United States about 'we need "dot dot dot"', speaking about the state. It's different in India with its 17 left parties, in West Bengal with its second international communism, M.N. Roy founding the Communist Party of Mexico, etc., and the way I have been guided by the *Frontier* group, the left of the left party critique of the parliamentary left. It is not the same everywhere, as in a colonial country where the state was not at the centre. The United States is not the model of the world. This is why I say that we have to think state-wise. I mean you just said in the US 'we need a party "dot dot dot"', because the left has been so defunct, whereas in India, I don't think a party is going to do anything. So therefore I think I will not be against you, but I will not put my faith in this. I cannot agree with Gramsci, whom I really like very much, that the party might be the modern prince. That was the anti-state argument – party.

Angela Davis: But if we can perhaps develop a new way of thinking about a formation that can have an impact on the state as you suggest. And of course this is a very practical question about, what do we do now in the US.

Gayatri Spivak: In the case of the Tricontinent, as the Bolsheviks and the Chinese communists used to call what we call the Global South, one is focused on the largest sector of the electorate, with whom the parties are really doing bad things. So, an alternative party for these millions of people, who are being violently pushed into voting, is a bicycle for a fish. In Africa campaigners go to campaign with the unsystematised mother tongues, so that right before elections you have ethnic violence. So one has to see that the party is not in itself an unquestioned good. In the United States, Cornel West pushes for a new party. Good … I like the United States, I have lived there for 58 years, so I understand where that comes from, but it does seem to me that one of the problems with the US is that sometimes it thinks it's the world, so that even the radicals adjudicate for what *the* party will be.

Angela Davis: You are absolutely right about that. And I think those of us who have spent most of our lives in the States have a responsibility to do the work of what Ngũgĩ called decolonising the mind, because even activists, radical activists, are not immune to US exceptionalism and the tendency to think that the US is the world. So I am thinking narrowly – not universally – about the specific predicament we face in the US, which of course has repercussions all over the world. But what do we do two years from now? Where do we go? We will not have another party by then anyway – and the Democratic Party doesn't seem like it's doing very well.

Gayatri Spivak: I wrote a little thing for Occupy Wall Street, because they asked me to, called 'What is to be done?'. It is very bold and rough, but I was talking about how even the states were trying to make Obama come forward to solve the 2007 crisis, when even the Congressional record commented on the insecuritisation of the loan syndrome, and Obama couldn't do anything given the exigencies of finance capital. So, those of us who remain Marxists have to see that electoral politics is not going to do anything anywhere *by itself* anymore, although it should still be used.

Angela Davis: I totally agree with you on that, I absolutely agree. I just want to bring the issue of indigenous people into the conversation. When we speak about postcolonialities, certainly we need to in the first place think about those who were subject to the colonisation process from the very beginning. I am listening to Gayatri and I am trying not to think about alternative epistemologies in the way you suggested that people are always looking for alternative epistemologies. But I do think that if we want to generate hope we might learn something from indigenous cosmologies. We might learn something from the ways in which many indigenous people think not in terms of the length of time of one lifetime, but think in terms of generations and hundreds of years and how the work we do today can guarantee the continuation of a movement that moves in the direction of what we have called freedom. And we cannot assume that we will accomplish that in our lifetime.

Gayatri Spivak: But let me also say something else, Angela. Indigenous people – there are three hundred-plus so-called Austro-Asiatic tribes in India – I work with them, but we must not mistake cultural conformity for revolutionary vision.

Angela Davis: Absolutely.

Gayatri Spivak: That's the thing that makes us go wrong. And again that is a legitimation by reversal. Those brothers and sisters of ours are, as we are, not untouched by social exclusion. One of the people I work with in Birbhum, a high school teacher, he has some land, etc. He is doing some collecting for us with our oral traditions. He goes out to collect and he is doing what Gramsci says about the subaltern intellectual. He is himself a songwriter. It is not easy to learn how they do their songs. Very carefully he has learnt so that they take him seriously as a songwriter and thus, through doing this cultural conformity from within, he is introducing new thinking: around gender especially. There is a line that he has: 'We demand a steel Sita.' If there is anybody here who knows anything about the Ramayana, then this line that he has written, which goes with the way their cultural conformity works, makes them think differently. They are not protected from historical change. That's something that we must consider, even as we celebrate them for ecological thinking and a different mindset. But that cultural conformity should not be mistaken for a revolutionary mindset.

Angela Davis: I am not trying to suggest that … you know, that conversation can go on and on, but I simply want to think about how to be critical of the neoliberal focus on the individual and how we can learn how to imagine the work that we are doing today as having an impact on generations to come.

Gayatri Spivak: And not according to our plan.

Angela Davis: And no, not according to our plan. We thought we were going to make the revolution in the 1970s. And look at where we are now. But we did bring about some change. Something did happen and I think that that kind of posture can help us generate the hope that we need.

Photos credit: Akademie der Künste

Angela Davis is Distinguished Professor Emerita of History of Consciousness and of Feminist Studies at the University of California, Santa Cruz. Gayatri Chakravorty Spivak is University Professor in the Humanities at Columbia University. Nikita Dhawan is Professor of Political Science and Gender Studies at the University of Gießen.

Notes

1. Spivak has been teaching and training local teachers at five primary schools and coaching high schoolers among the landless illiterate Dalits in West Bengal since 1986. This is how she describes it for tax purposes: 'a long-term research enterprise trying to solve an intellectual problem: is it possible to insert, through teaching and training community-based teachers and supervisors, the children of the very poor, the largest sector of the electorate, into the intuitions of democracy?'
2. Karl Marx, 'The Two Departments of Social Production', in *Capital: A Critique of Political Economy*, vol. 2, trans. David Fernbach (London: Penguin, 1992), 471–74.
3. Since this conversation took place, the Bundestag passed a resolution in May 2019 declaring that the 'pattern of argument and methods of the BDS movement are anti-Semitic'. Though non-binding (as yet), the motion, which calls for a halt to the funding of pro-BDS groups (rather than, as the AfD proposed, making them illegal), has already had a significantly caustic effect on critical discourse on Israel within Germany.

Reviews

Entrepreneurial subjectivity

Marina Vishmidt, *Speculation as a Mode of Production: Forms of Value in Subjectivity in Art and Capital* (Leiden and Boston: Brill, 2018), 254pp., £120.00 hb., 978 9 00429 137 9

When the Swedish artists Goldin+Senneby's *Eternal Employment* was chosen as one of the main public art works to feature in the massive rebuilding of the city of Gothenburg, a heated debate around art and labour took place. One art critic claimed that the Swedish Public Art Agency, by choosing and financing the work, had shifted from their historical task of supporting 'workers' art' to 'employers' art'. The debate sprang from the fact that the work involves the permanent full-time employment of someone, beginning in 2026, whose only job will be to 'clock in' at an employee-stamping clock placed at a tram station in the centre of Gothenburg. To pay them, the artists are using the budget they have received for the commission (6 million SEK, approx. £490,000) to invest in shares on the stock-market. The value of these shares is expected to grow at such a rate that the employee can be paid for life. Is this a perverse inversion of art and capital where neither finance capital nor wage-labour have been done away with? Or is it a radical way of rethinking new forms of art in the age of financialised capitalism? Either way, the act of speculation plays a central role here. The risk of the shares falling in value is built into the artwork itself. But what is the relation here between finance and art? And what is meant by 'speculation'?

In colloquial language, to speculate means to guess possible answers to a question or to 'trade' – to buy with the hope that the value of what you buy will increase and can be sold at a higher price in order to make a profit. In modern European philosophy, of course, the term has a more complex meaning – from articulations within the German idealist tradition to the more recent academic trend of 'speculative realism'. But despite the centrality of the concept of speculation to her work, Marina Vishmidt's book *Speculation as a Mode of Production* offers neither a genealogical reconstruction of the concept, nor

a philosophical critique of it. Instead, it should be seen as an attempt to present and problematise the relation between speculation as it appears in financialised capitalism and the role of art in this. One of the key problems is, however, that the book places speculation in finance and in art on a similar ontological level of meaning, as if they 'speculate' in the same way, thereby cancelling art's critical function in modernity. Like *Eternal Employment,* Vishmidt puts financial speculation and art next to each other in order to unfold their relationship. Yet despite the tendency to create a flat ontology between the two, the book is a real contribution to a deepened understanding of how financialised capitalism has fundamental and worrying consequences for the ways in which art and subjectivity are reproduced today.

The first core argument of the book is that the current phase of capitalism and of contemporary art are best described as speculative. The concern here is to 'draw a parallel between these two modes of speculation, between contemporary capital and contemporary art as they come to constitute the poles of a society structured around speculation'. The second core argument – which draws on Hegel's concept of speculation, and specifically Adorno's take on this – is that both speculative finance and art are driven by a negative force capable of transforming social relations as they currently exist. All speculation 'holds the speculative to its promise of transformation, rather than simple expansion – and consumption'. I read these two arguments as two methods or levels of the book – one descriptive and one more critical-philosophical. But the book is not structured in this way. Instead the two arguments weave in and out of each other across its four chapters.

To begin with Vishmidt's claim that contemporary capitalism is best described as a speculative mode of production: the underlying argument here is that capitalism, from the beginning of 'neoliberalism in the West', is characterised by financialisation and what Marx in the third volume of *Capital* terms 'fictitious capital'. Drawing on thinkers such as Christian Marazzi, finance is understood by Vishmidt as an 'intensification of capital's intrinsic tendency for future oriented growth', as it captures value 'which has not yet been produced, through instruments such as debt, options and derivatives'. Moreover, financialisation does not reinvest its value into the circuit of production, but 'generates profit in a self-enclosed circuit driven by the leveraging of risk using highly technologised financial instruments'. According to Vishmidt, this speculative financialisation of the capitalist mode of production has created a new form of subjectivity. This is primarily to do with the reduction of wage-labour, as value is produced not through the extraction of surplus-value from wage-labour, but primarily from 'debt, options and derivatives'. In the speculative mode of production, the subjectivity of the worker thus transforms from one structured around wage, the union and struggle, to one of 'entrepreneurial subjectivation'. In order to describe this shift, Vishmidt employs the term 'human capital', mainly connected with Chicago School economist Gary S. Becker, to describe how the subjectivity of the worker has gone from one 'supported by wages as the exchange-value of her labour-power to the subject as a site of return on investment'.

Another distinct feature of the speculative mode of production, intimately connected with the argument about subjectivity, is that it collapses the spheres of production and reproduction in qualitatively new ways. Vishmidt emphasises how value, in the speculative mode of production, 'is experienced not just in the determination of the labour market but in all life'. Following Joseph Vogl, she argues that '[f]inance can thus be viewed as the basic engine that extends accumulation to consumption and reproduction once these are sustained by debt, that is, the future-in-the-present'. Equally important to the reproduction of value in the speculative mode of production is what we might call the wage-less class, that is, the unemployed, students and pensioners who contribute to the production of value through credit card debts, student loans and housing mortgages.

Alongside the argument that financialised capital is speculative, Vishmidt also makes the claim that art

is speculative. Here it becomes rather more difficult to follow her argument, in part because of the conflation between 'art', 'artistic practice' and 'artistic subjectivity', which all seem to stand in for 'art' at a more general level, which is never really critically discussed as a historical category. Moreover, the identity between art and capital would seem to place them in an undialectical relationship to one another. So how is art speculative for Vishmidt? In the introduction, she summarises that art 'speculates on its territorial or institutional claims to expand or displace its space of possibility'. Further, artistic practice is 'akin to speculative thought – in the sense Adorno imparts to his "negative" revision of Hegelian speculation – in that art is not identical with its objects'. Finally, art is speculative because the artist and the viewer of art perform a speculative subjectivity, in the sense that the artist 'behaves as the prototype of the entrepreneur'. Vishmidt grounds the idea of art as speculative upon Kant's aesthetic judgment and emphasises in particular its indeterminacy. This aesthetic subject has striking similarities with the subject of human capital according to Vishmidt, a claim particularly developed in a section entitled 'Reproductive Potentiality':

> The reproduction of the automatic subject of art and the reproduction of the automatic subject of human capital are both ways of socialising the automatic subject of capital. Each produces nothing but the reproduction of the subject, and in this, the reproduction of the entire system of valorisation.

Vishmidt's point seems to be that there is a conflation of the subject of human capital with the aesthetic subject modelled by German aesthetics as one of reflection and speculation:

> The speculative subject, whether of aesthetics or labour-power, is thus key to understanding how capital in its current mode – a mode that has been defined in terms of 'fictitious capital' as well as a double decoupling between labour and capital – drives a re-orientation of art and capital.

But what is this re-orientation? The introduction states that 'With the hypothesis that there is a speculative identity between art and capital, a contrary position emerges: this speculative identity is a non-identity, in-so-far as identity thinking must be thought against itself, and yet thought cannot help but identify'. Vishmidt thus appears to be trying to claim two things at once: on the one hand, claiming that capital and art are identical, mainly in that they propose a similar kind of entrepreneurial subjectivity, but on the other, that art and capital are *not* identical with one another. The book wants to trace this double negation or movement through a 'labour of speculation', which I think allows Vishmidt to see art and capital as dialectically opposed to one another, or in other words, as fully dependent on each other in their separation from one another. Doing so, she follows a classic Adornian and Benjaminian position where art and capital are understood as historically inseparable from one another. But where other contemporary thinkers make this claim, partly through the emphasis on art as a non-productive sphere and on the idea of artistic labour as a different kind of labour from capitalist labour, Vishmidt takes another route. In financial capitalism, the characteristics of art – indeterminacy and creativity – become central, which is why art stands out as the exemplary form of financial capitalism. Whilst she on several occasions refuses to align herself with the Italian autonomist and post-Workerist tradition, her position is similar to someone like Antonio Negri who argues that contemporary capit-alism's move towards creativity will eventually make it impossible to valorise labour in the same way as during industrial capitalism, making all labour creative.

On the other hand, though, Vishmidt is claiming that both art and capital are driven by a force of negativity, precisely because they are both speculative. Art is speculative in the Kantian sense, whereas finance is only 'speculative within the defined parameters of risk rendered homogenous through its calculation and trade. Hence financial speculation, the speculation confined to the value-form, lacks the genuine negativity ... which would enable it to be actually speculative in the philosophical or aesthetic sense...' But if finance is not speculative in the sense that art is – nor in the sense that Adorno implies – how can they both be understood as being driven by a negative force? Or is the argument that we can think the relation between art and capital as we can think of the relation between concept and labour in Adorno's critique of Hegel? In other words, that we can think neither art, nor capital, without concrete labour, although both try to hide this? Yet however much I look for it in the book, I cannot find the *labour* of speculation that would point towards the negativity of art and capital today.

The main problem I have with the book is neither its aim nor its points of departure, but rather its failure to fulfill its task, which seems to be due to a conflation of methodology and argument. The book is characterised by an Austinian performative-speech act which goes something like: the argument is that art and capital are speculative because art and capital are speculative. With Adorno, we might say that this is the identity-thinking of *Speculation as a Mode of Production*. But at the same time, the method – which is extremely underdeveloped – is to think this identity between art and capital non-identically. Here the issue lies partly, I think, in the missed opportunity to work out some of the key concepts and categories – such as speculation and art – and the way they relate to one another critically and historically, within the book itself.

In her seminal study of Adorno from 1978, Gillian Rose distinguishes three ways of thinking in his works: identity-thinking, rational identity-thinking and non-identity thinking. The first is the normal mode of thinking in current capitalist society in which concepts are attached to objects in a way that creates meaning. In capitalism, however, society is explained and experienced through 'a structure analogous to the theory of value ... without any reference to a posited future society'. Adorno therefore also proposes rational identity-thinking whereby concepts are linked to their objects in their ideal or utopian state – a way of thinking in which the concepts relate truly to their objects. However, Adorno is mainly concerned with the third form, non-identity thinking, which exists within identical thinking and confronts thinking with what it is, i.e. the kind of negativity Vishmidt is also concerned with. Rose writes that '[t]he consciousness which perceives this is non-identity thinking or negative dialectic'. Rose's exposition of Adorno might allow us better to decipher Vishmidt's argument. Art and capital are identical and speculative from the perspective of identity-thinking. They seem to be doing the same thing. This is most visible in the 'figure' of the artist in which the mediation between capital and value has gotten rid of labour completely. But through non-identical thinking, they are non-identical in that finance is not at all speculative, if speculation is understood as non-identical whereas art actually is speculative. With Adorno, we might say that finance is speculative as identity-thinking and that art is speculative as non-

identity thinking. From this perspective, Vishmidt's book should then be seen as an attempt to take this negative dialectical thinking further into financialised capitalism.

But here comes another difficulty which stems from the relation between the non-identical and art in Adorno's work. As Vishmidt points out, for Adorno, art was the privileged cultural sphere, where the memory of non-identical thinking could be mediated through the form of the artwork. Following Vishmidt's argument that in the speculative mode of production (as identity-thinking), art and capital conflate in the production of value and subjectivity, this seems to no longer be the case. 'Speculation thrives on investing previously un-capitalised or indirectly capitalised domains with value logics and value imperatives. And art is exemplary here as a domain that is itself deemed to be "socially speculative".' If this is so, how is this visible or mediated in artworks and in the institution of art?

Although Vishmidt discusses a few artworks by artists such as Pilvi Takala, Mierle Laderman Ukeles, Tino Sehgal and the Artist Placement Group, the discussion of the mediation of art is almost entirely left out, as is a discussion about the general category of art. Is it because art, according to Vishmidt, has no form any longer? Is it not able, either institutionally or at the level of artworks, to produce forms that differ from forms of capital, forms that propose non-identical thinking? Vishmidt follows a modern, Duchampian logic, to be found in Adorno – and more recently in the work of Thierry De Duve – that art is special in its very non-specialism. But what mediates this then in the age of speculative capitalism? If Adorno is to be taken further, which is Vishmidt's aim, this surely must be taken into consideration?

Coming back to Goldin+Senneby's *Eternal Employment* and the debate that surrounded it, we can see a similarity: instead of debating what the artwork was, in the sense of what it mediated materially, the discussion focused simply on its practical and ethical aspects. But what form does *Eternal Employment* take and is this form able to say anything about the *real* conditions in which it exists? Or does art no longer hold this function? In other words, what, if any, is the role of art in the age of speculative capitalism? This is an important question that the book rightly tries to grapple with. Unfortunately, the question is largely left hanging.

Josefine Wikström

Who's a feminist?

Catherine Rottenberg, *The Rise of Neoliberal Feminism* (Oxford: Oxford University Press, 2018). 239pp., £19.99 hb., 978 0 19090 122 6

It is the best of times and it is the worst of times to declare oneself a feminist today. Presentations of that creature have been shape shifting for decades, though right now she suddenly seems more popular than ever, sometimes appearing as a celebrated media figure: her shiny long hair and designer clothes triggering little fear. Should she appear *en masse* at demonstrations, however, the media will usually retreat. It is true that the re-emergence of the women's liberation movement, half a century ago, always included a multitude of contesting voices. But nowadays they seem more divided than ever. Younger feminist militants can often be seen welcoming trans women, sex workers and supporting the proposed Gender Recognition Act (GRA), making life easier for trans people; while some older feminists perceive these moves as threatening 'women-only' safe spaces and priorities, angrily opposing the GRA. My own brand of Left feminists usually hark back to other forms of radicalism, when we worked (as, indeed, we continue to do) 'in and against' the state for a range of welfare and other resources that would enable all women to participate in social, political and cultural life on an equal footing with men, thereby beginning to undermine, or at least marginalise, the complex system of gender hierarchy itself, entangled as it is with capitalist class and racialised domination.

For many years after the rise of second wave feminism, 'women's libbers' – of any stripe – were mostly ridiculed in the mainstream. 'You're not one of those angry, resentful bra-burners are you?' This was the routine greeting that activists received; often from men and women alike. Ambitious, professional women did not embrace feminism in the days of its combative radicalism. They suspected, usually rightly, that it was more an impediment than an advantage to career success, while many home-based women ('housewives') felt threatened by its critical appraisal of their marginalisation in the wider world. We were, after all, fighting for social transformation on every front, including the meanings attached to 'womanhood' itself. Indeed, many who would later happily adopt the label 'feminist' remained dismissive of the heyday of women's liberation, including, for example, the influential columnist and writer, Polly Toynbee, who declared in 'The myth of women's lib', in 2002: 'the "women's movement" of the 60s and 70s never really existed'.

Others who did identify with feminism from its early days of militancy, such as the attentive sociologist Angela McRobbie, later mapped out what she saw as the deliberate 'undoing of feminism' and some of its early successes. In *The Aftermath of Feminism* (2009), McRobbie suggested that, by the 1990s, feminism was not so much rejected as 'taken into account', while, at the very same time, being disdained as outmoded and unnecessary. Feminism was depicted as unfashionable, irrelevant for the sexy and successful young woman, now living a 'post-feminist' life, where individuals and their choices were all that mattered. A few years later, however, and we can detect the further twist with which I began, as feminism (of a kind) now appears fashionable, even popular – in some ways, really for the very first time. The T-shirt 'THIS IS WHAT A FEMINIST LOOKS LIKE' was first designed by the Fawcett Society (the leading British charity campaigning for gender equality and women's rights), but was quickly snapped up by fashion designers globally, even appearing in Paris fashion week a few years ago. Feminism was once notoriously 'anti-fashion', disdaining make-up and high heels, refusing to be the 'custom-made women' that male designers wanted us to be. But we know times are changing when feminist slogans appear on global catwalks, worn by film stars as celebrity allure (from Natalie Portman to Rihanna), or briefly flaunted by politicians and corporate executives, including men.

But is this what we *want* a feminist to look like, some may well ask, wondering what has been gained and what lost in all this 'feminist' shape shifting. If so, it is time to turn to Catherine Rottenberg's riveting survey of the recent rise and mutations of new feminist discourses, which largely mirror the dominant neoliberal rationality of competitive individualism, even as they highlight its pressures and contradictions. In *The Rise of Neoliberal Feminism*, Rottenberg sees 2012 as a symbolic watershed, following the publication of Anne-Marie Slaughter's 'Why Women Still Can't Have it All', which quickly became the most popular article ever published in *The Atlantic*. It helped generate a global explosion of media discussion addressing the situation of high-achieving women, reflecting the deepening crisis between public and private life. Slaughter explained that she needed to create a better 'work-life balance' as the mother of young children, which is why she resigned from her pre-eminent role as Director of Policy Planning under the Obama administration in Washington to resume her former tenured position at Princeton University, enabling her to spend more time with her growing family. This last decade also saw the spectacular impact of Facebook's chief operating officer, Sheryl Sandberg, soon to become one of the most influential women in the world following her call for more women leaders. Sandberg's chart-topping manifesto, *Lean In: Women, Work, and the Will to Lead* (2013), sold over 4 million copies over the following five years, and is apparently still selling 10,000 copies monthly. Surveying the landscape on other media highways, the singer Beyoncé performed live for the many millions who watched the MTV video awards in 2014, backed by a stage set left bare apart from giant lettering: FEMINIST. Two years later, the self-declared feminist Hillary Clinton *almost* became President of the USA, winning the popular vote by nearly three million, despite being beaten when Donald Trump managed to secure more state votes overall through the antiquated system of the electoral college.

Being a feminist could now be paraded as a badge of strength, integrity and self-assurance. But its most distinctive feature, as Rottenberg analyses, is the singular commitment to women's personal empowerment, while its leading voices are those of exceptionally powerful and successful women. 'Neoliberal feminism' is the description she coins to describe this particular mutation out of 'liberal feminism' – a feminist stance that had fought for equal rights for women within existing social structures, but eschewed the need for more radical transformations. Rottenberg's examples of neoliberal feminism are drawn mainly from the USA, but as I write, our current (though soon departing) British Prime Minister, Theresa May – unlike Margaret Thatcher – has similarly declared herself a feminist, and even co-founded Women2Win in 2005 to help elect more Conservative women to Parliament. The title itself captures the fiercely competitive drive of this new brand of feminism, echoing precisely the neoliberal zeitgeist of winners and losers. The capitalist market has no firmer ally, it would seem, than this form of feminism, one that promises to deliver greater benefits for women when, and only when, they hone their individual skills in search of career success. This is what Cinzia Arruzza, Tithi Bhattacharya and Nancy Fraser describe as 'equal opportunity domination' in their recent manifesto, *Feminism for the 99%* (2019).

Rottenberg is aware of all the questions and paradoxes surrounding her analysis. Is feminism itself complicit with the ascent of neoliberalism, the two having emerged at much the same time? Some Left scholars, including Fraser in her much-cited article 'Feminism, Capitalism and the Cunning of History', have argued that the 'overall trajectory and historical significance' of second wave feminism showed a 'disturbing convergence' with certain neoliberal ideals and demands. Fraser suggests that feminism's stress on the recognition of identity claims over calls for redistributive economic justice, as well as its critique of the patriarchal state, resonated with the hyper-individualism of an intensified finacialised or deregulated global capitalism. Others, like McRobbie, reject this, describing feminism as having been appropriated and twisted in neoliberal discourses. Still others, like the British criminologist Lea Sitkin, simply claim that neoliberal feminism is an oxymoron: 'A feminism that is a handmaiden to capitalism isn't feminism at all'. However, Rottenberg's analysis is more complex and nuanced. She notes that since feminism has never had any unitary manifestation, we cannot understand the work of these recent self-proclaimed, media-promoted, elite feminists by simply rejecting their pronouncements as a brand of fake feminism. After all, feminists campaigned for 'Hillary' in vast numbers, and many black schoolgirls are moved and motivated by the inspirational messages of former first Lady, now best-selling author, Michelle Obama. But, as Rottenberg does, we certainly do need to look very closely at the work being done by those aligning themselves with neoliberal rationality in the name of feminism.

What Rottenberg suggests is that the purveyors of neoliberalism have themselves reinvented and reinvigorated this version of feminism in order to overcome

the obstinate contradictions of contemporary capitalism and thus assist its survival. Capitalism now needs feminism, or at least a feminism reduced to fantasies of self-management, to solve its crisis of social reproduction, now that market metrics have been slowly colonising every area of our lives. Drawing in particular upon the feminist political theorist Wendy Brown, Rottenberg emphasises that neoliberalism is not just a set of economic policies promoting privatisation of state assets and deregulation to extend the amassing of corporate profits, but also a way of producing subjects who monitor themselves at every turn as a type of 'human capital'. This means always attempting to pursue modes of conduct that might help ensure that they, and their children, become more flexible and hence desirable in present and future labour markets, entailing constant self-regulation and self-improvement that is always expressed and encouraged via the language of choice. This is why that doyenne of corporate neoliberalism, Sheryl Sandberg, declared her pithy text a feminist *manifesto*. *Lean In*, she cheerfully asserts, is dedicated to inspiring Western women, who happily have now won all their basic rights (unlike those in other, usually Islamic states, elsewhere)

to expand their goals and surmount their own 'internal barriers', aiming for the pinnacles of power. Most importantly as well, successful women must ensure they can find that 'happy' work-life balance along the way to enable them to function with maximum efficiency and apparent personal fulfillment in both their public and private lives. Such a stance is further necessitated by market requirements for a shrewd and capable workforce.

These elite women, therefore, not only tower above the rest of us, and help make feminism acceptable, but also crucially suggest that it is indeed *possible* to extend market principles into our home lives, once we start tailoring our performances to enhance our chances of success – whether as managers of home or workplace. As Rottenberg highlights, what is happening here is the spatial collapse of the traditional separation of public and private, with the private sphere now tailored to suit the public domain, as the 'liberated' woman knows she must accept full responsibility for her own well-being in both arenas. The world of care now transmutes into little more than yet another affective investment in the future.

In reality only a fraction of women can maintain any balance at all between these two worlds, when in recent decades most women, like men, are being forced to work ever longer hours in paid work just to survive, with wages falling or stagnant. Meanwhile, whether in the USA, Britain or increasingly elsewhere, the decline in welfare provisions and the ongoing ruthless reduction in community resources has made any form of domestic caring progressively more stressful. Unless commodified as a corporate concern, markets neither engage with nor value either reproduction or care work, while states have been shedding their responsibilities for maintaining domestic well-being. Hence the need to redefine 'motherhood' in managerial terms, making women, in particular, responsible. Despite fifty years of feminist challenges, motherhood, not parenting, remains emblematic of woman's lot and caring work generally, but must now be rendered potentially compatible with women making all the right 'choices' to enable them to maintain necessary paid employment.

In the name of choice, what we actually find is a drastic curtailment of many women's options. They must either delay or (perhaps unintentionally) forsake motherhood, in search of the perfect conjuncture, or they must fall back on the outsourcing of caring to others, which in practice further entrenches both racialised and class-based gender exploitation. As Rottenberg forecasts, coming into focus on this horizon is not just professional women freezing their eggs until the opportune moment for breeding arises, if it does, but renting a womb from what now emerges as a new class of 'disposable' women. In her succinct, if alarming, summary: 'Neoliberal feminism is not only shorn of all obligations to less privileged women while actually producing new classes of disempowered women, but it is also making alternative futures difficult to envisage, since it actively and performatively "forgets" the conditions that naturalise sexual difference and leaves us stunned in the face of a fading lexicon of critique.'

This much is true, and yet, as each day passes, things sometimes look better, and sometimes chillingly worse, for envisaging those alternative futures for which fractious feminists have fought. Impressively, in 2018 over five million women took to the streets of Spain on International Women's Day, supported by several politicians, as part of a 24-hour Global Woman's Strike, calling for an end to sexist oppression, exploitation and violence, while raising awareness of all the unpaid or poorly paid caring work done by women: 'If we stop, the world stops!'

Similar marches, study groups and grass-roots mobilisations, have been occurring around the globe, often led by women, fighting for more egalitarian, sustainable futures against the hurtling harms of the present. Many of them are addressing precisely the contemporary crisis of care, and the diverse exploitations of those women, in particular, made responsible for solving it.

We know from much feminist writing that even middle-class women with children or other dependents are struggling to advance or simply maintain careers and attend to loved ones in need. Meanwhile it can prove the very worst of times for those 'disposable' women whom they call upon for assistance, often part of post-colonial global care chains, perhaps far removed from their own children and support groups, while barely surviving their precarious employment. This is why Rottenberg closes her book by calling for the return to issues of inclusive social justice, invoking Judith Butler's concept of 'precarity' as a unifying factor for attending to the most marginalised of women. In this way, she hopes to turn around the 'unfortunate mutual entanglement of neoliberalism with feminism', eviscerating the alliance from within.

There are now, as there has always been, real possibilities for renewed feminist discourses, as well as for the most diverse of feminist practices, designed to resist the exploitation or diminishment of any woman, including trans women and sex workers (however contested our understandings of these categories are). Above all, this will involve revaluing the world of care women still shoulder in support of both male domination and capitalism. Nowadays it also means extending notions of care to embrace concern for the world itself, while once more invoking old feminist visions that always placed the world of love and shared wellbeing (social reproduction, in the Marxist lexicon) above that of production for profit. It returns me, once more, to those struggles in and against the state, the rebuilding of local communities, and the regeneration overall of popular Left discourses for that ever-daunting task of maintaining the broadest possible alliances against a reactionary populism now on the move, and especially targeting women. If we fail, it will not only be in Alabama that we witness the triumph of political formations that are lethal for many women, as for oppressed and exploited people everywhere, indeed, that threaten to devour the future of us all.

Lynne Segal

The monochrome and the readymade

Jaleh Mansoor, *Marshall Plan Modernism: Italian Postwar Abstraction and the Beginnings of Autonomia* (Durham: Duke University Press, 2016). 288pp., £80.00 hb., £20.99 pb., 978 0 82236 245 6 hb., 978 0 8223 6260 9 pb.

The title of Jaleh Mansoor's *Marshall Plan Modernism* provides a number of clues about the author's methodological ambitions. The juxtaposition of the term 'modernism' with an economic programme not only unsettles its meaning but implies an intention to cast a new light on this moment in the history of art. However, as always happens when two substantives are placed side by side, the semantic relationship between the terms remains obscure. The word order of Mansoor's title encourages us to treat 'Marshall Plan' as a qualifier and Modernism as the subject, but regardless of the way in which the sentence is structured, the title is made up of two juxtaposed nouns without preposition. From the outset, Mansoor implies that the relationship between the economic and artistic spheres proposed in the book will not be univocal.

Covering both art history and theory, *Marshall Plan Modernism* is a dense book which has developed from Mansoor's doctoral thesis. Mansoor's work is not entirely unfamiliar to an English readership, since parts of the thesis have previously been published as articles in the journal *October*. However, whereas the artistic practices considered in the book are largely the same as in the thesis, a new theoretical framework is in evidence. The references to French poststructuralist philosophy, which once characterised Mansoor's research and signalled its connection to the *October* school, have become sporadic, supplanted by a more materialist approach. Given that the object of study remains unaltered, one would expect the implications of this theoretical shift to be discussed in some detail, not least because the particular nature of the move – from post-structuralism to Marxism – calls for some 'grounding'.

Mansoor's research hinges on a body of artistic practices that emerged in post-war Italy, a country which was one of the main beneficiaries of the Marshall economic plan. Her analysis is predominantly concerned with a selection of works produced by Lucio Fontana, Alberto Burri and Piero Manzoni from the early 1950s to the late 1960s. What ties the three artists together, according to the book, is not a deliberate affiliation to an artistic current, but their attempt to recover and combine certain formal tropes associated with the early twentieth-century avant-garde, such as the monochrome and the readymade. In Mansoor's reading, this redeployment signals the unconscious resurfacing of failed revolutionary aspirations (monochrome), and a renewed drive for accumulation on the part of capital (readymade). In addition to identifying elements of the works that index these returns, the book also throws light on tropes marking a departure from the past such as the cutting and burning of the canvas. These formal features were absent in the earlier generation of monochromes, and would bear some relation to the forms of political resistance that emerged in Italy in the years of the economic 'miracle'.

In making this claim, Mansoor is heavily reliant upon Giovanni Arrighi's *The Long Twentieth Century*. The economist's account of the development of capital through long cycles of accumulation, in which each cycle simultaneously supersedes and recuperates aspects of its predecessor, is crucial to Mansoor's understanding of art history as a whole. In her analysis, the practices of the Italian artists are connected both to the long and recursive temporal trajectories of capitalism and its increasingly global scale. Their distance from indigenous artistic traditions, and their interest in tropes of the international avant-gardes, would demonstrate 'the obsolescence of the national state' and Italy's inscription within a broader capitalist space through the Marshall Plan.

By connecting the works of Fontana, Burri and Manzoni to contemporary macro-economic events, *Marshall Plan Modernism* challenges established art historical accounts and opens up new interpretative paths. In particular, the book marks a departure from the secondary literature on Alberto Burri, which tends to trace his burning of canvasses back to the violence he experienced during the Second World War. Yet while Mansoor's rejection of a narrow autobiographical perspective is a major strength of the book, she also overstates the impact that the international movement of capital may have had on post-war Italian artists, nearly obliterating historical and political factors immediately preceding and in geographical proximity to the production of the works of art considered. The termination of the fascist regime, for example, has to be acknowledged as one of the reasons for the tendency to privilege avant-gardist tropes over the national futurist heritage. After twenty years of policies which discouraged the importation of foreign art and favoured a return to indigenous sources, artists were eager to reconnect to an international scene. Mansoor's reading, however, suggests that Italy's incorporation within a broader economic capitalist space simply wiped out, almost frictionlessly, these historical wounds and cultural heritage.

In the introduction to the book, Mansoor appears to revive the debate on art historical method by situating her work in relation to other critical approaches. Her declared aim is to overcome the impasse between 'formalist autonomy' and 'social reflective history' by offering a 'third' way that might reveal the radical aims of the works under consideration. Nevertheless, the introduction and following chapters do not engage with historical debates on art historical methodology. Nor do they refer to more recent attempts to rethink the relationship between Marxism and art history. Given the introduction's bold declaration of intent, one would expect the author to expand on her own proposal in relation to the current state of the debate. After all, the schism between 'formalist autonomy' and 'social reflective history' which Mansoor declares she wants to surpass has already been replaced by more intricate methodological frameworks.

Mansoor appears more interested in critical approaches which originate outside of the field of art, such as those set forward by the literary critic Fredric Jameson. In the introduction, the author announces that she will adopt a definition of culture extrapolated from Jameson's *The Political Unconscious* (1981), and makes repeated use of terms such as 'symptom', 'unconscious' or 'aetiology', recalling the psychoanalytically inflected style of the latter. Echoing Jameson, Mansoor defines culture, and implicitly art, as 'the object [which] makes manifest the contradictions in the mode of production', and hints at an Althusserian notion of economic determination 'in the last instance', a key point of reference in *The Political Unconscious*. Jameson sets forward an interpretative model for literature that relies upon Althusser's critique of expressive causality and the presumed hierarchy between economic base and superstructure. As an alternative to the latter, Althusser had conceived a system made up of semi-autonomous levels, in which the mode of production does not amount to the underlying layer determining the others, but to the structure as a whole.

Jameson uses Althusser's work to call into question cultural and literary approaches that seek to establish homologies between the economical and the cultural. His final aim is to propose a new interpretative model in order to grasp the 'interdependency [between levels] in terms of a mediation that passes through the structure'. Jameson's method consists of three phases of analysis, which successively 'reconstruct' the object of study. The phases can be imagined in spatial terms as concentric frameworks: the first and narrower one coincides with the study of the individual literary work and its specific political history; the second treats the text as an example of a broader and antagonistic discourse of social classes; and the third places the work within the 'ultimate horizon of human history as a whole', conceived in Marxist terms as a sequence of modes of production.

Returning to Mansoor, we can see how Jameson's method could be of help in overcoming a reflective theory of history. However, such a framework is not applied or investigated in detail across the book. Her use of the Jamesonian concept of the 'political unconscious' can be considered a case in point. The latter is mobilised to link the violence of the post-war imperialist project to the physical and metaphorical assaults upon art, but the analysis remains confined to the work of three artists and does not address how the political unconscious was mediated more broadly by the language of art and culture in the context under consideration. What is glossed over is the second stage of Jameson's method, which approaches the text – or work of art – as a *parole* of a broader system of language before placing it in relation to the mode of production.

The absence of this intermediary passage leads, paradoxically, to the reinstatement of an analogical relationship between the artistic and the economic. For example, as Mansoor puts it: 'the violent expenditure of accumulation made manifest in war of a new scale, the atom bomb, and the ensuing continuation of that war in the excess of expenditure … finds its way into Fontana's slashes'; or again, Manzoni's 'work operates as a forensic device through which to understand the transitions occurring in the capital-to-labour relationship'; and finally, Burri's 'decision to experiment with one destructive process after the other, from ripping to exploding, responds fairly starkly to the sudden eruption of an accelerated, world-market-oriented productivism'. The book establishes a reciprocal relationship between artistic and economic spheres: just as works of art symptomatise the specificity of capital in the historical moment under consideration, so this latter is 'understood against' bodies of artistic practices. It remains partly overlooked, however, how this mutual influence would work in practice. Except for the account of Manzoni, the connection between Burri's and Fontana's work and the shift occurring in the political and social field is explained in fairly metaphorical terms.

Marshall Plan Modernism's dense analysis of artistic practices in post-war Italy considers both their link to capitalist restructuring and to the political struggles that emerged in response. The works of Manzoni, Burri and Fontana are interpreted as a 'form of resistance … against the very same historical conditions they symptomatise', and as such they are juxtaposed to other, and more direct, expressions of political dissent that arose in the same period. In particular, Mansoor seems to draw a parallel between the gestures of the artists and the political theories and struggles of the Autonomia movement, which are explored in detail. It is important to observe the author's conspicuous interest in Italian Heterodox Marxism, and in the debate around autonomy that originated in that milieu. Her foray into the terrain of Marxism has a precise purpose: finding aspects which could be deployed to cast a new light on modernist notions of aesthetic autonomy. This attempt signals a certain impatience with the restricted disciplinary boundaries of art history and a desire to place art at the very core of socio-political transformation. Nevertheless, the question remains open as to whether borrowing concepts from political theory and philosophy can challenge art's marginal position and revamp its ossified discourse, or simply risks re-instating the precedence of theory over artistic practice. Any new notion of aesthetic autonomy can, perhaps, only be thought immanently, from within art's own terrain.

Luisa Lorenza Corna

Geopolitical antifuturism

C. Heike Schotten, *Queer Terror: Life, Death, and Desire in the Settler Colony* (New York: Columbia University Press, 2018). 241pp., £81.00 hb., £27.00 pb., 978 0 23118 746 6 hb., 978 0 23118 747 3 pb.

When George W. Bush threw down his infamous gauntlet in the aftermath of the attacks of 11 September 2001 – 'Either you are with us, or you are with the terrorists' – he intended the apparent choice presented in this imperative to offer no choice at all. In *Queer Terror*, Heike Schotten flips around the apparently self-evident nature of this choice to ask how anyone committed to the destruction of settler colonial empire could *not* choose the terrorists. There is something both audacious and limiting about the symmetry of this logic. Audacious, because we are invited to offer our allegiance to the very forces and discourses that empire finds most threatening. Limiting, because our choices seem, well, limited to those offered by this self-same empire. Yet whatever choice one makes or refuses to make, the dilemmas elucidated by this provocative work are ones that are likely to endure, making an engagement with its arguments both fruitful and inescapable.

Schotten attributes the persistence of 'war on terror' discourse to a 'civilisationalist moralism of life and death that underpins, motivates, and defines the US imperial project', the purpose of which is to sanctify settlement and empire as good while vilifying resistance to it as evil. *Queer Terror* offers an anatomy of this moralism, in an attempt both to rethink the biopolitics of empire and to sharpen resistance to it. Central to the book is the claim that the notion of 'life itself' is not a self-evident, natural or biological category, but an ideological one imbued with moralised content. Against the tendency to think of life in biologised terms, evident in the contrasting treatments of 'bare life' offered by Arendt and Agamben, Schotten demonstrates how the Hobbesian commitment to the preservation of 'life' against the putatively nihilistic threats posed by everything from indigenous 'savagery' to 'Islamist terrorism' is an intensely moralistic endeavour that seeks to shore up settler colonial civilisation. For 'life', then, always read 'our way of life'.

In temporal terms, Schotten reads the settler colony's commitment to the preservation of 'life' as a commitment to futurism. In an illuminating reading of Hobbes, Schotten suggests that in looking for a mechanism by which 'life' might be preserved forever, the Leviathan is engaged in an obviously futurist endeavour. Indeed she goes further, arguing that the Leviathan brings the state of nature to an end in part through the creation of a sense of temporality and, specifically, futurity. This is because the ceaseless struggle of each against all to secure one's present existence in the state of nature makes the past irrelevant and the future unimaginable because it is so tenuous. The state of nature is characterised not only by the ever-present physical threat of death, but also by the psychic condition of hopelessness, diffidence and despair. The sovereign brings war to an end by securing the possibility of a future. Much later, game theorists would deploy this insight to argue that rational self-interested actors could be induced to cooperate through the lengthening of the shadow of the future.

How better, then, to destroy the settler colonial social order than to refuse the future, and not merely *this* future but the future per se. Enter queer theory – and, in particular, Lee Edelman's singular antifuturist manifesto *No Future*. Widely hailed as helping to inaugurate the antisocial turn in queer theory, Edelman attacks the ideology of what he calls 'reproductive futurism' which, in his view, invokes and deploys figurations of the Child as a representation of the innocence that must be protected from the perversity and narcissism thought to be embodied by queers. Rather than working to disabuse this ideology of its moralistic and relentlessly negative view of queerness, Edelman urges queers to embrace the role ascribed to them as destroyers of the social fabric and to become the very exemplars of negativity and death that it most fears. Schotten proceeds by way of analogy with Edelman's argument, while also enlarging its scope and shifting scale. Thus, where Edelman takes aim at reproductive futurism, Schotten's target is a more general logic of futurism underpinned by the supposition that the body politic must survive. What makes futurism

oppressive, Schotten explains, is its insistence that everyone accede to its moralistic mandates and its relentless queering of those who do not. Just as 'queerness', for Edelman, names not an identity category but a structural position marking those who are abjected as standing in the way of the future of the Child, 'terrorism' for Schotten is not an analytical category naming a particular kind of violence but the epithet with which resistance to empire and settler colonialism is illegitimated. We might think of *Queer Terror*, then, as a reading of the geopolitical implications of *No Future* in the era of the 'War on Terror'.

Schotten is acutely conscious of the critiques to which *No Future* has been subject in the fifteen years since its publication. Disavowing any intention to defend the text against all of these, she nonetheless focuses on two. Critics such as Jack Halberstam have worried about *No Future*'s too easy slippage from the antisocial to the apolitical. After all, Edelman's Nietzschean critique of the freedom-denying effects of moralism also extends to the moralism of revolutionary desire, so that the only 'better' future (if it can be called one at all) is the death of the social order as well as the calls for justice that em-

anate from it. In response, Schotten argues that we do not need to take Edelman at his word when he claims to reject politics per se. As she astutely points out, to advocate for anything at all, and to do so in a text that adopts the rhetorical forms and conventions of a manifesto by purporting to answer the question that all manifestos do (what is *to be* done?), is to adopt a future-oriented position. A politics of no future is therefore both a politics and a future – one that advocates neither capitulation to, nor compromise with, futurism's mandates, but instead urges us to accede to its worst nightmares.

José Muñoz, among others, has pointed out that the antisociality of Edelman's polemic is achieved at the expense of viewing sexuality as a singular trope of difference, uncontaminated by gender, race and other particularities. Muñoz does not recognise queer of colour children in the sanctified figural Child in whose interest futurism operates. And we might wonder, with him, whether only those queers most able to inhabit the present can afford to disavow the future. This is why Muñoz thinks of the future as queerness's domain, as a temporal space that might offer refuge from the injustice of the present. Recognising the force of this critique, Schotten argues that while the concrete referents for queerness in Edelman's text are primarily white, gay and male, because queerness is treated as a structural position, his thesis is not incompatible with the now substantial queer of colour scholarship demonstrating how as privileged queers assimilate into the mainstream, queerness becomes displaced onto other figures such as the Muslim fundamentalist and the illegal alien. Importantly, she concedes that futurity and survival do not mean the same things in canonical theory as they do in traditions of the oppressed. The problem is that Schotten does not give us much of a sense of these 'traditions' and of how they might compel us to alter our views of futurity and futurism.

The implications of this become more apparent in the final chapter of the book, which situates its thesis more firmly in contemporary 'war on terror' discourse. Here Schotten applies her understanding of queerness as naming the position of those abjected by the social order, and the praxis of queerness as entailing the affirmation of that abjection rather than flight from it, to the question of 'terrorism'. Offering a genealogy of the concept in political discourse that reveals it to be less an analytical category than a term of illegitimation, Schotten argues that if 'terrorism' is the name that the imperial settler state gives to its existential nightmares then resistance to it entails affirming 'terrorism'. In her words, 'If the only options are, as Bush says, to side with a futurist, settler, and imperial "us" (whether as avowed advocates of empire or its collaborationist liberal compromisers) or with a queered, "savage", and "terrorist" other, the choice, I think, is clear: we must choose to stand with the "terrorists".' But are these the only options? In *The Intimate Enemy*, Ashis Nandy long ago suggested that the most subversive responses to colonialism were those that did not simply negate or invert the binary options offered to them by colonial discourse but deconstructed and refused them altogether.

What Schotten intends to suggest, I think, is that these are the only options that are legible to Bush, and, by extension, imperial settler colonialism, and that the affirmation of the 'wrong' option within these terms is deeply threatening to that order. This becomes clear in her narration of highly mediatised instances of con-frontation in which Muslim US activists have frequently been invited to choose between 'us' and the 'terrorists' and have typically found it impossible to render their opposition to US policy legible in any terms other than 'terrorism'. Here Schotten is rightly suspicious of liberal attempts at compromise, which invariably produce insidious differences between 'good' and 'bad' Muslims thereby retaining the sense of Islam as a potential problem. And she is also right to be pessimistic about prospects for the expansion of the terms of mainstream discourse given the all too familiar structural constraints of state regulation and corporate media ownership that frame these conversations. Yet her argument makes me wonder what might be lost in its insistence on offering resistance in terms that are legible to the imperial settler state. Why be the opponents that it wants and, in some sense, creates? Might sovereignty not be threatened far more by what it does not and cannot know or understand, by the 'unknown unknowns', as Donald Rumsfeld might have put it?

And what would it mean for us – 'us' who stand against settler colonial empire – to embrace our status as 'terrorists' rather than to protest that we are 'freedom fighters'? What are the consequences of naming and understanding ourselves – of becoming legible to ourselves – entirely in the terms imposed by the coloniser? Fanon was deeply preoccupied with this question, theorising the epidermalisation of inferiority as the result of self-recognition in the terms offered by the dominant other. Indeed we might understand the enduring hunger for alternative world-making, of which the surge of interest in Afrofuturism is but one manifestation in our own time, as the reparative dimension of this Fanonian insight. Schotten is right that all futurisms are destined to fail because the future can never finally or fully arrive. But if some futures are more emancipatory than others, then their failures also mean very different things for the world. A manifesto against futurism that hesitates to enter into these distinctions for fear of reintroducing moralism, this time in the guise of appropriately revolutionary desire, may have the virtue of logical consistency. But it threatens to bracket a great many of those questions that we have come to call political.

Rahul Rao

Jazz as a credo

Fumi Okiji, *Jazz as Critique: Adorno and Black Expression Revisited* (Stanford: Stanford University Press, 2018), 160pp., £58.00 hb., £17.99 pb., 978 1 50360 202 1 hb., 978 1 50360 585 5 pb.

During a public discussion to mark a 2018 career retrospective show at The New Museum in New York, John Akomfrah was asked a question about the function of music in his film works. Having addressed the importance of post-punk and dub to his early practice, Akomfrah then said the following:

> The side that I've learnt the most from though is jazz, and free jazz in particular, because free jazz is not music, it's a credo. It's a credo because it's about an approach to not simply the sonic, but to that great big slab of the philosophical that we call time. It's an approach to time. That's what free jazz is. It's about the splintering and reordering and reconfiguring of time. Once it's told you that, you never forget it.

For Fumi Okiji too, jazz is a credo, and to grasp it as such requires taking on another 'great big slab of the philosophical': the work of Theodor Adorno.

Adorno's essays on jazz have long been a source of tension for those who recognise his standing as a powerful thinker of western art under conditions of capitalist modernity, or who understand jazz to be *the* world-historical art form of the twentieth century. Readers of Adorno with an ear for jazz have sought to contextualise his weak judgements on jazz music in order to rescue the remainder of his corpus. Within Black Studies, by contrast, it has become commonplace to undertake extensive theorisations of jazz without feeling the need to take seriously Adorno's philosophical aesthetics and their relation to the debilitating nature of life under modernity. Okiji does not appear to want a stake in either of these games, and thus she is able to avoid either mild censure or simple avoidance in order to take Adorno to task for his wilful mishearing. Organised around the desire to 'meet Adorno partway' – by virtue of the ways in which his account of the double character of radical art appears on the surface to 'rhyme' with the drive of the music – Okiji is also able in *Jazz as Critique* to detail the precise nature of his failings.

One such failing is Adorno's transposition of the jazz solo onto the individual bourgeois subject. As Okiji explains, the central tenet of his thinking was that the bourgeois individual was the most advanced subject under modern capitalism, and thus any assessment of aesthetics and politics had to move through it. This conceptual prefiguring was what allowed Adorno to, firstly, fetishise the solo as the apex of the jazz work, and secondly, to hear in the solo form a type of regression and complicity with the administered world which at best meant jazz only offered an accurate image of the 'embattled individual'. Okiji suggests that Adorno's mistake in privileging the solo as his point of attack lay in his general devaluation of proletarian consciousness, and thus his inability to understand that the historical formation of the individual as an image of the bourgeois was antithetical (hostile even) to the social composition of jazz:

> We find reified fragments of poorly formed ideas, bordering on caricature, which add false depth to Adorno's jazz critique. There is an implication that the modern black has, in a sense, previewed, under a distinct set of circumstances, the disenfranchisement of the bourgeoise under monopolistic capitalism. Adorno invites us to read jazz as a fable through which we can grasp the predicaments of bourgeois subjectivity a little better.

Adorno's inability to account for the difference between the unique mode of racial proleterianisation that forged jazz as black music and the formation of the bourgeoisie points to a further error on his part, and for Okiji, his most grave: that is, his refusal to historicise jazz through the experience of black diasporans in North America. As a communal mode of sonic experimentation, jazz's history was indivisible from the history of slavery. Okiji argues that Adorno displayed an unwillingness to comprehend the implications of slavery as it fused with (but was never reducible to) the making of jazz. If he had done so, he would have realised the slave had no access to the veneers of self-determination which duped the modern bourgeoise. For the slave, and the free blacks who followed them, exploitation and violence were natural and material. Thus, in response to Adorno's judgement of the music as one of 'obedience and unreflective servitude on the part of slaves', Okiji states, by contrast, that the propulsion engine for jazz can be found in the intense social contradictions of black life in North America. If Adorno had taken the requisite care to consider such extra-musical factors, he would have realised using European art music as the model for assessing jazz was a fruitless task. As such, the central flaw in his method of structural listening is not technical but ethical, in that structural listening relies upon the idea that a musical work has an internal logic equivalent to the individuality of the bourgeois subject:

> Moments like these – attempting to reconcile Adorno's indispensable insight on the dehumanising tendencies of Western Civilisation with this aggressively exclusionary approach to music – give me pause to consider the limits of his self-cognizance. It recalls other such indefensible moments but, more seriously, points to a fundamental flaw in a body of work committed to the reconcilement of humanity, scholarship driven by a desire to allow suffering, the nonidentical, and the unthought, to speak. It is impossible to dismiss as an aberration an essay devoted to the supposed regressive character of jazz, which proceeds to silence the music in order that it fit a wholly inappropriate formalist agenda.

Despite what feels at times like an excoriating admonition of the jazz essays, there is, however, a meta-critical provocation implicit in Okiji's decision to read Adorno so closely. The choice to organise a book which seeks to make a series of arguments about the blackness of jazz as a mode of radicalism through such a careful interpretation of Adorno causes trouble for some recent promotions of more diverse citation of sources as a means to address structural inequalities in knowledge production. Much like the opening chapter of Gayatri Spivak's *An Aesthetic Education in an Era of Globalisation* (where she moves through Kant, Schiller and Bateson), Okiji's problem with Adorno is not that he is European and male. The issue is that despite his own deeply held ethical convictions, Adorno was brutally misguided when it came to jazz, and therefore black life. At the same time, precisely because he could be so illuminating when diagnosing the many fractures of modernity, Okiji feels it is her duty to take him apart for his own failings when it comes to blackness. As Fred Moten has said, the only people who give out citations are the police, and Okiji moves within the same vein. Instead of editing him out of existence,

she embraces Adorno, holding him tight enough to whisper into his ear both her criticisms and her case for jazz as a credo.

It is when making the case for the credo that *Jazz as Critique* comes into its own as an intellectual undertaking. Moving beyond the task of pointing out Adorno's shortcomings, Okiji develops an enriching theorisation of the nature of jazz as the aesthetic imperative of the black radical tradition. Perhaps her key insight in this area concerns jazz's poverty. According to Okiji, attuning to the poverty of jazz requires two tasks of the listening congregation. One is that poverty is not understood as the basis for the music's debilitation, but is its resource. The other is that poverty as resource is not a narrative feature of jazz (it is not about tales of nobility found in poverty), but that poverty is its defining formal characteristic. Pointing to the twelve-bar blues as a primary instance of poverty as formal resource, the wealth of this organising principle lies in its openness and usability which allows for seemingly infinite adaptations. Thus the impoverishment of the twelve-bar blues operates as an instance of the 'mascon' – or the massive concentration of black experiential energy (a formulation borrowed from

Stephen Henderson) – whereby the 'propensity towards deviance … the gathering of contribution that makes up a standard is a celebration of aberration.'

The formal impoverishment argument allows Okiji to assemble her second major insight. For her, if encountered with the level of generosity and attention that goes into the making of the music, what soon becomes evident to the listening congregation is that jazz is not a musical repertoire but a means for the non-coercive organisation of life. Jazz is both fed by and nourishes modes of socio-ethical orientation that contour an over-riding homelessness. The historical fact of the unavailability of ownership (in its multiple forms) for the masses of black people has meant that jazz enacts a concrete alternative to the dominance of the private sphere: 'A reclaimed, subprime, matrofocal, fractal compound or extended home'.

It is in the interplay between impoverishment and homelessness that Okiji makes her case for the blackness of jazz. The significance of these claims lies not only in their novelty, but the means by which she puts them together. A notable feature of the theorisations of jazz as a

modality of blackness in this book is Okiji's break with the modernist reliance upon heroic figures. She does not get caught up in the trap of lionising exceptional artists, but instead braids her analysis with numerous instances of jazz's radical operations (Charles Mingus, Bessie Smith, Louis Armstrong, The Art Ensemble of Chicago, Thelonious Monk and Billie Holiday), as well as extra-musical figures who have their own orientations towards blackness as impoverishment and homelessness (Nathaniel Mackey and Saidiya Hartman).

All of this thinking is presented in a manner which folds back into Okiji's repeated reference to jazz as 'sociomusical play'. It is evident from the opening pages of this book that it has been handled by a person, with all the beauty of scars running across the surface of the writing. Which is to say that *Jazz as Critique* is the rare type of text that has a voice and is willing to use that voice to make an argument, as opposed to the now standardised model of text as hermetically-sealed object engineered in the hothouse of a graduate school program.

Dhanveer Singh Brar

Narcos (and their discontents)

Laurent De Sutter, *Narcocapitalism: Life in the Age of Anaesthesia (*Cambridge: Polity Press, 2018). 140pp., £41.50 hb., £9.99 pb., 978 1 50950 683 5 hb., 978 1 50950 684 2 pb.

In *A Contribution to the Critique of Hegel's Philosophy of Right* Marx remarked that religious devotion performed a fundamental role in the reproduction of nineteenth-century capitalist societies. Following Novalis's poetic intuition that 'religion works simply as an opiate: stimulating; numbing; quelling pain by means of weakness', Marx argued that religion should be understood as a sedative and a painkiller like morphine: 'the sigh of the oppressed creature, the heart of a heartless world, and the soul of soulless conditions. It is the opium of the people'. Religion, in other words, is a *symptomatic pharmakon*. It is 'the expression of real suffering and a protest against real suffering', but it does not eliminate the real, material, structural causes of misery and despair. Marx recognised that scholastic theology played an important role in driving the working class towards religion – just as he recognised that 'to push the sale of opiate is the

great aim of enterprising wholesale merchants' – and yet he was adamant that religious practices and rituals performed a *real* function, anaesthetising the working class against the physical and psychic pain experienced throughout the process of production and reproduction of its material life.

Today, after Nietzsche's 'death of God' and Lyotard's 'loss of faith', opium is all that is left. Already Marx, in a prophetic footnote to *Capital, Volume I*, stressed that 'in the agricultural as well as in the factory districts the consumption of opium among the grown-up labourers, both male and female, is extending daily'. Similarly, Engels, in *The Condition of the Working Class in England,* noticed that 'English working-people increasingly consume patent medicines to their own injury and the great profit of the manufacturer', attributing the commercial success of Godfrey's Cordial – 'a drink prepared with opiates, chiefly laudanum' – to the break-down of traditional family structures and the growing need to impose an artificial silence in working class households. Now narcotic drugs, whose consumption has been gradually simplified, depreciated and democratised, are the lynchpin of a post-hegemonic system of pharmaceutical management of the suffering masses: opiates themselves are 'the opium of the people'.

The surging pharmacological order is not itself void of contradictions, metaphysical subtleties and theological niceties. It also confronts us with a whole new set of political issues and conundrums. Only two years ago, Trump declared a national emergency under the *Public Health Service Act* in order 'to respond to the crisis caused by the opioid epidemic'. This declaration of emergency followed the guidelines indicated by the *President's Commission on Combating Drug Addiction and the Opioid Crisis*, whose interim report estimated that '142 Americans die every day from a drug overdose', with a majority of those deaths caused by opioids. We are told this is 'a crisis', a 'health emergency' requiring exceptional measures and extraordinary powers beyond the law. But this should not obscure that it is also a *structural crisis*, rooted in a long history.

In *Narcocapitalism* Laurent De Sutter continues this classical line of critique, offering a captivating genealogy of our 'age of anaesthesia'. 'Narcocapitalism', he writes, 'is the capitalism of narcosis, that enforced sleep into which anaesthetists plunge their patients so as to unburden them from everything that prevents them from being efficient in the current arrangement – which means work, work and more work'. Like a postmodern Virgil, De Sutter guides us through the hellish circles of our contemporary 'Prozacland', telling the story of how a pharmaceutical technique, which revolutionised chirurgical practice in the nineteenth century, gradually became the key technology of neoliberal subjectification, the material instrument through which our fatigued bodies are increasingly adapted to capital's endless cycles of accumulation. According to De Sutter, the dawn of the new chemical age is to be found in the first inhalations of diethyl ether vapours in the contained space of the clinic, where it 'would produce a state of nervous insensitivity' in the patient, while allowing 'the surgeon to work without causing discernible pain'. And yet, with a narrative twist that readers of Foucault's *Abnormal* and Deleuze's 'Postscript on the

Societies of Control' will not fail to recognise, De Sutter insists that 'the logic of anaesthesia' has now abandoned the disciplinary walls of our medical institutions, in order to infest the entire social field.

The capitalist city never sleeps. The heart of capital beats faster than any biological clock. The capitalist subject, dancing to the ever-accelerating rhythms of capital circulation, is leaving behind 'the cyclical ecology in which the human being has evolved until now'. A condition of 'general somnambulism' – buttressed by a growing number of pharmacological props and chemical crutches – is the new norm and the new normality. How did we get to this point? According to De Sutter, the invention of chlorpromazine represents the hinge of this fundamental shift. 'Chlorpromazine,' he writes, 'essentially transformed the person taking it into a passive spectator of their own mental state, incapable of feeling that they had been affected by the emotions passing through them. It was no longer a question of anaesthesia in the surgical sense of the term, but of a much more profound operation – anaesthesia in the sense of the ablation of the relationship between a subject and their sensations, and the elimination of their enjoyment.'

While *Narcocapitalism* may be read as a short history of anaesthetic technologies – or as an analysis of the contemporary medicalisation of everyday life – it is first and foremost an attempt to perform what Foucault once defined as 'a critical ontology of ourselves', a *political introspection* 'in which the critique of what we are is at one and the same time the historical analysis of the limits that are imposed on us and an experiment with the possibility of going beyond them'. De Sutter's diagnosis is clear and consistent: our contemporary era is defined by a generalised condition of induced indifference, social anhedonia and sexual impotence, insisting that 'the absence of desire characterises our psycho-political condition'. De Sutter's analysis confronts us with an uncanny, disturbing image of contemporary capitalism, which suddenly appears as a monastic, penitent regime; a colourless world populated by a marching multitude of narcotised, chemical Buddhas: 'in the age of anaesthesia', he insists, 'there is no existence except as psychic asceticism'. Against Marx, he affirms that contemporary capitalism is no longer driven by the contradictory logic of endless accumulation, but rather by the 'logic of anaesthesia'. Against Foucault, De Sutter discretely revives the repressive hypothesis, describing the emergence of a 'psychopolitics' that 'ablates' desire and confines the 'old biopolitics of the body' to 'governmental obscurity'.

There is more than a grain of truth in De Sutter's account: the consumption of narcotics has dramatically risen since the late 1990s, as have the number of days we spend under conditions of induced anaesthesia. As Marx could already glimpse in the 1840s, the growing consumption of opioids continues to be driven by the objective economic interests of 'enterprising wholesale merchants', but it is also rooted in widespread subjective experiences of pain, suffering, anxiety and depression. Modern medicine – whose aim is to eradicate the pathological sources of pain – is increasingly accompanied and substituted by the practice of algiatry, i.e. indefinite 'pain management'. It is in its conclusions, concerning the 'ascetic' nature of contemporary subjectivity and the relation between power and desire, that De Sutter's narrative breaks down, revealing the limits of a perspective that ultimately obscures the contradictory logic driving the increasing consumption of narcotics in advanced capitalist societies. De Sutter's otherwise agile book – just over one hundred pages divided into 51 fragments that mimic an Agambenian style - is at once too modest and too ambitious: too modest because it limits our view to the history of one class of drugs (focusing on anaesthetics at the expense of an analysis of the parallel, growing consumption of euphoriant, empathogen and serenic drugs such as ecstasy, phenethylamine and MDMA); too ambitious because it extrapolates from this partial history a set of general conclusions about the essence of contemporary capitalism. The history of anaesthetics leads De Sutter to a conception of capitalism driven by 'the logic of anaesthesia'. And yet, a very different conception of capital would have emerged from looking exclusively at the history of stimulants, or at the history of euphoriants or at the history of psychedelics and hallucinogens.

Ultimately, the main thesis presented by De Sutter is theoretically unconvincing, and politically perilous. Certainly, our desires are often repressed but they are more often stimulated, incited and aroused. Entire industries – from marketing to pornography – are aimed at the systematic production of desire. Can we really affirm that contemporary neoliberal subjectivity is characterised by 'ascetism' and 'absence of desire' when shopping has become an ubiquitous obsession and a medicalised addiction, which subjects experience as an 'irresistable urge'? Can we really say, in a society dominated by ubiquitous advertisement and endless appeals to the passions of the consumer, that the fact 'that an individual might no longer feel or desire anything seemingly poses no problem for doctors or public authorities'? A lack of desire has been denounced and medicalised since the nineteenth century, and today flibanserin – a drug specifically designed to target serotonin receptors and boost sexual drive – is regularly precribed and sold to women affected by 'hypoactive sexual desire disorder'. If the introduction of chlorpromazine in 1950 established the logic of anaesthesia at the centre of modern narcocapitalism, one could say that the commercialisation of flibanserin is symptomatic of contemporary capitalist practices aimed at the artificial stimulation and production of desire on a massive scale. Should we then speak of a 'hedonic phase' of capitalism, characterised by the systematic stimulation of the neural structures of the human reward system and the incessant titillation of the hedonic hotspots that mediate everyday pleasure reactions?

Though it presents only a partial history, De Sutter's account nonetheless represents an important chapter of a much larger work yet-to-be written, which would probe the multiple relations between pharmacracy and capitalism. We neither live in a narcocapitalism of universal anaestheticisation, nor in an hedonic capitalism of universal stimulation, but rather in a normalising society in which a multiplicity of drugs are deployed differentially, targeting each individual according to their peculiar characteristics and their specific social role.

Amedeo Policante

The promise of a pantheist politics

Saul Newman, *Political Theology: A Critical Introduction* (Cambridge: Polity Press 2019), 180pp., £15.99 pb., 978 1 50952 840 0 pb.

In *The Crisis of Parliamentary Democracy*, first published in the midst of political turmoil in Weimar era Germany, Carl Schmitt attempted a theoretical amputation of liberal parliamentarianism from democracy by excavating the contradictory principles on which each was based. Some thirty years after Schmitt's death, it would appear his prophecy has been fulfilled. As Saul Newman writes, today 'a major rift has opened between liberalism and democracy', a rift manifest in the prevalent demand for 'closed borders and a strong state', two marks by which national sovereignty is known. Newman writes that the return of this 'spectre', the 'phantasm' of sovereignty, is symptomatic of our 'increasingly abstracted and virtualised form of existence'. Yet, in his rejection of the abstract and virtual, (a rejection Newman finds in Max Stirner and anarchist thought), do we not hear, perhaps unexpectedly, a faint echo of Schmitt's own demand for the concrete, for *reale Möglichkeit*? Rather than solving the 'politico-theological problem', Newman argues (against Schmitt) for a profane politics that refuses to be drawn towards political power, and instead works around and outside it.

Newman's *Political Theology: A Critical Introduction* can be grouped with a number of recent texts offering contemporised readings of 'political theology', including recent works by Adam Kotsko, Elettra Stimilli and Mitchell Dean, amongst others. These explore a number of closely related questions on the theologico-political significance of contemporary issues, ranging from debt and indebtedness to democracy, sovereignty and power. While many of these works draw heavily from the same sources – Schmitt, Foucault and Agamben are central to most – Newman's text is unusual in its attention to the anarchist theoretical tradition and includes significant discussion of Max Stirner and Mikhail Bakunin, whose critical engagement with political theology is often overlooked. In doing so, this work returns to questions Newman had explored almost twenty years ago in *From Bakunin to Lacan: Anti-Authoritarianism and the Dislocation of Power* (2001).

Newman's central thesis is that 'the problem of political theology is really the problem of power itself'. This problem is approached through a staged confrontation between conservatism and anarchism. On one side, Donoso Cortés and Schmitt represent the conservative attempt to immunise the state against anarchism through the sovereign moment of transcendent lawlessness. On the other side stand Bakunin, Proudhon, Stirner and Agamben, who deny the need for transcendence and demand an immanent anarchist politics. Yet, as Newman notes, these two positions offer a 'curious mirror image' of the state as an absolutist structure. While one side affirms it, the other wants to abolish it. Newman's core problem, then, is one that also plagues the works of Agamben: how to provide an account for this alternative non-politico-theologico conception of politics?

Central to Newman's book is the ambition to 'explore the crisis of liberal politics and political theory through the problem of political theology'. The 'problem of political theology', or the 'politico-theological problem', as Newman describes it, is ostensibly that political concepts 'are influenced, shaped and underpinned by religious categories' – although precisely why and for whom this is a 'problem' is at times difficult to grasp. Despite Newman's univocal nomenclature, there seem to be a number of distinct problems that arise according to particular points of view: for secularists, it is a problem that their concepts are not secular enough; for Schmitt, it is a problem that secularists ignore the importance of sovereignty; and, for anarchists, the problem is manifest as the persistent demand of the general populace for substantial identity/unity in the form of transcendence. However, ultimately each of these points of view is equated with the 'problem of *power*'.

This calls to mind Mitchell Dean's *The Signature of Power* (2013), where, guided by Agamben, Dean attempts to develop an account of power encapsulating both sovereignty (Schmitt) and governmentality (Foucault). Newman, however, is concerned rather more with the former than with the latter. Newman emphasises the religious

dimensions of the Schmittian sovereign, referring to it as a 'sacred concept', the 'redeemer and saviour of the people'. He acknowledges that 'Schmitt is right in pointing to the structural recurrence of the problematic of sovereignty, which is revealed every time a social order undergoes a crisis of legitimation.' But for Newman, sovereignty is a phantasmic object of desire. It is a 'paranoid dream of identity – national, cultural, religious – asserted against any universalism'; a desirable but ultimately unattainable moment of transcendence that arises whenever the present order is threatened. Today, such a desire for transcendent authority derives from the demise of the technocratic neoliberal consensus, but in the 1920s it was the end of the nineteenth-century aristocratic constitutional monarchies, and before that it was the disruption of political consensus caused by the Reformation.

A key premise adopted in Newman's work is Claude Lefort's claim that 'modern democratic society ... is structured by a symbolically empty place of power, left vacant by the absent body of the prince'. Utilising Lacan's psychoanalytic nomenclature, Newman writes that religion fills this structural deficit, no longer in the symbolic register, but today in the imaginary. The result is a constant, insatiable desire for a point of transcendence, a

new form of power. Through a series of short vignettes, Newman recounts the central debates of the twentieth century on the subject of political theology, orienting each towards his question of power, and its vacant place in politics. The opening chapter alone includes a detailed account of Schmitt, a commentary on Schmitt and Strauss and the conflict of reason and revelation based largely on Meier's reconstruction of their 'hidden dialogue', and the theological responses from Peterson and Taubes. However, the real value of Newman's work lies in his retrieval of a number of anarchist responses to problems of politics. Eschewing Schmitt as a starting point, he returns instead to Bakunin's 1871 critique of Mazzini. Bakunin's criticism is that religion and idealist political theories begin by posing an abstract transcendent set of moral principles against the 'materiality of life'. For Bakunin, it is such pessimistic anthropologies that must be confronted with a materialist, atheist international socialism.

This is followed by a rehabilitation of Max Stirner, who believes 'the whole of secular modernity to be haunted by the spectres of religion it had believed itself to be rid of.' For Newman, the value of Stirner lies in his attempt to free 'subjectivity from the fixed forms of identification' which are characteristic of political theology, but also contemporary 'identity politics'. On this point, the contemporary intervention intended by Newman's work becomes apparent. In fact, one thread running throughout the book deals with the logical proximity of today's identity politics to the Schmittian problematics of political theology. This critique of liberal identity politics is introduced through a rehearsal of Stirner's critique of Hegel and Feuerbach, culminating in Stirner's distinction between insurrection and revolution, also discussed briefly by Agamben in *The Time That Remains*. Stirner fails to offer a 'programme' for politics, but he does offer some 'useful concepts', Newman argues. Yet is Stirner's critique of essentialism really valid as a critique of Schmitt's conception of 'the political'?

One weakness of Newman's text is its inadequate attention to 'the political' as such. In particular, he neglects the relativised conception of *politische Einheit* (unity/entity) on which Schmitt's works are based. Instead, the field of possible positions is reduced to a dichotomy between essentialist homogeneity, on the one hand, and radical singularity, on the other. This simplification overlooks Schmitt's attempt to theorise a more flexible and relativised homogeneity, insofar as any distinction can be 'intensified' to the level of a properly political distinction. For Schmitt, it is only this relative conception of identity that is necessary for the properly 'political' existence of population. Without some form of unification or alignment, is there any room in Stirner's egoistic politics for large-scale collective projects, such as, for example, the Roman aqueducts or Britain's National Health Service? The recent works of the anonymous collective The Invisible Committee, which pursue some parallel ideas, are similarly haunted by a kind of new Malthusian problem of scale, which Newman's ecologically-inspired politics also cannot easily ignore. Are the localist and syndicalist politics advocated by these groups really an ethical solution in the face of the scale of contemporary populations and the ecological and agricultural pressures of the coming years?

In a chapter on the body of the sovereign, the *corpus mysticum*, Newman struggles with this problem. He traces the sovereign body through Hobbes, Schmitt, Kantorowicz and Walter Benjamin, critiquing identity politics as a demand for 'sovereignty at its most ideological, phantasmatic'. The desire for ipseity, self-hood and autonomy manifest in the Brexit slogan to 'take back

control' is present on both the right and left; in the latter, as a demand for greater democratic control. The only exit is to be found, for Newman as for many others, in Benjamin's controversial 'divine violence', identified as a 'pure means', despite the fact that, for Newman, it offers a rather specific goal in the form of a 'messianic promise of the redemption of life.' In any case, it is in Benjamin that Newman finds the concept of a 'spiritual anarchism', central to his final vision of an escape.

Shifting to the power located in government, Newman turns to Foucault and Agamben. Foucault's lectures on pastoral power lead to a conception of ethics as care of the self, while Agamben's archaeology of economy provides a link with contemporary capitalism. These are supplemented with Jacques Ellul's writings on technology and his religious mysticism. The aim is a rejection of technocratic visions of the machine-man of La Mettrie, which form the basis of the liberal technologist religion of progress. But here Newman struggles to align positions that remain in an uneasy tension. Newman embraces the demand 'to break down this economic-technical-theological machine [of modernity] ... and bring it back under human control', but must distance himself from any secular humanism of the kind criticised by Stirner and ignore the fact that the demand for human control is itself a demand for a certain kind of transcendent sovereignty.

In the final chapter, Newman offers his alternative: a profane politics, which is worldy but spiritual. He writes of a theology of immanence and evokes an ecological pantheism that embraces contingency, indeterminacy and multiplicity. Despite the religious register, Newman's proposal has much in common with Agamben's destitutive politics. Profane practices simply refuse to be drawn into the game of power. They embrace aspects of asceticism, self-discipline and apostolic poverty as a means to 'foster greater personal freedom and autonomy'. This also leads, however, to a disappointing turn to localism, in which 'local traditions and ways of life' are the defence 'against the abstractions' of today's capitalism.

Political Theology: A Critical Introduction ties together disparate concepts with a practiced ease. Yet it is a curious text. As the subtitle suggests, it is intended as a 'critical introduction'. But can an introductory text ever offer a meaningful platform for critique? In only 170 pages, the reader is offered a hasty tour through an impossibly dense region of theory and historiography that stretches from the nineteenth century to the present day, but which takes as its object of study the entire history of Judeo-Christian civilisation. As a result, there is an unavoidable tension between Newman's intention to provide introductory sketches of entire oeuvres and his aim to offer a critical perspective upon positions that, due to the requirements of the form, lack nuance and depth.

At times, Newman's writing exhibits rather less conceptual rigour than is required. This is particularly evident in his use of the terms 'theology' and 'religion', which seem to be used almost interchangeably – an obvious problem given the object of his study. Terminological imprecision and rushed abstraction occasionally seem to be the real basis for some apparent 'paradoxes' unearthed. For instance, when Newman writes that the 'state's abandonment of religion' 'leads only to the religion of the state' is there not a quite fundamental distinction between particulars hidden by his use of the abstraction 'religion'? Given his own Stirner-inspired distaste for such 'abstractions', the lack of attention to the singularity of the problems of western state-church relations seems inconsistent. A related difficulty concerns his conception of politics itself, which in a text such as this deserves special attention. It is unclear precisely what marks the political as political for Newman. Clearly he rejects Schmitt's friend/enemy criterion, but no alternative is offered beyond some vague references to community.

In his first chapter, Newman skirts a little too quickly over a perennial problem for anarchist politics, the paradox of the 'corruption of man'. Newman writes that, 'for the anarchist, man was inherently good and therefore could be trusted with freedom and self-government', it was only 'the sovereign who was corrupt and whose intervention corrupted the lives of men.' But the tricky question is then, of course: is the sovereign not also human? What was the original source of corruption? On this point, we should return to Schmitt's reading of Hobbes' anthropology, and to the distinction between the Catholic claim that man is inherently evil and Hobbes' weaker alternative that man is merely dangerous. Is there really such a gulf between the anarchist position that man is corrupted by power, and Hobbes' assertion that the cause of war in nature is ambition?

Luke Collison

A clash of spatialisations

Chris Hesketh, *Spaces of Capital/Spaces of Resistance: Mexico and the Global Political Economy* (Athens, GA: University of Georgia Press, 2017), 240pp., £76.95 hb., £23.95 pb., 978 0 82035 174 2 hb., 978 0 82035 284 8 pb..

In *Spaces of Capital/Spaces of Resistance*, Chris Hesketh provides an overview of the possibilities and challenges for anti-capitalist politics in Mexico. As the book convincingly demonstrates, such an overview is only possible if one grasps both the historical and spatial dimensions to revolutionary transformation, through what Hesketh terms a 'historical-geographical sociology'. To aid him in this project, Hesketh draws on a range of Marxist thinkers, especially Henri Lefebvre and Antonio Gramsci, as well as his own fieldwork, which allows him to explore processes of 'uneven and combined hegemony' that put questions of scale at the centre of analysis. One of the great strengths of the book is its attention to scalar detail, too often marginalised in radical geographical work that has tended, in recent years, to privilege the flat ontology of flows and networks, and in so doing has eschewed the actually existing politics of scale that governs so much political and social life. As Hesketh shows, political struggles over state formation involve an articulation across local, national and international processes that shape and constrain practices of resistance and domination. As such, struggles in and through territory also assume a central role in the kinds of political struggle recounted throughout the book.

The history of anti-capitalist struggle in Mexico has played out through a 'clash of spatialisations', in Hesketh's terms, as alternative spatial practices confront each other at key moments in the restructuring of capitalist relations. For example, the Zapatistas' understandings of territory, as a space of collective self-governance and *power-to*, have directly clashed with those of the state. Such alternative understandings of space are also directly lived, thus generating different 'spatial practices'. In Chiapas, the Zapatistas' alternative ideas of space were materialised through the everyday production of new institutions and structures of governance (for example, legal systems) that not only questioned the state's understanding of territory but directly challenged its capacity to exert its sovereign power over space. In response, the Mexican state has used a range of strategies to re-territorialise their top-down vision of state sovereignty, thereby leading to an ongoing dialectical struggle in and through space. Although these clashing spatial practices have been traversed by the ongoing formation of the Mexican state, the constant has been the autonomy of grassroots struggles in which the indigenous have been central protagonists. Hesketh's book is framed around two of the most paradigmatic cases of autonomous resistance in the region in recent years, which have also been the source of ongoing inspiration for large sectors of the anti-capitalist left: the Oaxaca uprising (2006) and the Zapatistas.

The first question thus revolves around the extent to which these forms of struggle, based on insurgent spatial logics that clash with hegemonic spatial projects, could and should inform the current political juncture that Latin America confronts. Since the election of Mauricio Macri in Argentina and the impeachment of Dilma Rouseauf in Brazil in late 2015 (which led to the election of President Bolsonaro), the region appears to be entering a dramatic rightwards turn. This regional turn of events is leading to reflections on the strategies of the left in Latin America more generally, although much more is still needed in this regard. Hesketh's book is useful in providing an assessment of two of the most successful cases of grassroots political projects that have eschewed state-based strategies. It is worth noting here that during the period of analysis discussed in the book, Mexico was not part of the so-called 'Pink Tide' and was in some ways a regional outlier. Nevertheless, Zapatismo has remained a constant in the region that both precedes the institutional turn to the left and has outlived it. Despites their many limitations, the Zapatistas' institutionalisation of alternative spatial practices provided a vital set of infrastructures that would not otherwise exist. This institutionalisation includes not only new structures of autonomous governance and law but also core services such as healthcare and education, all of which attempt to provide the necessary resources for Zapatismo to reproduce its radical political project. One lesson for the region is that when clashing spatial projects fail to institutionalise themselves (or *territorialise* themselves) with a certain level of autonomy from the state, they will be left in a vulnerable position when trying to survive any turn to the right. Hence, immediately after rising to power in Argentina, Macri imprisoned one of the country's most important indigenous leaders – Milagro Sala – and deterritorialsised her movement that had reconstructed everyday life in a Northwest province based on grassroots utopian spatial practices.

One of the reasons why Lefebvre is so important to the narrative of Hesketh's book is his insistence that revolutionary transformation only makes sense to the extent that is also a spatial transformation. Territorial *Autogestión* in everyday life and counter-hegemonic spatial forms must arise and take root if other worlds are to become a reality. Chapter 4 of the book is extremely insightful in this regard, detailing both the revolutionary potential contained within new ways of imagining the city of Oaxaca and its spatial relation to the rest of the state, as well as the incapacity of the Oaxacan uprising to effectively scale-up its struggle. Key to this has been the protagonism of indigenous movements within Oaxaca and the successful mobilisation of the city as a node for establishing new relations, as well as deepening existing ones, across diverse political organisations. Nevertheless, while the 2006 uprising did manage to politicise everyday life in the city for a brief period of time, there was a failure to establish a lasting form for ongoing political coordination. Once again, these experiences suggest that although social movements may fear or dismiss strategies of changing the world via state power, the production of (counter) institutions remains unavoidable and necessary. Autonomous uprisings that fail to institutionalise themselves, to establish a means through which they can reproduce their spatial practices, are likely to suffer the same fate as Oaxaca. Successful experiences of ongoing everyday territorialisations of struggle within a network of social infrastructures and practices thus provide one of the more hopeful readings of autonomous spatial projects that attempt to clash with dominant spatial forms.

One thing that Hesketh could not have foreseen when writing the book, but which has the potential to reorient strategic questions about the future of the left in Mexico, is the rise of AMLO. In July 2018, Andrés Manuel López Obrador (AMLO) won a landslide election, twelve years after his first attempt ended with widespread claims of electoral interference. Hesketh's reading of Gramsci's passive revolution proves useful here, as do Hesketh's writings with Adam Morton on Bolivia, in outlining a possible future path that may unfold in Mexico. Yet Mexico seems to insist on being a regional outlier and its turn to the left, if indeed we are happy to understand AMLO in such terms, must thus be read through a close sociological reading of Mexico's own historical-geographical development. *Spaces of Capital/Spaces of Resistance* opens the way but also leaves us hanging at this pivotal moment in Mexican history.

Hesketh ends by highlighting the central challenge for spaces of resistance in Mexico: 'the need to "scale up" their activism while avoiding becoming reinscribed into the state apparatus and neutralised via means of passive revolutionary activity'. My sense is that many, if not most, of the book's protagonists would see AMLO as more of a threat than ally. As such, it may be that new movements arise that are better placed to articulate the relations between insurgent, autonomist demands and the messy institutional politics that goes with strategies seeking to redirect the project of state building. Yet, a strength of the book is its placing of local struggles within the context of a global political economy and this will be a hugely determining factor in the outcomes of AMLO's government, which faces a very different context to the start of the progressive tide some two decades ago.

We will need more rigorous, multi-scalar and political economic analyses such as those provided in this book in order to make sense of the political transformations unfolding in Latin America. Politically, the region will also need a greater articulation between different grassroots strategies that are likely to approach the Mexican state from contrasting (and conflicting) vantage points but with similar anti-capitalist ambitions. I hope that Hesketh's analysis can be drawn into discussion with scholars and activists from different backgrounds who are currently debating the recent past and future of Latin America, and who will benefit enormously from the historical-geographical sociology provided in the book.

Sam Halvorsen

Kept afloat by the generous support of our patrons

www.patreon.com/radicalphilosophy

Michel Serres, 1930–2019

Lucie Kim-Chi Mercier

In Serres's works, the table of method is the method, the idea is its own image, the code is already overcoded. Serres cannot be commented but only stuttered. A repetition won't add anything to a text that knows better than anyone how to repeat itself in its innovations, or how to innovate by repeating itself.

Régis Debray[1]

Michel Serres passed away in Vincennes, on June 1 2019, at the age of 88. Much appreciated by the French general public, he was one of the most unclassifiable characters of the generation of French philosophers who came of age in the 1960s. Serres was born in Agen, in the South-West of France, to a modest family of peasants. His father worked as a sand dragger on the Garonne river, and, as Serres would often state, his early years followed the rhythms of the Garonne river, which was at the root of his long-standing curiosity not only regarding navigation, but all questions of transport. An outstanding student, Serres was a pupil of the Republic and moved from one public boarding school to the next. After a brief attempt to join the navy he went back to Bordeaux to complete a Licence in mathematics, and then to Paris to join the philosophy section of the prestigious Ecole Normale Supérieure. Serres would always emphasise this dual training, and highlight that although he ended up choosing philosophy he remained attuned to the mathematical developments of his time. As he wrote in a letter to Canguilhem, 'As a mathematics student I would read Bergson and Plato, as a philosophy student I would study Bourbaki.'[2]

He entered the ENS in 1952, the same year as Jacques Derrida, and placed second in the philosophy aggregation in 1955. It is little known that, like his former classmate, Serres spent much time reading and commenting upon Husserl: in particular, 'The Origin of Geometry', a reflection on the philosophy and historicity of mathematics, to which he would periodically return until his 1993 book *The Origins of Geometry*. Up to the 1990s, Serres's interest in the sciences would remain a foundation of his philosophical works, evolving through several different phases – including structural mathematics, information theory and thermodynamics, chaos theory, biology and ecology. While his scientific references changed, however, his philosophical companions would not alter much through the years: Lucretius and Plato, Leibniz, Comte or Bergson.

In 1958 Serres moved to Clermont-Ferrand to teach in the philosophy department directed by Jules Vuillemin, where Michel Foucault was also working at the time. There he composed his doctoral dissertation, which was initially focused on the philosophy of topology and ended up as a 900-page long monograph on Leibniz, *Le Système de Leibniz et ses modèles mathématiques*, which he would publish shortly after its defence in the hot days of June 1968. Engaging with Leibniz's systematicity not as 'dream' but as realised 'structure', the monumental study reflects Serres's evolving rapport with French structuralism, moving from a strong formalism grounded in Bourbaki's definition of mother structures towards a 'transformational' structuralism in which the principle of identity gives way to a principle of translation. In the prologue of his thesis, Serres thanks his teachers: George Canguilhem, Jean Hyppolite and Yvon Belaval. Like Foucault, Serres enjoyed a particularly privileged relationship with Canguilhem, and the ambitious methodological apparatus of his PhD thesis is replete with his master's epistemological themes: the role of the scientist and the role of the philosopher, science, truth and normativity.

In many ways, Foucault's retrospective labelling of this period as that of the 'philosophy of the concept' as against the philosophy of 'consciousness' is relevant to

Serres's own earliest philosophy, albeit according to a different orientation than Foucault. For Serres, this entailed a return to the classical philosophical concepts of *form* (Eidos/Morphe) and *relation* (as methodic path between two points or systematic connexion) through the lens of the scientific inventions of his time, such as the axiomatisation of mathematics by Bourbaki, the second principle of thermodynamics, the discovery of the relationship between information and entropy, or the determination of the structure of DNA. The first *Hermès* volumes located themselves at the frontier between the history and epistemology of science and structuralism, delving into the question of a 'history of truth' which, arguably, haunted his generation as a whole. Puzzled by Husserl's intentional account of idealities, Serres helped to stimulate reflection not only on the historicity of scientific notions but on the languages spoken by science; the uncontested reference for which was still the work of Gaston Bachelard. From the beginning, Serres's confrontation with the latter was open and explicit, as he chose to focus on impurity by mixing scientific discourse with the language of rites and mythical narrative. For his minor thesis, published as *Hermès II, L'Interférence* in 1972 – less to the liking of Canguilhem than his study of Leibniz – Serres undertook to rewrite the 'new scientific spirit' into a theory of 'interference'; that is, into a philosophy of networks (epistemological and cybernetic) and a theory of transdisciplinarity.

From the start, Serres's epistemology was programmed to dissolve itself, not in the autonomy of each self-regulated science but in the heteronomy of 'interobjective' communications: objects *speak*: 'Here I enter the circuit only by integrating the fundamental communication network drawn up by the object-object diagram. When reflexive epistemology becomes intrinsic, the transcendental field turns objective.'[3] Through this bold choice, he announced his divergence from French epistemology. For going beyond a modest theory of the history of science, Serres's ambition would be to recover and narrate the philosophy of science in the making, seeking to situate himself ahead of the contemporary. And indeed, at the same time as the publication of his doctoral thesis, he started publishing volumes of essays on the philosophy of science, culture and literature under the title *Hermès*. The series comprises five volumes in total, and it is widely agreed that they contain some

of Serres's richest intuitions and densest philosophical essays.

As an epistemologist and a structuralist, Michel Serres developed a philosophy of *models*, working on the history of science outside of disciplinary constructs and rethinking it from the standpoint of triptychs of figures: point, plane, cloud; vectors, transformation, information; Diagrammes, trees, networks. The five *Hermès* volumes bore titles that summarised different models of relations, brought to bear on different objects. Scientific modernity doesn't depend on stupendous inventions but on the slow progression of a moraine of knowledge, which gradually transforms into entirely new landscapes. There is no authentic and inauthentic science, no obstacles nor mistakes, but cultural formations, which obey mutating forms of order and disorder. Enthralled by the classical question of beginning(s), Serres remained forever attached to the threshold he set for himself from an early stage, between a new epistemology of models and a metaphysical topology or topography of the universe.

Against the 'masters of suspicion' of criticism, Serres's philosophy was not a polemical one; he didn't intervene much into conceptual debates and offered very few philosophical references to anchor his discourse. Yet, through this early reversal, his philosophy stayed in some relation to critical philosophy, since he kept on raising the question of the 'objective-transcendental', of how to establish the conditions of possibility of knowledge – even non-knowledge, or, in a Leibnizian idiom, 'obscure knowledge' – in objects. The topology or 'science of the qualitative' uncovered in Leibniz remained crucial throughout, as it enabled him to reconceptualise the distance between cultural and scientific formations. He raised the question: 'How shall we take into account forms in history, without bringing these forms back to the concept?'[4] For Serres, this required practicing a genuine science of the qualitative, a rigorous aesthetics which would 'radically pluralise the traditional unicity of *a priori* forms.'[5]

A seasoned alpinist, Serres compared philosophical work with travels or hikes across landscapes: the figure of the messenger, who relates, communicates, translates or heralds, is a permanent one in his oeuvre. His boldness cost him Canguilhem's friendship and, indeed, that of the French philosophical institution as a whole. After partaking in the short-lived Vincennes experiment, he was invited by the Sorbonne not as a professor of philosophy but as a professor of history of science, which he would always consider as a *de facto* exclusion from the community. Serres attributed his fate to his role of mediator, which, instead of giving him a share of two worlds, alienated him from both. 'I was lucky enough to remain alone for thirty years and work on this passage in indifference and silence. I'm standing in the empty intersection between two groups, ... White space without stakes nor battles ... Why draw on the history of religions to examine a corpus in physics or geometry; could we imagine that literature is a domain [réserve] of science rather than its exclusion?'[6] This solitary path, however, remained his general theoretical orientation, for he would characterise his subsequent books as such admixtures: sociology and astronomy (*Origins of Geometry*); politics and physics (*The Natural Contract,* 1990); technology and the anthropology of death (*Statues,* 1987); and so on.[7]

Thanks to his friendship with the anthropologist René Girard, Serres started working in the United States: invited first to Johns Hopkins University in 1971, he would then become a professor at Stanford University in 1984, where he taught for nearly thirty years. A prolific writer and speaker, Serres published over sixty books and became, from the 1990s onwards, an unavoidable figure on French radio and television and in the press. He received several official accolades and was elected to the illustrious Académie Française in 1990. Serres's late period, during which he produced an impressive number of programmatic, often self-referential texts on moral, cultural and political questions, alienated him a little more from the French philosophical community. Because of this gradual move away, in style and content,

from academic philosophy, French commentaries on his works have remained extremely scarce. In the Anglophone world we are still lacking translations of many of Serres's foundational writings, in particular of his earliest books, including the thesis on Leibniz, even though these are crucial to the legibility of his better-known books (*The Parasite, The Natural Contract, Genesis*). Moreover, his own self-marginalisation from the French philosophical landscape has made readers forget the complex ties that bound Serres to his contemporaries. In fact, Serres's philosophy of the 1960s and 1970s offers some powerful reflections on the most important questions of his time, including those concerning structure and subject, truth and historicity, language, information, nature and the social and political role of technology.

His Sorbonne lectures, punctuated by his inimitable, almost prophetic way of speaking, were always packed with students and auditors. Serres was undoubtedly a stylist, a 'poet of the concept',[8] who believed in the power of analogies and questioned the criteria of philosophical 'rigour' in the name of a broader conception of rationality and a return to great narratives. At a time when the limits between science and the sacred are questioned anew, when local human mastery over the earth has become 'a possible global hell',[9] we can hope not only that Serres's works will be better read, but that his fearless attempt to grasp the human and political facets of the sciences and technologies in their contemporaneity will acquire new resonances.

Lucie Kim-Chi Mercier is a member of the Radical Philosophy *editorial collective.*

Notes

1. Régis Debray, 'L'ard du feu', *Critique* 380 (January 1979), 16. Translation mine, as are all subsequent translations.
2. Letter from Michel Serres to George Canguilhem, Archive Canguilhem, CAPHES, Paris. Cote 40.1 Michel Serres.
3. Michel Serres, *Hermès II, L'Interférence* (Paris: Les Éditions de Minuit, 1972), 99.
4. Michel Serres, *Hermès V, Le Passage du Nord-Ouest* (Paris: Les Éditions de Minuit, 1980), 72.
5. Serres, *Hermès V*, 73.
6. Serres, *Hermès V*, 17.
7. Michel Serres and Bruno Latour, *Conversations on Science, Culture and Time*, trans. R. Lapidus (Ann Arbor: University of Michigan Press, 1995), 151.
8. Debray, 'L'ard du feu', 16.
9. Serres and Latour, *Conversations*, 171.

Lightning Source UK Ltd.
Milton Keynes UK
UKHW05081724 0919
350314UK00005B/34/P